AMERICAN SOUL

D1445857

To Dorothy Schurmann

AMERICAN SOUL

FRANZ SCHURMANN

foreword by Richard Rodriguez

Mercury House
San Francisco

Published in the United States by Mercury House, San Francisco, California, a nonprofit publishing company devoted to the free exchange of ideas and guided by a dedication to literary values.

United States Constitution, First Amendment: Congress shall make no law respecting an establishment of religion, or prohibiting the free exercise thereof; or abridging the freedom of speech, or of the press; or the right of the people peaceably to assemble, and to petition the Government for a redress of grievances.

Mercury House and colophon are registered trademarks of
Mercury House, Incorporated

Printed on recycled, acid-free paper
Manufactured in the United States of America

Library of Congress Cataloging-in-Publication Data
Schurmann, Franz, 1926–
American soul / by Franz Schurmann ; foreword by Richard Rodriguez
p.   cm.
ISBN 1-56279-068-4
1. Civil religion—United States. 2. National characteristics, American.
3. United States—Religion. I. Title.
BL2525.S34 1995
155.8'973— dc20   94–15727
CIP

5   4   3   2   1

TABLE OF CONTENTS

ACKNOWLEDGMENTS

Many people helped form the thoughts, writing, and shape of this book. Listing names always seems to imply a hierarchy, but the Chinese long ago discovered how to arrange everybody without regard to status—by seating them at a round dinner table. Thus the following list is alphabetical by first name so that someone appears as higher or lower only for trivial technical reasons.

I am especially indebted to my family, my colleagues at Pacific News Service, and my friends: Andrew Lam, Anita Nones, Beatriz Johnson-Hernandez, Hugh Pearson, Bilal Hyde, Chen Jie, Jim Armistead, Kevin Chan, Ling-chi Wang, Mahadeo Patel, Lisa Margonelli, Ma'mun Fandy, Maggie Ballard, Mark Schurmann, Michael Kroll, Nell Bernstein, Pao Saechao, Percy Hintzen, Peter Schurmann, Richard Rodriguez, Robert Guerra, Sandy Close, Bob Beyers, Stefan Brecht, Stuart Miller, Tosun Aricanli, Walter Truett Anderson, and Yoichi Shimatsu.

I also wish to thank those who helped get this book into print, especially Esther Cohen, who gave the manuscript its first read; my editors at Mercury House, Tom Christensen and David Peattie, who provided invaluable help on every aspect of the book; Ann Edelstein, my agent; and Peter Solomon and Rick Whittaker, who edited early versions of the manuscript.

Finally, I want to share the names of those thinkers and writers from whose work I have drawn inspiration: Amano Motonosuke, Shih Cheng-chih, Calixta Gabriel, Chen Shih-hsiang, Francis Cleaves, Hans Urs von Balthasar, Hsüan-hua Fa-shih, Karl Korsch, Maryse Conde, Padre Alejandro Cussianovich, and Zeki Velidi Togan.

FOREWORD

There is peasant blood in my veins.
You cannot astonish me with peasant virtues.
—Anton Chekhov

On the walls were huge, faded photos of Shanghai harbor. Unkempt waitresses pushed steaming trolleys up and down the aisles between plastic-covered tables at which sat grandmothers, babies, cousins, nephews. Green bottles. Red sauces, mustard sauces share yin-yang porcelain bowls. From a large glass case of brackish water, fish considered the species that would sooner or later devour them.

Franz Schurmann writes: "It is common, in Chinatown, to see a Caucasian man sitting alone in a restaurant, looking out a window." And that is where I often find Franz—toward the back of the room, alone at a table, reading an Arabic newspaper. And that is where I like best to talk to him. Professor Schurmann, the famed sinologist, surrounded by the din and the smell and the effort and the necessity of China. Talking about the French Enlightenment.

Franz Schurmann thinks he looks Chinese—"Chinese or like a Portuguese from Macau." Chinese waitresses and busboys seem unsurprised when he addresses them in Mandarin.

There are slogans on the walls. There are slogans stamped onto the fluttering red ribbons attached to potted plants. It amuses Franz when I ask him to translate the slogan on my red menu. "Believe me, you don't want to know. Behind all the mysterium of Chinatown is banality." Very well. He decodes: WITH HARD WORK, COMES . . . He removes his glasses to wipe his eyes . . . CONTENTMENT.

A theme that recurs in Franz's table talk is that he comes from peasant stock. "I'm a peasant, from peasants. Where would the world be without peasants?" is both boast and self-deprecation. He grew up among people who tempered fear of the future only with a desire for more money.

So, at some moments, Franz turns away from the banal reality of China—Chinatown—it's the same thing for him. The village culture of China reminds him of Hartford, Connecticut, where he grew up. China, Chinatown, is a civilization of the valley. Generations sleeping together in a few small rooms; fat and fur; carnal knowledge; suspicion of the world outside the family. ("Whereas Tibet—Tibet is visionary, a place of nomads, people of the mountains; they see more than what is in front of their faces.")

His house in Hartford was a house of immigrants. His father was too timid to learn to drive. As a boy, Franz hung maps on the walls of his bedroom and dreamed of escape. Schurmann's memories of childhood are voices—the awkward English sounds of his parents and relatives. Only an American kid can be so embarrassed. Only an American kid would entertain such a vision of himself advancing. His family's accents represented all that restricted him. Language—linguistic assurance—would be his passport. At eighteen, Franz left the maps on the wall for the army and then Harvard, traveling through thousands of books, entering the languages of the world.

Franz speaks of the war years as liberating, the chance to travel. Of course, he would end up in California. In the 1950s, it seemed to him that every traveler in America was headed for California.

Movement. The word recurs like a mantra in these pages. A holy word. A textual freshet. A good. "I don't think there is anything more extraordinary in the contemporary world than the unending movement of people."

After one of our lunches, we walk along Stockton Street in China-town, jostled by quilted, padded bodies, assaulted by smells of mothballs and garlic and by the quacking of grandmothers. "Biology," Franz says triumphantly—indicating the movement of peoples—stopping, half-turning in the street, he momentarily diverts the current of humanity, which now flows round us and re-closes: "Biology."

"Biology," in the Franz Schurmann lexicon, is a way of talking about life at the bottom—the crowd, the poor, the peasant, the stew of humanity. The "South" is another metaphor—in counterdistinction to the "North" (settled nations of the Northern Hemisphere where pale, reasonable people speak quietly in large rooms about overpopulation). The North is also the "state." By the "state," Franz means to imply all who are on top—the government planners, the academics, the politicians, the Founding Fathers.

The florescence of California in the 1950s was biological, a triumph of energy from the bottom, bubbling up—a triumph of "society" over the state. In the 1950s and 1960s, Professor Schurmann concerned himself only with "higher things"—politics and matters of state. Not coincidentally, he lived in a house in the Berkeley hills. He was a renowned professor of sociology and history, an antiwar activist, traveling throughout Southeast Asia. He says, from the distance of this afternoon's Chinese restaurant, that the state in the 1950s and 1960s was capable of much that was evil and much that was good.

The state materialized the California Dream of the 1950s. Politicians in Sacramento built freeways allowing individual ambitions free range; the University of California system was expanded to promote meritocracy. Politicians even made water run uphill.

By the time I met Franz, in the early 1980s, he was already turning away from the academic career. No longer the participant at international conferences, no longer "sucking at the teat of New York foundations." Intellectually, as well as bodily, Franz drifted from Berkeley, which had come to represent stasis to him—"the sifting of information; nothing to do with knowledge."

Franz moved across the bay to San Francisco. With Orville Schell, he founded the Pacific News Service. In its earliest years, PNS had an academic cast and a leftist political stance.

Franz became a walker in San Francisco during those years. The city of small shops and small businesses, of jostle and endeavor, mesmerized him. San Francisco was becoming an Asian city.

"God was moving his wand from the realm of the state to the realm of society." When Franz speaks in this way, he is not echoing the Berkeley leftist for whom society is an odorless abstraction. For Franz Schurmann, society is abrasive and noisy, carries a bag full of cheap oranges, steals your seat on the bus. The realm of society includes the dry cleaner, the bus driver, the waitress ("ooh-wahhh") with her trolley of hot pork buns.

Franz is unlike any intellectual I've known. He seems to find everyone he meets worth listening to. He listens to my parents as he listens to a Pakistani journalist. He regards the priest with the same awe that he holds for the Filipina midwife. Everyone a teacher; everyone a student, . . . which is not to say he cannot pull an academic diva out of his bag on occasion.

We first met at a party. We talked about Mexico City. His wife, Sandy, borrowed five dollars from me. When we next met, weeks later, the first thing Franz asked about was the five dollars. Had Sandy repaid me? (She hadn't.) Franz embodies the working-class scruple. Five bucks is five bucks. Before we could become friends that transaction had to be put to rest.

When I walk with him, he is always reading shop signs and peering through the windows of restaurants; a sucker for churches. Years ago, in Hartford, "doing lower things" meant staying home and hanging around in the street. Now, he does much the same thing, though walking is also the occasion for thought.

Chinatown in San Francisco is a continent away from Hartford. Franz never forgets that most Chinese kids hate Chinatown and want to get out. Freedom and confinement often have the same address, he reminds me. Within this irony is the dialectic that has preoccupied Franz for the last decade. How to understand stasis and movement.

"I love to walk the same streets again and again. How un-American! I have become a place-bound person."

The wanderer has an address. He lives on 29th Avenue on a charmless block, near the leaden sea. ("I have always wanted a room facing west where I could work.") It is the same street my parents live on, a middle-class neighborhood that has become an immigrant neighborhood.

Franz writes: "In 1970, my international traveling more or less stopped. Two years later my first son was born. I was forty-six years old at the time. Soon I started walking with the baby, going ever longer distances." Franz was not merely walking, he was traveling. He was teaching himself Arabic and Spanish as he pushed the pram through the city.

The U.S.A. is in decline. America—the dream, the ideology—is triumphant all over the world. California in 1994 is luring immigrants from Asia and Latin America. Native-born Californians (the children of the 1950s) worry about the future. The University of California system is crowding with "Asian whiz kids." The University of California is running out of money. Eminent professors are offered "early retirement." Thus did Franz Schurmann retire from the Department of Sociology and History last year, the same year he traveled at last and for the first time to his beloved China.

Only to return to say: "It was okay, but now I'm more interested in Latin America—the final things."

What makes *American Soul* such a distinctive book is precisely the knowledge that comes from 29th Avenue. It is not a book written in a high tower. It is not a book of abstractions . . . Well, it is, but ideas are always redeemed by mundane considerations. This book comes from a life that is lived, not conjectured, not graphed, not extrapolated or poled. Picture Thomas Aquinas with a wife and two kids. The *summa* of the diaper pail: slamming doors and shouting matches, ringing phones and bad report cards, and *You forgot to get the goddamn birthday candles.*

It is Franz Schurmann's great fortune that he was brought down from the Berkeley hills by this tribe of savages, his family. These are the ruminations of a father with two sons, about whom he frets like a mother-dog. These are the ruminations of a father with two sons who have two dogs, and an extended family of Filipinos with improbable names, living close by.

The book exemplifies a mind's movement toward God. No observation or argument is knotted on the underside of the text or weighted with footnotes in standard academic fashion. The design flows—permutations and transmigrations of rumination spiral and swirl, like the summer fog off the Pacific, flowing from Asia toward 29th Avenue.

Secular readers will feel betrayed by the religious conclusion, annoyed by Schurmann's reliance on the existence of soul, especially because he will not use that word metaphorically.

Over lunch, Franz will tell you that he disowns his academic life and the books he wrote. But the mature ambition of *American Soul* has Franz looking for the unity of his own life. The task of these final years of the twentieth century, he says, is to to reconcile the state and society. What that means for his own life is to see his life whole. How is Hartford related to Berkeley? Chinatown to China? Or China to heaven? How is it that Franz Schurmann, the antiwar activist, who later wrote an apology for the Nixon years, would end up, like a comic character in an Indian novel, reading the Bombay newspaper in the isolated comfort of a warm bathtub, steeped in banality, oblivious to the pounding at the door?

I remember the day our favorite dim sum restaurant on Pacific Avenue closed. (The closure had been rumored for weeks throughout Chinatown.) On that last day we went to lunch and spent much of the afternoon talking, talking in the manner of this book, which is a pretty accurate approximation of Franz Schurmann's conversation.

Around four o'clock, Franz abruptly stood up, said his Chinese good-byes. He tipped the waiters and waitresses extravagantly. (The peasant's ultimate tribute.) Life is impermanent, the great saints try to teach us. That, and movement is pilgrimage. The man who had traveled the world in imagination, in text, and in body, finally wept at the closing of the Chinese restaurant on Pacific Avenue. This was his parish, his club, his British Museum.

"Okay," he said. "Let's go"—barging out into the late afternoon sunlight.

Richard Rodriguez
July 1994

AMERICAN SOUL

✧

INTRODUCTION

In the 1970s a sense of America's decline began to spread among American intellectuals. To those on the left—where I positioned myself—the decline seemed inexorable, a postmodernist drifting.

These same intellectuals earlier had excoriated an America whose imperialist reach had led to the Vietnam tragedy. After Vietnam, that image was succeeded by one of an America in decline.

In *Logic of World Power* (1974) I examined how America had wielded its power in the world, particularly during the 1950s and 1960s. The sequel to that book, *The Foreign Politics of Richard Nixon*, theorized that America's role had shifted from hegemony to centrality, meaning that America was the chief unifying force in the world. My globalist view of America was quite the opposite of the nationalism implied in the view of an America in decline, which holds that America's importance and direction are waning. The globalist view, however, holds that America continues to have importance and give direction in world history, although its role is changing. I felt converging leftism and nationalism were moving in one direction while my own globalist and universalist views were moving in another.

In the 1970s neoconservatives vigorously disputed the notion of an America in decline and preached a militant globalism intended to spread American ideals—primarily democracy and free-market economics—throughout the world. Libertarian in economic inclination but politically authoritarian, the neoconservatives believed that the latent American pioneer spirit only had to be unbound to fly again.

During the 1980s the Thatcher-Reagan revolution seemed to confirm the neoconservative position. The American economy revived;

yuppie elites emerged. The arms race fueled by Reaganite re-armament, along with the Soviet Union's "Vietnam" in Afghanistan, they believed, were crucial factors in breaking the back of the "evil empire."

I was attracted to the neoconservative affirmation that America was not in postmodernist decline and to their stress on the market, which shifted the locus of creativity away from the state to society. But their neohegemonism, which was linked to the conservatives' traditional awe of authority, did not appeal to me.

Libertarians hate and distrust authority, while conservatives love their kings and presidents. Libertarian and conservative inclinations co-exist uneasily within the American right. I distinguish *power*—the capacity to force compliance from others—from *authority*—compliance given willingly by people to those whom they hold in awe. I think the state is losing authority. When neoconservatives talked about authority, they really meant power, raising the image of hegemonism in rawest form.

In the 1980s Francis Fukuyama came out with his "end of history" thesis. He held that history had reached a pinnacle where all the principles had been found and what remained was only to implement them. That meant finishing the task of spreading American civilization over the world.

My gut reaction to that thesis was disagreement. I believed history was a continuing flow of collective human experience from past through present into the future. How could it end? The collapse of communism was only the end of a chapter. But upon reflection I realized that in one sense history did end; it ended for the state. The modern state has been shaped for over two hundred years by Enlightenment ideals and American action. American civilization is the product of the modern state. It has been spreading downward from a higher plane of great European theory and magnificent American praxis.

I regard the state as consisting of government as well as the vast public sector that includes "the information society." The great domain in which information is produced—schools, media, entertainment, and so on—is a central part of the state.

American civilization has lost soul. By *soul* I mean a force that gives direction. Individuals with a sense of direction feel themselves moving on a path of meaning in their lives and possibly beyond; people who have a sense of direction feel themselves going along with history. The possession of soul therefore is a sign of the flow of history. When soul is lost or exhausted life consists only of the interplay of body and mind. There is no future.

American civilization began with an enormous force of soul, unleashed by Europe's far- and deep-reaching religious, intellectual, and revolutionary movements. But as modern civilization yearned more and more for stasis, it lost that soul force. When the state, particularly under socialism and welfare capitalism, became the chief instrument of settling everything down, it moved toward ending its own movement, thereby producing an end to its own history.

Until the mid-seventies virtually all my writing had been on the state. I am a sociologist and historian by profession, a sinologist by training. In *Ideology and Organization in Communist China* (published in 1966), I analyzed what I believed was a radical transformation of society by a revolutionary state. The mandate given by history to modernism was the transformation of entire societies through states operating from the top down.

My political philosophy changed radically in the aftermath of the Vietnam war. I lost my awe of the state even in its relatively benign form in America. I began to regard society as a great creative force. My viewpoint has been influenced by Chinese thinking—undoubtedly strengthened by the fact that I have long lived in San Francisco, soon to have an Asian majority. China is like a massive sun exerting powerful gravitational attraction on all who come into contact with it. It is the oldest continuous civilization. Its long history has been shaped by a continuing philosophical concern with the interaction of state, society, and the individual.

Although I have only recently made my first visit to China, China has come to where I live. The entire west coast of North America is becoming part of a vast Asian-Pacific region whose contours are being shaped by a melding of American civilization with a renaissance of the great East Asian civilizations, especially that of China.

The great achievement of Chinese civilization is its melding of state and society. And in that melding, society has primacy. Third century B.C. Chinese philosopher Mencius wrote, "People are the roots." For more than two thousand years Chinese leaders have always kept this teaching in their minds even when they violated it in practice.

Taoist thinking, strongly associated with the *Tao Te Ching* of Lao-tzu, is concerned not with roots but with unending movement. Though often thought of in Western stereotypes as an immense, static civilization, China has a history of great movements of people and ideas. The intermingling of Confucianism and Taoism throughout Chinese history has been marked by a search for harmony between rest and movement.

American civilization has produced movement on a scale the world had not seen before. But the ideal of this civilization—evident in the character of the "American Dream"—has become one of settling down, of peace—to replicate the stability of the village on a much higher plane. Marx called it *communism*. But in this postmodern, postindustrial world, movement occurs on a scale not even imagined a few decades ago. The notion of a place—having a fixed address—is increasingly obsolete. The mammoth scale of migration is an indicator of a new human condition. The home is being replaced by the house.

If there are no longer to be homes, we end up homeless. Direction reduces to accelerating circular movement driving individuals and peoples mad. The madness will vanish only when a sense of history and a belief in the future return.

States guided by American civilization have performed impressively when they had a sense of flowing with history. America did so in the nineteenth and through much of the twentieth century with the notion of "manifest destiny."

History may in the end only be for those who imagine themselves in higher planes, above ordinary mortals, reaching upward to the state and higher. In society, people seek rest, a sense of belonging, roots. It has been the genius of Chinese civilization to seek the melding of rest and movement at the lower plane. For Confucius the process began with the self-consciousness of every individual, then continued with society, and finally revitalized the state with a sense of history or "divine mandate." He described the process as "first knowing oneself, then ordering the family, and finally making the realm peaceful."

By the mid-1980s I felt more than just a new chapter of history was beginning for the world—a new book was about to be written. This book begins at a time when there have come into being a world economy, a world culture, a world consciousness. In this new "world-oneness," history's new book is formed by the melding of an already older American civilization with a newer one, growing up in East Asia and elsewhere in what once was called the third world. In this new history, society will initially be more important than the state. History's challenge is to meld social formations with the unending movement that will remain a mark of the human condition well into the next century. The new roots will move as roots have moved, contrary to Western stereotypes, for so long in Chinese history.

The West responded to the challenge of movement with individualism. East Asia is responding by meshing society with movement. And, in the Confucian spirit, once endlessly wandering individuals believe if they know themselves and their families are ordered, then peace can be made in the realm of the state.

If that response succeeds, then—as happened in China—the new states of the next century too will regain a sense of direction and meaning and a future. And if the new states are local, national, and global, they may be very different from the kind of massively bureaucratized architectural states we now see around us.

When I first wrote in earlier books about America's centrality it was only with a vague sense that America would continue to be a key force in world history. Now, after having further thought about two key founders of American civilization, Jefferson and Hamilton, I realize that the two currents they left behind have been pulling America in opposite directions.

Hamilton—indeed, the whole strip of thirteen colonies on the Atlantic seaboard—looked to Europe. Jefferson looked westward with imperialistic eyes. America sought to dominate those it found to the west, crushing the Indians, sweeping the Mexicans aside, and taming East Asian empires. Jefferson (toward whose current I was drawn) was a republican, a democrat, an imperialist—political attitudes more closely connected than I had previously thought. With imperialism now waning, many conservatives, liberals, and globalists have become politically nationalistic, often without losing their cultural imperialism.

I was attracted to Jefferson's grandeur. I felt the tragedy of Hamilton's life (he died insolvent, leaving a widow and seven children behind) but did not consider him important. Later in life during my travels, I began to become fascinated by trade and money. I realized they were central to ancient, medieval, and modern empires. I began to see Hamilton in a different light. Born in the then rich Antilles, fluent in French, and brilliant in his understandings of trade and money, he was so convincing in his advocacy of a strong federalist government to assure a sound currency and a prosperous trade that the resisting states accepted the controversial new constitution. Many discussions of empire in this book reflect a Jeffersonian influence, but the spirit of chapter seven, "Capital," is essentially Hamiltonian.

Hamilton looked not only eastward toward England and Europe, but also southward toward the Caribbean. Those islands, now so impoverished, were then the richest parts of the Western Hemisphere. The triangular trade between England, the Antilles, and the American colonies mainly benefited the former. Hamilton advocated strong government, active trade, and sound currency so that the new United States would be the main beneficiary.

I started looking southward in the 1970s because new social forces were arising throughout the "South." I was fascinated by the rising tide of religion in the South and began to see all great religions as southern in origin. The children of Israel were southern, as were the Arabs from whom Islam arose. Confucius melded northern rationality with southern spirituality. Lao-tzu's taoism is southern. The Hindu religion is southern. The evangelical sweep of Latin America and the Caribbean is southern. The spread of Islam in the United States, especially among people of African descent, is southern. This tide sends a message to postmodernist American civilization: for all its brilliance and despite the attractions of "civil society," it cannot ignore the worldwide rise of religion and the attendant rebuilding of society.

Maybe it is historically significant that both Jefferson and Hamilton were southerners. Even today much of the American South is still called the "Bible Belt" religion and trade remains the lifeline of the Caribbean peoples. For the past five thousand years the single richest part of the world were those lands lying along the shores of the Indian Ocean. That wealth came through trade.

I see American secularism—shaped by European intellectuals after the French Revolution—as northern. Secularism and the state go together, but so do religion and society.

Through trade-driven diplomacy an "Asia-Pacific" world, comparable to that of common-market Europe, is coming into being. If America allows itself to become part of that new world, it can learn to value society as it now values the individual and the public sector (the state). And then it will be able to use society to meet its challenges as it now uses the state and the power of individuals.

But the smaller America (the U.S.A.) is also becoming integrated with the larger America of the Western Hemisphere. South-of-the-border states are not strong nor are its societies. Below Latin America's states and societies inherited from Iberia lies a past embedded in Native American soil. Religion is very much a part of Latin America's past and its present. The rapid spread of evangelical Christianity may be linked to that soil's receptivity to religion. And in the Caribbean and Brazil, Africa has seeded that soil with its own religions.

If America looks eastward, then history will indeed have ended for America. If it looks westward and southward, then a new book of history will begin, and America will have a central place in that book.

PART I

AMERICANS

Americans are a distinct people, easily recognizable sauntering along anywhere in the world. They may be brown or white or black or yellow or red, but they are unmistakably American. Maybe newly naturalized Americans have difficulty passing, but few of their children will.

One can see Americanization happening in immigrant kids six or seven years of age. The language their parents chatter becomes jerky in their mouths; the sentences become hybrid, filled with Americanisms. Soon enough, the kids respond in English when the parents address them in the old language. A little later, the kids wish the parents would just speak English as other parents do.

It is not only a conquest of language—their gestures, looks, behavior become American. They'll dress in faded jeans and walk with a limp look that's supposed to shroud an inner toughness. The kids will act as if they own the place. And they'll be disgusted by their parents in a way few children in other cultures would.

Today's immigrant kids, like those I grew up with in Hartford, Connecticut, are moving fast at early ages to become part of the American race. In my childhood we did not think of this process in racial terms, for there were few blacks and browns around to compare ourselves to. Rich people, whom we heard about but rarely saw, were supposed to be unique. They weren't even fully American, maybe. (The Amish still refer to Americans as "the English.")

By becoming American we triumphed over our bumbling parents. They could not respond to us in the tongue of that powerful people and place—American English.

To anyone who travels, it is remarkable how Americanized the world has become. I saw in an Arab magazine from Kuwait a picture of the Nairobi airport, with hundreds of tourists, almost all white. It was not the fact that they were white in a black country that struck me, but how similar the airport and the people looked to what one sees in the San Francisco airport.

Why are so many people all over the world aping Americans? In Germany they play at being cowboys. In Japan they sing country and western music. That is only on the surface, one might say. Deep down they remain German or Japanese or what have you. Yet the surface is where American civilization resides. And, as mathematicians have shown, a simple trick can turn a volume equation into one of surfaces, and vice versa. Americans are a conquering people—they conquered the Germans and the Japanese. Perhaps it is inevitable that the conquered mimic their conquerors.

A CONQUERING PEOPLE, AN IMMENSE CIVILIZATION

Throughout history conquering peoples have been imitated. Consider Muhammad's new converts, who stormed out of the desert trading town of Mecca to conquer much of Asia, Europe, and Africa. In a short time an obscure Semitic tongue, Arabic, became a world language. Even more startling, the religion Muhammad founded garnered millions of converts, even though the early Muslims saw themselves as a small elite whose proudest possession was the faith revealed to them.

The Chinese like to think of themselves as a peaceful people, yet their might has expanded in all cardinal directions save north. They too were imitated. Ultimately the Chinese so impressed the multifarious conquered that the latter abandoned their old ways. The Romans spread their language throughout the western Mediterranean and even into eastern Europe, Dacia, modern Romania. And the mighty Bantu spread across Africa with their superior agricultural technology and convinced those whom they conquered to adopt the Bantu language and Bantu ways. (The Mongols were an exception; they conquered much of the civilized world in the thirteenth century but left behind no civilization.)

Americans have created and spread an immense civilization that is garnering more and more converts worldwide. Americans are like the Romans and the Chinese, forever struggling to make others more like themselves. The American middle class, with its consumer affluence, its beckoning to every person to become an individual ("to be oneself"), and its great public arena of participation in street, forum, cultural, political, and state life, is the single most powerful cultural force in the world.

After World War II, it was common for American tourists to be treated with extraordinary deference when they traveled abroad. If the American tried a few phrases of the indigenous language, broad smiles of appreciation would follow. Americans were never arrested—it would be bad for the tourist business. If an American broke his leg in a car accident it made the news. Americans were special.

In the world pecking order, Americans still remain on top, though others rank highly too. Western Europeans do, by virtue of their history as conquerors and the nineteenth-century elevation of white skin to high status. Japanese are not white, but have fought their way to the top (in South Africa they have long been "honorary whites"). Israelis, too, are up there: when one of them dies it makes news, but it is only news when at least a hundred Palestinians die. We know that when killer cyclones roar from the Bay of Bengal into Bangladesh, hundreds, even thousands, may die, and that makes the news, usually on inside pages.

But Americans are different from Japanese in one important way. Outsiders cannot become Japanese, as many Koreans have discovered. Only Jews, really, can become Israelis. But anybody can become American. In this Americans again resemble the Romans and the Chinese. No outsider could become a Mongol, but anyone, almost, was able to become Roman (Paul of Tarsus was a Roman because his father, a Jew, became Roman). Almost anyone can become Chinese. Likewise, Islam is surely the most open of all creeds (so many blacks have become Muslim because they find it a creed freer from racism than any other in the world).

In Africa, black Americans are Americans first, and then black. In Israel, American Jews stand out from the others; many are shrill. In Japan, the Japanese who have been to school only in America are dismissed as "Americans." Mexicans born or long resident in the United States are called *pocho* in Mexico, meaning thin, washed-out Mexicans. Russian immigrants, arriving in increasing numbers, are eager to become infected with the strains of American civilization.

The world is full of examples of people who, for many generations, have lived among other peoples and barely understood their neighbors' language. Eastern Europe used to be full of such minorities. Franz Kafka was a Jew who wrote in German in the city of Prague, which, for him, was a German city. He spoke only a little Czech. How many South African whites speak any Xhosha or Zulu? I remember an old one-legged American in Paris in the late 1940s who had married a Frenchwoman after World War I; he stayed in France and ran a hotel, even during the German occupation. He understood French perfectly but barely spoke it. To him the Americans, his people, were the conquerors, and so theirs was the language to be spoken.

In Israel, many Palestinians speak Hebrew; aside from Jews born in Arab lands, few Jews speak any Arabic other than curses. If you are a member of a conquering people, then you expect the conquered to understand you.

Civilizations take a long time to a rise. Roman civilization grew up over many years from its Greek and Etruscan roots. China's civilization had a long gestation process. Mecca had no distinct civilization, but Islam has deep roots in Judaism, which it resembles, and Christianity. The Mongols had no civilization. American civilization generally had roots in Europe, but in practical terms, meaning how it affects our everyday lives, the roots of the civilization must be understood in terms of the revolution that brought about the entity known as the United States of America.

Our word *civilization* comes from the Latin *civitas,* or city. To be civilized meant to live in a city. Similarly, the Arabic word *hadhara* was used by the fourteenth-century philosopher of history, Ibn Khaldun, and meant "a quality of settled rather than nomadic life." The Chinese word is modern yet characteristically Chinese: *civilization* is "life with writing and enlightenment."

The American Revolution was the first in history that sought to do more than create a new order of power. It thought in broad ways about creating an entirely new and better way of life for people. The notions of life ("quality of life"), liberty ("I want to be myself"), and the pursuit of happiness ("I want it all") became the elements of our civilization. The revolution was about a vision that could be realized here, in this world, now.

In ancient China people were urged to work hard and rulers admonished to go easy on their subjects so that the realm could be enriched. In eighteenth-century France the Physiocrats preached that land was the source of all wealth. But in America the message became: go out and seek wealth. This was a message for would-be conquerors. The Spanish conquistadores went out and stole and killed. The Americans did that too, especially to Indians. But the Revolution also conjured up a vision that hovered in the air, always beckoning. Beckoning to anyone who wanted to try his luck. Anyone could get rich if he or she hustled, moved about, shook things up, played the game.

When I was a kid, we immigrant people thought of Americans as hustlers. They had names beginning with "Mc," and came around peddling insurance. The worst were the hoboes with their American flags. We considered ourselves decent people who worked hard, had nice homes. Who knew what kind of homes the Americans had?

Our Founding Fathers were drenched in the spiritual fermentation of the Enlightenment. That is why the Declaration of Independence became such a visionary document and why the Constitution of the United States of America, far more than that of any other country, acquired a status close to that of the Bible or the Qur'an. Even now in this "postmodernist" age Americans act as if the Constitution is The Book. (Many foreigners do not understand why there are so many lawyers in this country. One reason is that the religious/visionary spirit is so strong here that priesthoods are always arising, and no priesthood has been more durable than that of lawyers, American mullahs who gather their charisma and power from The Book.)

The ancient Romans worshiped Fortuna, the greatest goddess of the early empire; when Americans are lucky, they feel that somehow God has a special plan for them.

Historians would agree that all great civilizations have had mighty religions. We know they were mighty because so many people held them in common, whereas for other peoples religious sentiments, like languages, differ from valley to valley. What is the religion of America? There really is no common religion, unless you accept the accusation of the fundamentalists that it is secular humanism. Secular humanism means that humans, not God, are the source of all values. In America, laws are not only rules, but values as well, a concept intrinsic to the three great western religions: Judaism, Christianity, and Islam. The Book is the source of values, placed there by the representatives of the people, not as a revelation from God.

PEOPLE OF VISION

Of all Americans, Californians are the most visionary, to the point that they have become a joke, a subject of derision to East Coast intellectuals. In California there are no settlers. There are just Americans. Cults abound. Millions of Californians are among the tourists who seek Old Provence, Ancient India, Eternal Rome. Californians are never still.

Americans wear pants so that they can walk fast. (A museum exhibit of the history of American clothing showed how suddenly, after the Civil War, men began wearing clothes fitted for rapid movement, and how suddenly after World War I women began to wear short skirts so that they too could move fast.) In New York people walk fast; in California they jog, ride, hike, move from house to house, partner to partner, job to job. Californians began as gold seekers in 1849; then they came to San Francisco where, in the astonishingly short space of five years or so, more than the outlines of the current city came into being. When water from the Owens Valley was made available, Iowans poured into Los Angeles.

In human life, important things sometimes produce their antagonistic opposites. In San Francisco, "Old Chinatown" is what California is not. China values rest, not movement. That is why so many young Chinese hate Chinatown. Behind its mysterious ideographs is a banality that those who are daunted by them cannot imagine or will not admit. Everything is practical, commonsensical, usually mercenary. Yoichi Shimatsu, a friend, says the West has the tree of knowledge and the East has the tree of life. In Chinatown the tree of life is so full of leaves, bark, boils, gaudy flowers, smelly compost that the language has become rich in words, but not a wisp of a vision thrives. It is common, in Chinatown, to see a Caucasian man sitting alone in a restaurant, looking out the window—maybe tired of movement and seeking rest.

California-style visions are not doctrinaire. They take the form of cults, passions, obsessions, happenings, free-flying imagination. You can worship Satan and not be considered out of the mainstream. You can hike in the mountains and believe you are in and of something religious. In California you do better if you have some kind of vision and let people know you think in such terms.

When I first started teaching at the University of California in the late 1950s, a young student said to me, when I asked her why she was going to Europe: "I am going to find myself." I have forgotten what she looked like except that she seemed Californian. I also remember a learned man remarking that we have only begun to scratch the surface of what it means to be an individual. That is the California vision—the search for the Holy Grail of the self.

If Americans are a conquering breed, then it is in good part due to their technology (the list of lethal and benign technology Americans invented or perfected during World War II is long). All conquerors have had a technological genius. That of the Macedonians and the Mongols was purely military, and so they quickly latched on to other civilizations. But the Romans also had it, as did the Chinese, Japanese, Indians, Incas, Aztecs, and others.

In America technology conjures up for me the image of somebody tinkering with a car in a garage, at night, lit by a single bright lamp. Of course, swarms of researchers, technicians, and workers will then manufacture the technology in "teams," but the American word *team* implies a group that comes and works together for one purpose. When that purpose is accomplished the team dissolves into its component parts—individuals. Vision is translated into product, followed by conquest in the market, and then the visionaries and their soldiers return to everyday life.

American technology is as visionary as it is practical. That has been the American genius. Americans built flying machines, and within a few years we had combat aircraft, and shortly thereafter commercial aircraft. Americans had the visionary drive to land on the moon. Maybe Americans need this magical trinity of the visionary, the practical, and the lethal to keep their technological innovation moving.

Perhaps to be American is to have a flair for the visionary, the practical, and the lethal.

PEOPLE OF MOVEMENT

Like all conquerors, Americans are people of movement. We are nomads; many are also peasants.

The Pilgrims who first came settled around Plymouth, but then some moved on to western Massachusetts, and then on and on, until they settled in Oregon; others went on to Hawaii and Polynesia and—as missionaries and merchants—to China. There are descendants of the Pilgrims who today live in Bangkok.

Could American consumer capitalism have developed if Americans had not been a people on the move? In the post–Civil War period, an American invented and mass marketed the cigarette, and made millions. Cigarettes are for fidgety people whose minds, like their eyes, flick back and forth, people who are ready to get up and dash off somewhere after inhaling a deep breath of smoke.

One of the things that impressed me as a sociologist a long time ago was an article about "succession" in American housing patterns. Americans "move" a lot. (The French say *déménager*, to undo a household.) Immigrants would move to America and settle in houses near the port. As they earned money, they moved farther out. Newer immigrants replaced them. A generation or so later, their grandchildren would move even farther out, while the children of the later immigrants moved into the intermediate zone. And so on. Gradually a stratification could be observed, going from poorest in the oldest homes to the richest in the newest. Sociologists called this "social mobility."

One cannot understand this American urge to move unless one realizes that in history nomad and peasant have been the two great life-style alternatives. In many lands, these were the chief life-style differences: peasants lived in the lowlands, and nomads in and out of the hills. The historic dislike between Chinese and Tibetan is due to this life-style difference. Tibetans are one of the great visionary people of the world, and historically the Chinese were among the least. Christianity, then Westernization, then Marxism, and now American civilization hit the Chinese hard, but starting in the mid-1800s they began developing a visionary streak, different from the old-fashioned antivisionary characteristics.

Why do some people want to move on all the time? Why do Gypsies or Tinkers or the Hmong, who wandered around doing slash-and-burn farming in the Lao-Thai-Burma hills until they ended up in Fresno? Nomads do better in cities than they do among peasants—even nomads who practice farming, as many do. Very few nomads are purely pastoral. For many centuries, as Ibn Khaldun wrote, nomads fought with civilization to shape history. Nomadism is a way of life, a frame of mind, not only a mode of production. It is an addiction to movement. When movement and civilization coincide then visions—individual and collective—often arise.

Even if you are old-stock American, you become fully American only when you enter the middle class. You enter it by moving into it. You are not born into it. If you arrive as an immigrant, you strive to move into the middle class. You are given visions—those of affluent suburban consumer life. Or you can "be yourself," be free, become what you want to become. You can try to make it in the great democratic American public arena, as a doctor, a lawyer, or other professional, and make a name for yourself and your family. You become an American by having fantasies and dreams that you believe you can eventually attain. As children in a worker's family we regarded Americans as different from us because none of us saw himself as special. When you become an American, you become an individual.

In Europe they used to have bourgeoisies. These were the inhabitants of the cities. In Japan, these same people were also bourgeois, the word being *chōnin,* which means townspeople. The chōnin, we were taught in Japanese history courses, were utterly despised by the noble samurai. The samurai had no fear: they saw themselves as the friends of death, a man being at his finest when he prepares to die. The chōnin, however, as portrayed in so many films, were sleazy operators cheating their way through life. Marx's view of the German and French bourgeois was not much different; neither was Balzac's. Yet some Japanese scholars now believe the chōnin did have higher moral, religious, and philosophical concerns. That was, and is, also true of European bourgeois, despite the views of Marx and Balzac.

The American middle class contains the bourgeoisie and the chōnin, but its set contains more. If it didn't, there would be no American civilization. There would have been no American civilization to pour over Japan in the wake of World War II and give rise to a Japanese middle class. The people one sees walking down the Ginza are not modern chōnin. They are people who have roots in that earlier bourgeoisie but have been reshaped by American middle-class civilization. They have visions and fantasies and think and dream about futures. They are taken in by American "secular humanism." In some ways this pseudo-religion, which was and still is driven by forces characteristic of charismatic religion, is shamanistic because it is like a spirit coming into people's bodies and minds that makes them do strange and wonderful things.

Historically Americans have been not only movers—whence have come the visions—but also settlers. In the movies, ranchers and farmers fight with each other. When the moviemakers are in a conservative mood, the farmers are the good guys. But when the moviemakers think heroic, the ranchers are the heroes, their lone cowboys ever wandering like samurai *rōnin* (ones with no lord to serve). Americans want to be both movers and settlers. They want to be both nomad and peasant, like people in "open marriages."

Settlers, by definition, have no roots. They develop roots. But roots take time. Property can be claimed fast. I stake out something and buy it—a legal order, the state, certifies that it is mine. It is surface, not volume, as roots must be. Property gives the illusion of roots but does not necessarily contain them.

Capitalism means attachments to people, things, property. The state recognizes attachments such as marriage, obligations to children, ownership of material things. Governments like to create more and more claims, for, while claims can cost money, they also provide stability, a condition any ruling group wants. But too many claims can stifle innovation, and so it is the genius of American middle-class civilization that it also provides for vision, or "enterprise," which means imagination and generally a cutting loose from roots. Too many roots can be bad for the throbbing of any capitalist system, but too few can be dangerous. And so fears are produced, generated, instilled into people.

Fears are deadly to visions. Those with visions must in a way be unafraid of death. The samurai had only visions, no fears, and he was a loner, an individual making his way into battle; if he came out alive then he walked off into the sunset, just like the cowboy. But those with claims, property, attachments (as the Buddhists say) are terrified of death, loss, pain, being humbled, embarrassed, and so on down the list of things that people—that is middle-class people in their bourgeois aspect—are afraid of.

Politically, Americans are usually divided into liberals and conservatives. And while the words have taken on many connotations different from their root meanings, those root meanings still have force. To be liberal means to seek freedom. To be conservative means to keep intact, stash away, maintain as is. Do I want to say that liberals are movers and conservatives are settlers? Maybe it is the other way around: liberals are settlers and conservatives are movers. I have been struck by how much the old class-oriented left has become taken in by notions of giving people security—helping old folks, the sick, pregnant teenagers, and so on. Those are good, heart-warming, conservative notions. And then Ronald Reagan, in his "conservative" rhetoric, called for more free enterprise, risk taking, communist battling. Reagan looked like a mover, with his full head of dark hair and his athletic torso. Jimmy Carter, despite his jogging, looked like an anguished man, and Walter Mondale looked like a Kwakiutl totem, stuck in the ground. In 1980 Americans voted for the visionary Reagan.

But whoever is what, the sense that this country has oscillated between poles of movement and settlement is old. It goes back to the founding days of the republic, probably farther, deep into the colonial period when those who became Americans appeared to be frontierspeople and loyalists were mainly townspeople, many of whom settled in Canada. Americans were the movers then, and the American British were those who had made a new home here.

SUBURBS AND VILLAGES

The Americans were an unruly bunch, probably quite nasty, maybe not that different from the brawling Australians who turned up in California at the time of the gold rush. But then schemes of settlement arose. President Jefferson sent Zebulon Pike and the famous Lewis and Clark far out into the West, not just to explore and claim territory for the United States but to find land suitable for settlement. *Settler* even became the name of those migrants who headed out West.

Most Americans believe that the home should be defended by arms. America is a heavily armed country. The right to bear arms is written into the Constitution. Hunters abound. Kids love guns. The murder rate is high. A very high percentage of Americans favor the death penalty. Even many liberals came around to supporting the death penalty in the 1970s when they felt crime lapping at their doors.

Real conservatives love the word *authority*. French renegade priest Marcel Lefebvre—he broke with the Vatican over Vatican II—made authority into a keystone of his traditionalist movement (he wanted a return to absolute monarchy). Property needs authority to maintain it (conserve it). There cannot be a middle class without KEEP OUT signs. And behind every KEEP OUT sign there is a frightened man or woman with a gun.

Conquerors must be visionary and brave. Samurais die before they have a chance to become cowardly. The cowboy fades away into oblivion—no one wants to think that he has ended up a middle-class wimp in Peoria. (The Random House dictionary defines wimp as "a weak, ineffectual, dull person—origin uncertain." Could the word have come from Popeye's pudgy, amiable, sponging pal Wimpy? Could Wimpy have been Popeye's alter ego, another *I* who walks alongside? Are the hero and the coward two sides of the same coin?)

Let us remember historically how bourgeoisies were formed. They arose as merchants and created wealth, which then drew peasants into the cities where they became artisans. The artisans wanted to reproduce their villages, but this time in wealth and not poverty. We can see this process in the way Japan's brilliant urban civilization arose. In its Japanese reading, the Sino-Japanese character for *chō* (whence *chōnin*, "bourgeois") is also pronounced "machi." The ideograph represents a strong man next to a rice field. Every Japanese city is full of *machi*, neighborhoods that make up the grid of a city map (there are no street names, so every address is a number in a neighborhood in a ward in a district, and the numbers are not arranged in any numerical fashion). So the memory of the village is built into the reality of modern urban Japan.

What are suburbs but attempts to create a village in wealth rather than poverty? Kids play outside on the grass-lined sidewalks with parents who hope it will be like some village four generations ago in Bohemia where everybody knew everybody else. The grass is as green as it was in Bohemia, but there is no smell of shit. And the kids dream of leaving it for New York City, where all is movement and there is no rest, or need for it.

This is the peasant side of America, and in this respect American bourgeoisies are little different from those anywhere else. They give the illusion of stability, yet unlike peasants who know what killing is from marauding soldiers, suburbanites only fear it could happen and do everything they can to make themselves secure. They are people of fear who work hard, think hard, and generate the immense energy that filled out American civilization. They are the "silent majority" of Nixon's Vice-President Spiro Agnew.

America's royalty—movie stars—are movement people. They are glamorous and witty and are always doing something new and interesting, such as showing up with new mates. They are like the nomads who appeared on the exquisite Persian miniatures of the thirteenth century, going on hunts, disporting themselves in palaces. As in India, where every member of a lower class worships those a rung above, in America the lower classes crave the middle classes' security, and the middle classes want to be movie stars and roam around on stunning steeds, to be elegant ladies eyeing handsome heroes.

The American throb is still there, a craziness that erupts again and again even as suburban fear seeks to quash it or turn it around by making it comical (as in television shows.) Blacks have given America an immense dose of movement and genius. And what about WASPs? The electrical current from their Pilgrim forebears still vibrates as they continue to seek and feel with an astonishing universality, aspire to royalty and beyond, and remain a conscience and consciousness for the country. The danger of decline is there, but the throb remains, and with that the urge to keep moving, to find a new direction.

THE AMERICAN DREAM

The people I lived among growing up were mostly immigrants, and most of them had a "nationality" that was not American. "Americans" lived farther away in the better parts of town, and they had English names. In high school I got to know some of these Americans. One or two became friends. When I visited their homes I noticed that their parents spoke differently from the way my parents spoke.

I guessed that these Americans came from old stock—ultimately, I supposed, from England. They lived in nice houses but clearly were not rich. They just seemed fundamentally decent in a way my people did not. They seemed to say and do the right things.

I sensed that Americans, unlike other people, were involved with higher things; and while I admired that, I felt a kind of tribal loyalty to being with "lower" people and doing "lower" things. Even later, when I did "higher" things, I still clung to the "lower," as I do now. Doing lower things means staying home and hanging around in the street. Doing higher things means heading out, and the farther out you go the more alone you become and the riskier it gets—but maybe there is a pot of gold at the end of the rainbow.

Like most countries, the United States has more or less definable regions. There is the South, New England, the Midwest, Texas, the Southwest, the West, and the Northwest. And then there is California.

CALIFORNIA DREAMING

When people think about the region of their birth, they often become nostalgic. Region connotes roots, as does the thought of the "old country" for immigrants. But when people think of California they rarely become nostalgic. California is special. Its air is different. It is like a promised land even to those who have lived in it for a long time.

Geographically, California is almost a self-contained nation. Great mountains separate it from Nevada, whose own near-total desert surface separates it from other states. In California's southwest, deserts separate it from Arizona, which once was largely desert as well. Its northern parts remain thinly populated and forested, melding into another thinly populated state, Oregon. One has to go much further north to come to another major settled region, the Portland-Seattle-Tacoma area. California, however, is unique. It is the classic land of the American Dream.

Is Burgundy a dream for the French, or Szechwan for the Chinese? No; rather they are memories, beautiful ones in both cases. To the modern tourist, Burgundy seems rich and its capital, Dijon, splendid. And most literate Chinese remember Tang poetry with its evocations of a rich province that goes from fertile plains to towering mountains. But even as a recollection California remains a dream. To Americans for whom California is a memory (by which I mean a serious concern with the past), it is in all likelihood a bad memory. California is fresh like newly picked lettuce, but lettuce spoils fast, and so does California. California does not age well.

The suburb was invented in California; it spread from there to the rest of the country and then to many foreign countries. White South Africa now lives largely in suburbs. The blacks are crowded into "townships," with the other races somewhere in the interstices. American-style suburbs have arisen around European cities and even in Japan, modified to fit into the jumbled real estate patterns of nations with long histories. Manila boasts a typical American suburb, Forbes Park.

California is a special place, but it is not like Burgundy or Szechwan. It is an American place with no American past and a future that is already evident in the present. Suburbs have no past, only a present, and the hint of a future that will be much like the present.

Despite all the sincere devotion to racial equality, Americans, like most people, like to live among their own. And if they are white, they want to live alongside whites who are like themselves, as little different from them as possible. So they decide to live in suburbs, where, surprisingly, housing is often much cheaper than in cities. When they shop in the shopping malls, they are part of a sea of white faces and figures doing familiar things, smiling and grimacing in familiar ways.

The suburb is a place where white people can settle down to something like an older small town. They may sally forth regularly, often on long commutes, but they can come back at night, sink into a comfortable chair, and know they are among their own kind.

Although Americans are fearful, restless, and endlessly on the move, as one can see from traffic congestion growing at an exponential rate, they also crave rest. They want to settle down. Americans divorce a lot, but they like to remarry. After working all day outside the home they like returning to the peace and warmth of a house with polished wood, smells of a gently browned roast from the kitchen, maybe the sound of one kid coming from the den, a well-behaved dog or cat curled up in front of the fire, and no phone calls. Home is where bodies can relax and minds can empty themselves of all thoughts except those that tickle intellectually or sensually.

That is what the American Dream promises—a house, a car, health, and enough self-respect to convince you that what you have and are is legitimate. You are entitled to your comfort. California invented that promise, though it borrowed the elements for implementing the promise from elsewhere—for example, from Detroit, which gave us mass-produced automobiles.

Burgundy and Szechwan were rich places, but they never promised wealth and privilege to any other than their own kind. California is a rich place and promises wealth and comfort to all who come (although now it is wavering on that promise). California imported the European concept of comfort (which was for the privileged, of course, as in fancy, expensive hotels) and promised it to all. You can have a nice house in the suburbs, own several cars, and look and feel decent enough to enjoy what you have gained without getting ulcers.

MOVEMENT AND REST, CALIFORNIA-STYLE

When non-Indian people first came to northern California, they tried to make money by panning for gold. When Iowans started pouring into southern California in the 1880s, they too came to make money. But the white immigrants coming into California were also part of that great stream of settlers who had been going from east to west ever since the Pilgrims first landed on American shores. Settlement was spurred by land grants such as the Homestead Act, which was passed by the Union Congress during the Civil War to spur military enlistment.

People migrated not just to keep moving, but to settle down. The speed with which the settling down occurred in California can be traced from early pictures of San Francisco. Until 1849 San Francisco was just Yerba Buena, "good grass," a small Mexican settlement on the bay. Six years later much of downtown San Francisco had the outlines it has today. A decade later it had become a major city, a place for wandering performers to come to and make money. Old photographs show solid citizens watching them.

Cities throughout history have been marvelous combinations of movement and rest. When markets were finally allowed inside them, the swirling of commerce became part of the daily life of city people. But when city people began to build solid houses not just for the wealthy but for ordinary burghers as well, and even for some poorer people, they showed a common desire for settling down. Already by the early 1860s it seemed San Franciscans wanted to show they were settling down, quitting their rowdy past.

And by the 1860s thousands of Americans had also settled in California valleys to farm. There was no water, and makeshift irrigation had to be devised; later, a program of waterworks stretching over much of the state was begun, which has made of California the most stupendous example in the world of large-scale irrigation. If peasant populations in the world have become fruitful, it is in part because water has been made available to them, by their own efforts or some external agency such as a benign government. Nomads, however, must search out water, and so they wander with their flocks and their kids in tow.

In the late 1800s great waterworks were built to bring water from the Owens Valley to Los Angeles. That was the beginning of the American Dream. The water fed the farming, the farming created wealth, and the wealth overflowed into real estate developments out of which the suburbs arose, radiating out in ever wider circles from the small Mexican quarter in downtown Los Angeles. The Los Angeles landscape presents an aerial sight of millions of small one-family houses with greenery around them, a palm tree or two in the front yard, and so much sunshine. "It never rains." And then early in this century came the car.

If water made settlement on a large scale possible throughout the southern California desert, the arrival of the automobile early in this century started the creation of a civilization based on a union of settlement and movement. Collusion between the new and fast-growing Detroit automobile companies and those who had power in Los Angeles succeeded in wrecking the city's great rail mass transit system, built when water first came. The schemers wanted to get people to live in suburbs and buy cars to get back and forth between home and ever more distant work.

In this way the second element of the Dream was added. You could now move in an American way, speeding along endless freeways, all the way down to San Diego or Bakersfield. You could know that there always was a home—if not a real home then a home away from home: a motel, also a California invention.

When Alexis De Tocqueville visited America in the 1830s most Americans lived in small towns. Neither villages nor cities as in Europe, they seemed to combine the best of both: the freedom and self-sense of bourgeois and the rootedness of villagers. But life in small American towns bogged down, especially as so many peasants from Germanic countries flocked to the United States. The Germans, the Dutch, and the Scandinavians became solid farmers all over the Midwest and gave many of the rural towns they settled into a village flavor. Even today many can trace their roots in those towns back for several generations.

The New England towns were different. There the townspeople continued to be restless—maybe because big cities were closer by than in the Midwest—and wherever they migrated they brought that yearning for movement with them. The suburbs that arose rapidly in the Los Angeles region at the beginning of the century were modeled after small Iowa towns that had origins in Yankee New England towns as well as in the villages of central Europe. The new Los Angeles suburbs had spacious green lawns. They had the space of rambling farmhouses. They had something really innovative: garages for automobiles. And in Los Angeles more and more of them had swimming pools. They looked rural, which was understandable in that much of the region was agricultural at the time. They were close to new roads with that alluring smell of fresh tar. They reveled in water.

In addition, California understood that the new vision had to feature bodies and minds. Beautiful people. Clever people. The movies showed stunning women and men, not just with fine speech and intriguing eyes but with a sense of certainty, of knowing who they were. They were idolized in movie theaters all over the world. In Los Angeles, where the sun shone all the time, you were supposed to look beautiful, especially with a bathing suit on your sun-bronzed body. You were supposed to talk with wit, assurance; to never be gloomy; to always talk as if you were on the move and in control. If you could achieve that, then you not only got respect from other Californians, you also began to respect yourself. You never stood straight, but you walked with flair.

The house, the car, and the perfect individual. That was the California Dream out of which the American Dream grew. That was the higher life in America, an ideal that California opened up not just to an aristocracy, old and new, but to everyone. Just as sex, the supreme experience of joined body and mind, was available to everyone, so was the California Dream.

IMPERIAL CALIFORNIA

In the 1920s a number of Marxist scholars, influenced by a renegade communist named Karl August Wittfogel, argued that all societies did not evolve through the same stages, as their grand totem, Karl Marx, had taught. There were Asian empires that developed quite differently from Europe. And the key factor making for the difference, Wittfogel wrote, was the existence in those societies of great state-controlled waterworks. Marx once wrote that there might be an aberrant formation he dubbed an "Asiatic mode of production," and Wittfogel obediently used that term to describe such societies. Those societies, such as China or India or Mesopotamia, had certain common characteristics. They were marked by political centralization and a high degree of bureaucratization, and they were imperial.

The last place Wittfogel might have thought his thesis applied would have been easy-going, democratic California. The empires he wrote about were all despotic. How could California governors be considered despots? But California has one of the most powerful, extensive, and centralized governments of the fifty states in the United States. California has a government that is much like that of an independent nation. Like those Asian empires, it gained much of its power through its control of water. And its unassuming political demeanor masks a true imperial self-consciousness.

California's government acquired that power by acting as a grand builder of large-scale infrastructures of waterworks, transportation, education. In fact more than any other state, California as it exists today is in good part the creation of government. The ancient Asian empires made the deserts bloom. So has California's government. Without that grand building few people would have come to live in a state that was half desert and half wild mountainous regions.

The gold-crazy adventurers who came to California in 1849 were headstrong individualists. But a few decades later powerful political figures in Los Angeles and Sacramento started the process of using government to build a paradise, a task that many Easterners and Europeans believed would be possible only under a socialist regime. The key move was the great engineering project that brought water from the Owens Valley to the Los Angeles desert. That started a century of building that saw great dams go up, that covered the state with irrigation canals, that created the most extensive network of motor roads in the United States, that pioneered "freeways," meaning grand highways for the use of which motorists did not have to pay tolls as they did in the East, and that gave the state the world's first academic empire, the University of California.

Government made the California Dream, and later government would make the American Dream as well. During the 1920s when all of America was rollicking in fun during what seemed to be an unending economic boom, the California paradise began entering the national consciousness. Movies, shown in theaters built to look like palaces, were the conduit.

Then came the Great Depression. The East, South, and Midwest were battered by the Depression, but sunny California was brimming with hope. California, with its many progressive institutions and general egalitarianism, became a model for many young closet socialists in Washington.

General affluence returned to America after World War II. Capitalists built factories that poured out the good things, and workers worked hard to make them. But what made the affluence available to so many people—those who came to form the great American middle class—was government. Government made it possible for home ownership to become manageable for almost two-thirds of all Americans. And most of the homes were solid, spacious, decent. Government made it possible for people to buy cars because it made the credit system possible. It built the roads, and it kept oil prices low. In fact government made it possible for the five essentials of any consumer society—food, energy, housing, medical care, and education—to be affordable or even "free." If prices were subject to "market forces," the government manipulated those forces to make sure the prices stayed low.

THE DREAM PUT INTO ACTION

In the 1920s the American Dream was something you had to go after yourself. In 1933, however, FDR began to preach a different tune. To the frenzied anger of conservatives, he argued that it was the duty of government to help citizens not just to overcome the suffering of the Depression but to move ahead on the road to attaining the American Dream.

His presidential predecessors contributed to the architecture of the Dream. His immediate predecessor was a California engineer, Herbert Hoover, whose administration pioneered several policies later adopted by the New Deal. Hoover showed how the powerful tools of government could be used to help people in crisis. He had organized a vast famine relief program for Russia just after World War I. Before Hoover, the small town New Englander, Calvin Coolidge, had said, "The business of government is business." He asserted that whatever good was produced in America came from the economy. And although Roosevelt may have distrusted the business class, he nevertheless agreed with Coolidge on that proposition.

I was six years old when Roosevelt became president. I remember his voice coming through the radio. My mother's relatives hated FDR because they were fascists, East European peasants transplanted to towns and cities where they became workers. They were people who knew their place, as southern whites said of nice "nigras." They were determined to rise as far as they could within that place—make it to foreman in the factory. Some then retired to Florida. They did not to my knowledge even know where California was. I lost contact with them and have no idea what their children or grandchildren are like. I was a dreamer and a mover. General George S. Patton, on the eve of the American invasion of Italy, addressed his troops of German and Italian descent: You shortly will be fighting your cousin, maybe your brothers—kill them—they are slaves since they elected not to come to America—you came and became free—you are now different races—kill them.

When the time came to be drafted I went willingly, gladly, not to risk death in a war but to go to where some raggedy visions of mine had already reached (if no farther than the American South, where it was warmer, with palmetto trees and even a few palms).

In the 1930s many kids, and not just in America, had their dreams aroused for political purposes. In Nazi Germany, Josef Goebbels invented propaganda. He borrowed the word from the Catholic Church and realized that the media could be used to seduce young people into joining the Hitler Youth or the army and go marching forth to give Germany victory. Simultaneously in the Soviet Union, people began to realize that all the brilliant but elitist articulation of the 1920s was doing nothing to advance the cause of socialism or the power of the Soviet state. So the Soviet communists shifted to propaganda.

In America the propaganda came from Hollywood and spread forth an American vision for all to see—perfect and beautiful people living in wonderful houses and driving stunning cars. Karl Marx had abstractly preached the potency of socialism to create affluence for all, but only in America did it become a powerful ideology. All over the country the children of immigrants began to dream of making money to buy a car and a house, of becoming perfect and intelligent and beautiful—of getting a part of the American Dream. No pie in the sky for the afterlife. There was no reason for Americans to risk revolution for the fulfillment of a vision that the powers that already were in America were thrusting on them.

In the 1930s my father bought a house in the poorer outskirts of Hartford, Connecticut. The price was brought down because it was next to a cemetery. But we bought a *new* car, a Chevrolet, which my mother drove because my father was too timid and nervous to drive. My father had acquired two elements of the American Dream, and if they are to be seen as the apexes of a triangle then sooner or later the third angle, the vision—an exciting picture in your mind of a possible future—would come into place, as it did not in him but in me. So it was with many American families.

When I first went to California as an eighteen-year-old soldier in 1945, the ethereal quality of the country (I thought of California as a country) both enthralled me and gave me a sense of direction so powerful that it has guided me for all these years—not in any specific direction, but it gives me a feeling that if I'm not going anywhere, I must always find out where I should be going. And when I was in other arid parts of the world, such as Central Asia with its seminomadic, semisettled populations, I also had a visionary sense, maybe coming from the water of mountain springs and irrigation ditches.

Wittfogel understood that strong governments arose in lands where there were great waterworks, but alas, his mind was blocked to visions and his prose was heavy, and iron-willed, like that of the Russians.

The University of California, where I taught, was founded with a land grant in 1868. In its mandate the University of California is decscribed as the research arm of the state, and not long into its history it became the place where innovative ideas for agriculture were developed. Its county agent system, under which scientifically trained agronomists were sent out to farms all over the state to inform their owners of new technologies and market conditions, taught them how to be farmers rather than peasants. Thus California became the premier agricultural state in the union. Its vast central valleys have become models for modern farming throughout the world, far more influential and successful than Soviet state or collective farms. These California valley farms began producing varieties of fruit that until then grew only in the Muslim paradise.

California agriculture put onto the market canned cling peaches drowned in a heavy syrup that was nectar to young boys in Connecticut.

Giant corporations like Del Monte produced the peaches and made hefty profits, but the dream that produced those peaches came from the state.

In America *state* indicates one of the fifty that make up the union. In Europe *state* refers to the higher entity that reigns or hovers over societies. The state is a higher domain; society is a lower one. The sultan/caliph sits at the heart of the state. At one of his sides is a soldier, at the other a learned man. Learning, in those ancient empires, was always in the domain of the state. It still is in California, if for no other reason than that in the great land-grant universities all salaries are paid by the state, as is the rule in Europe.

The state leaders in Sacramento knew how important education was, just as the great sultans of the medieval Arab empires did. In California brilliant physicists led in the development of the atomic bomb, just as the imperial artisans of Chinese emperors and Muslim sultans pioneered in the development of military explosives.

We Americans have become accustomed to, addicted to, the American Dream. First California exported it to the rest of the country, and now it has spread over the world. But the vision can be sustained only if the state keeps conjuring it up, supporting it, making it possible, and above all, convincing people it is good.

The vision tells us that we can be nomads and peasants at the same time and also have a spiritual life. That is what it means to live in a democratic arena. In earlier times, peasants cowered in their huts. It was not for them to go outside and speak; they even spoke little at home with each other. It was an effort to go to the market where the clever Chinese or Jews were waiting to trick them with their golden tongues. In Turkey it was the clever Greeks, who spoke Turkish better than the Turks. But here in California we all go out into the street and school arenas where we talk, talk, talk. At the Berkeley campus of the University of California students talk incessantly, sometimes about very sophisticated things.

Many of their great-great-grandparents were peasants who cowered in huts.

And women? What woman dared speak in earlier times, except secretly to other women? Beware of nuns and charmers, a stern Chinese man in the tenth century wrote in a manual of family instructions, because they have glib tongues. Women are to remain silent and suffer, for that is their lot, men told them; pleasure is for the man since it is only his pleasure that drives the seed into her womb and makes birth, and so greatness, possible.

In California, the vision said it can be otherwise; all can climb into the arena of democracy. And if you have the gift of talk, then you get respect. The "strong, silent type" is now dismissed as a relic from village days. You are nobody today if you cannot talk. In California the house you own in a suburb gives you place among your own kind. The car gives you mobility, and the vision gives you direction for the future and confidence that it will be there for your children—sun children lying on the sands of Santa Monica beaches.

CHALLENGES TO THE DREAM

The triumph of the American Dream did not come without challenge. In the 1930s the Depression sparked a great movement of revolt against capitalism. It was also a revolt against the 1920s, a time of easy money, personal liberation, and private intimacies made public by the movies. It also was a turning against women. The rebels wanted to force women away from the flapper model of the 1920s back to being sweet and innocent, to claim the home as their domain. Kaiser Wilhelm said women should take care of the children, do the cooking, and go to church. Women in films swooned waiting for strong, tall men to save them.

The working class led this revolt against the California Dream, the American Dream. It wanted the houses and the cars, but it detested the vision. And there were plenty of intellectuals to feed this hatred. Socialists, communists, and unions came on to the political stage in force during the 1930s, and they and their intellectual allies swarmed into Hollywood. They substituted reason for vision and called for organized political struggle to give workers their due. "A car in every garage and a chicken in every pot" was socialist Upton Sinclair's campaign slogan in his 1934 California gubernatorial race.

In Europe industrial workers and bourgeois intellectuals joined together to bring socialism, communism, and fascism into being. The workers wanted to be called "sir." In all the European languages the word *mister* is the word for lord: *Monsieur, Signore, Señor, Herr, Mijnherr, Pan, Gospodin,* and so on. They wanted no American Dream, California style. They wanted to be little lords: a man's home is his castle. They wanted property such as the lord had, a house they could own.

The worst class conflict in any society is that between the near-poor, those who have just made it out of the filth of backwardness, and the really poor, who are at the bottom of the social ladder, close to being untouchables in the eyes of the near-poor. Fascism was espoused by the near-poor. Communism was fed by the poor. The poor became its soldiers, helping intellectuals like Lenin gain power. Not surprisingly, communism flourished in the poorer countries of the world while fascism remained mainly European.

In World War II communism destroyed fascism. Then for forty years communists thought they had a vision for the future. But in 1989 they finally abandoned that illusion. What undermined the so-called working class was their own children who, first in the United States and then elsewhere, began to hunger for visions and often adopted just those visions that their fathers detested. I remember having a vague premonition of this when, in the early 1960s, I saw Soviet premier Nikita Khrushchev— the Archie Bunker of Soviet history—on television looking at some modern art and exploding with obscenities. I wondered whether he had any children.

The working class was European because feudal traditions were still so strong there that, despite industrialization and modernization, there was little opportunity for working one's way up into the bourgeois class. There were (and are) patches of a traditional working class in the eastern and midwestern parts of the United States. But there never was a working class in California. Those who were drawn to California felt middle class the moment they crossed the border into the state. Many of them considered themselves "lower middle class" back East, but once in California not even that euphemism was necessary.

But some of the people who came to California did not fit this model. They were farm workers from south of the border who had no such visions in their heads. They came for the jobs. They were part of a class of workers that those in the East knew well: the poor. No working man, however strapped financially, would ever consider himself truly poor. When I came to California I did not even know there were farm workers. And even now only distant echoes from the valleys filter down to me, mainly through students who have miraculously fetched their stories up to the university.

People who considered themselves workers in Europe and the European enclaves in the United States despised California and the American Dream. I knew such people. At best, the visionary essence of the Dream didn't matter much to them. It was irrelevant, fluff on the surface of what was really going on. These workers were more Eurocentric than many elites. In Marx's day there seemed no doubt that Europe emitted the only light that mattered in the flow of world history and led the world in the imperialism and colonialism of the day or would do so in the socialism and communism to come. For them the civil war in Spain was of world significance, whether they supported the left or the right. The countries that counted were Germany, France, Britain, Italy, and Russia. Japan was just a curiosity. The working class was racist. White workers, even if they were communist, believed in the superiority of the white race.

Those who considered themselves of the working class, and the intellectuals who considered themselves their leaders in the drive for power, had their own visions, plans forged from iron and logic through which they would seize the state. Their leaders would rule, and they would get jobs in the bureaucracy; and if many still had to toil in the factories, at least they would be lesser nobles in the workers' state.

NEW PEOPLE AND NEW VISIONS

Socialism has failed and capitalism has prevailed—California has triumphed against Europe. But now in California new visions are forming, especially an environmental vision. They are challenging the old American Dream. Environmentalists maintain that nature is paying the costs of consumer capitalism, that scarce, irreplaceable resources are being gouged out of the earth, and that the environment that sustains all humans is being destroyed. Those resources are "potential," like the potential for electricity inherent in the water of a river flowing oceanward or oil deep in the ground. As the environmentalists see it, we delude ourselves into believing we get free labor from nature's energy. Some day, they warn, we will pay dearly for this supposedly free lunch.

East Coast intellectuals carp at the California life-style and are now eagerly embracing the new conservative vision. But their own life-style stems from the American Dream and is similar to that of middle-class people elsewhere. American civilization reigns supreme in the world, even if new people and new visions are clouding the Dream's future.

In 1840 the few people in California were mostly Indians, a few Mexicans, and even fewer newcomer Americans. Then came the immigrants, gold seekers, settlers, Chinese, Australians. They brought with them a tremendous energy. As most of us in big cities know, immigrants work hard—harder than native populations.

The immigrants never stopped coming, even when exclusionary and restrictive immigration laws cut the immigrant flow from other countries. Then they just poured in from other parts of the United States, drawn by jobs and by the California vision. Immigrants rarely became morose or resentful, wondering why they came. They were enthralled. They absorbed the vision and radiated it to others.

The California Dream depends on immigration, and so does the

American Dream. The middle class has to be replenished. It cannot survive as a caste that rigidly hands down its power, wealth, and privileges to its descendants. Immigrants come with dreams. They work hard. Their kids go to school where many of them shine, just as immigrant children did earlier. They provide the labor that a vision requires. They are like soldiers who work, sometimes brilliantly and at the constant risk of death, for a pittance.

America has continuously been nourished with immigrants since the coming of the Pilgrims from England. In the eighteenth century immigrants came from Germany; in the nineteenth century they came from all over Europe. Toward the end of that century California cut off immigration from Asia but at the same time attracted great flows of immigrants from the rest of the United States and Europe. In 1924, for the first time in its history, the United States cut off the flow of immigration even from Europe. In 1931 the full force of the Great Depression struck.

During the 1930s the New Deal began to pursue place-oriented social policies similar to those of European socialists. Many progressive measures were adopted. But World War II saw a resumption of movement on a grand scale. As white men went off to war, black men began migrating northward and westward. Mexicans came into the southwestern states. After the war, the California Dream resumed its attraction and millions of easterners, southerners, and midwesterners poured into the state. Later the flow covered the entire sunbelt, the southern tier of the states. In the early 1960s Congress lifted immigration restrictions, and the great immigrant flow from all over the world began again.

The newly hegemonic postwar United States offered the American Dream to its humbled enemies, Japan and Germany. They responded with such gusto that they have become American-style economic giants on their own, giving painful competition to their American parent. The American Dream has transformed Europe and made the East Asian rim capitalist. Middle-class enclaves shaped by the Dream have grown up all over the world, islands of prosperity in oceans of poverty and misery, like green oases in brown deserts.

I still remember when, in the 1940s, I saw California for the first time: the green in winter, the pastel-colored stucco houses, the way young men and women walked without the New England slouch, the general cheerfulness in contrast to eastern querulousness, the smell of the brine-tinged fog at Ocean Beach and Santa Monica, the cars zooming up and down streets, the smell of *taquerías.* California was special for those who had always aspired to be in the middle class, like myself. I wanted to flee from stagnation and rest to vision and movement. That is what California middle-class life meant to me. In California everything moved. Like Chuang-tzu's great bird and great fish, I would just fly and swim along. Like a soldier in battle, I would not ask where I was going. I would have faith that, somehow, I was on the right path.

THE DREAM
AND THE HIGHER PLANE

The 1960s are widely seen as a major epoch in American history. People went crazy, as they do when revolutions strike society. I did crazy things —like endanger the goose that lays the golden eggs, in my case a tenured position at a prestigious, rich, tolerant, well-meaning, major American university. Why? Vietnam.

In Oliver Stone's film *Platoon,* all the dramatic action is between Americans. During the film one American kills another, and, in the end, the former is killed by a concerned American observer. Our own Civil War, the bloodiest war of the nineteenth century in the Western world, was fought out of bitter hatreds between northern and southern whites, with the blacks serving largely as pawns and bystanders.

Freud saw the warfare between the id (humans' unconscious urges straining to burst through skin and constraints) and the superego (the forces of fathers and faith wrapping the skin in armored constraints) inevitably straining families to the breaking point. The American Civil War was a necessary war in the service of individuation. For Marx, warfare was the normal condition of society.

Civil wars are psychologically devastating because they sunder the family. Cain killed Abel, and the Judeo-Christian world has never forgotten it. How can one member of a family turn another over to an enemy to be cruelly tortured and killed?

TWO CURRENTS IN AMERICAN LIFE

In the 1960s, those on the left sensed but didn't understand the fierce hatred that existed between themselves, a motley array of educated city kids, and the other side, hard-hat-wearing white workers who, if they had been given a come-on, would have slaughtered thousands of those screaming smart-asses, as Mexican troops did in October 1968 (killing a half thousand students in the Mexico City district of Tlatelolco for protesting many of the same things that the American students were).

Civil wars are marked not only by hatreds among members of the same political community but also by clashes of ideologies and religions. The bloodiest wars in the world have been ideological and religious wars. Europe's wars of religion during the sixteenth and early seventeenth centuries took the lives of as much as a third of the population in France and Germany. In the mid-nineteenth century, millions of Chinese were slaughtered in the Taiping rebellion aroused by a charismatic leader of modest social origins named Hung Hsiu-ch'üan, who proclaimed himself the younger brother of Jesus Christ. In the recent civil war in Lebanon, which lasted from 1975 until 1990, two hundred thousand died among a people who share a common culture and language but not a common religion.

The hatred tearing the American people apart in the 1960s began to take on the characteristics of potential civil war. In the spring of 1968, America's political elite split in emotional and ideological ways—a sure sign of civil strife. Angry students finally felt they had an emerging leader, Bobby Kennedy. The enraged hard-hats looked to George Wallace. Blacks looked to Martin Luther King, Jr., who was allying himself with Kennedy. The year 1968 was a violent year. King was killed, then Kennedy. Lyndon Johnson dropped out of the presidential race and began peace talks. In the November elections, Wallace won almost ten million votes. In my book *The Foreign Politics of Richard Nixon,* I gave credit to that strange figure for having steered the ship of state through the dangerous shoals of incipient civil war. He could have tried to create a bloody right-wing regime that would have done to the American left what Augusto Pinochet (aided and abetted by Nixon himself) did to the Chileans after September 1973.

A civil war seemed to be arising between those who felt at ease in

America and those who did not. To make some sweeping generalizations: hard-hat workers loved America; their parents and grandparents had come from some godforsaken village in Europe, and now these workers were making good money in a Detroit factory. With kids in college, they hoped their sons would become engineers, wear clean suits and shirts, and do better than the old man. They were similar to German and French workers who in 1914 went cheeringly off to war against each other only weeks after their pompous socialist leaders had promised that none of their workers would ever heed the call to war. What counted for the German and French workers was the flag, as sacred a piece of cloth as any the church draped over its altars.

The flag also counted mightily for American workers in the 1960s. They voted for Johnson in 1964 and would have done so again in 1968. They were ready to take on the flag-defiling kids at home, and local police forces were just itching to get at the commie bastards. All they needed was a Führer. Love America or leave it, and we'll be happy to help you get out.

And then there was the broad mainstream American middle class who would have appreciated it if the hard-hats had beaten the students bloody (with some trepidation that a few of the students might be their own kids), just as "good Chileans" appreciated what Pinochet did. Good Germans liked what Hitler did—after all, he was so thrilling to listen to, and joining the party was certainly not like becoming a red. We have it good in America, our middle class thought, better than anywhere else in the world, and those students, most likely manipulated by communists, were "shitting in their own bed," as Charles de Gaulle said when he saw French students by the thousands screaming for his removal.

What else was fascism in Europe but the promise of order, so that decent people could settle down again to a secure existence of hard work and modest reward? And what else did communism turn out to be, as Hannah Arendt understood, but the promise of order by removing the internal and external enemies of the system? Fascism mirrored the cleanliness values of a middle class (or petite bourgeoisie in Europe).

Communism reflected the more slovenly habits of the working class, as one can see in the disorder so evident in everyday Russian life. Socialists liked the heavy architecture of bureaucratic organization; this was true of communists too, as became evident when they emerged from the Stalinist madness.

In Europe class lines were sharp, mirroring a long feudal history. Peasants were at the bottom in the rural areas, workers at the bottom in the cities, above them the burghers, and finally the nobles. England used to have three kinds of public drinking establishments separated by class: pubs for the workers, private bars for the middle class, and saloon bars for gentlemen.

In America the gap between the middle and working classes was smaller than in Europe. Blue-collar (that is, dirty) workers know they are, or could be, on the track to becoming white-collar (that is, clean) middle-class people. In 1968 the middle and working classes wondered whether a sizable cabal of subversives aligned with frightening blacks was about to try to seize power over decent Americans. The radical rhetoric blasted forth day after day.

America in the late 1960s had a tool to avert civil war that many other nations lacked: its mighty economy. Once again the economy was pumped up (as of December 1970), and houses and automobiles were being built at a fast clip. The massacre of demonstrating students at Kent State in May 1970 seemed to be the opening shot in a possible civil war. Yet the radical movements ebbed. A lot of their energy was then absorbed by the politicians, some of whom, during the early 1970s, began to sound as radical as some of the students had in the late 1960s. Radicalism was not squelched but was taken into the system and began to move in some surprising new directions. Far-reaching, officially sanctioned, and even supported, movements for all kinds of "liberation" arose: liberation of blacks, women, browns, Native Americans, gays and lesbians, the handicapped, animals. The unexpected victories showed that radicalism had gained wide support in American society. At the same time, Spiro Agnew's "silent majority" remained an equally powerful force. As in any potential civil war, the two opposing sides divided the society into two big segments.

In the fall of 1964, students lashed out in fury against the administration of the University of California at Berkeley in something called the Free Speech Movement (FSM). Youthful rebellion, it was thought. Yet something deep had offended those students. What it was I remember very well. It came in the form of 500 black-clad, helmeted, working-class cops ready to wade into the mass of sitting students with truncheons at a spot a minute's walk from my office. And though plenty were beaten, discipline held the police in check. A real fascist governor would have told the police to go ahead and kill 'em. But those cops were fascists and the students felt it, and with that willingness to die so characteristic of young people, they told the "pigs" to come ahead. For the students, the cops were but the arm of the ruling class—nice, friendly men extending their velvet-gloved hands, while underneath was an iron fist.

In Berkeley's Barrows Lane and on Sproul Plaza, in the days before Vietnam became a widely known word, vision and antivision clashed. The students had their vision, and the cops fought back. The vision gave the former the courage to taunt the latter into striking them, and the antivision gave the latter the white-hot anger needed to contemplate massacring them. The cops came from Alameda County, then white-ruled, suburban, and rural, except for Oakland. Most of them had close relatives who fit the usual working-class categories. Workers were passionate and angry and also had a peasantlike conviction about their own values. They were much more conservative than many wealthy businessmen or people from the old American aristocracy. They had old-fashioned values, often identical to those of deeply conservative religions. They had strong ideas about their children's shining futures that made them work hard. They were proud of their origins, and memories of the past figured strongly in their minds. They were racist—they felt that no matter how meager their incomes, their white skins gave them status above those with dark skins.

Racism was embedded in the American industrial-era worker.

Because they regarded poverty as wrong, they feared and hated it. And because so much poverty existed among blacks, they hated blacks. If a black man worked hard alongside white workers, they may have liked that black man, but not enough to invite him home to dinner. They liked him because he appeared to be trying to act like a white man.

They had strong loves and often equally strong hatreds. They hated pink-faced students with weak arms and inflated brains. The Alameda cops looking out from beneath their helmets saw the students as something they particularly hated: freaks with power (as did Nazi storm troopers and the Buenos Aires police). And they sensed that, being on the campus of a great university with far more connections to power centers than they themselves had (workers know how powerless they are and therefore worship power with as much passion as they hate enemies), the students were perhaps even dangerous.

The right-wing passions of the Alameda County police and the left-wing passions of the Berkeley students were but extreme reflections of two profoundly different philosophical currents in America. A great gap was opening up in the body politic of America, first on its coastal extremes and then (as at Kent State) in its hinterland.

STIRRINGS TOWARD A HIGHER PLANE

Try to visualize a young soldier who made it through World War II alive. At the beginning of that war, he and his own kind were as far from the American Dream as ever. Twenty-five million unemployed. Tough to buy a car, tougher to buy a house, and workers knew they were at the bottom of the respectable heap, only inches from falling into poverty. But when the worker became a veteran, he was adulated. He got the GI bill to go back to school; he got a GI home loan; he could hitchhike with his old uniform on and get picked up; he might even get to move out to Yonkers, or go all the way and head for Los Angeles. After the magnificent war was over, the ladder upward and the path outward, especially in California, were wide open. You could look up and see the blue sky above you, with clouds beckoning.

Only a short time after the Free Speech Movement erupted in Berkeley, the Vietnam War began. American planes started bombing Vietnam in February 1965. That summer American troops were sent there. Middle-class people, naturally, "supported the war." Why not? At worst it would last as long as Korea (three years). Most likely it would end sooner. Anyway, "the people in government knew what they were doing." Nobody really believed the Vietcong were going to come marching down Market Street in San Francisco, as the "tap dancer," Senator George Murphy, kept on saying. What counted was winning one for the good old U.S.A.

There were plenty of jobs around. Lots of good cars. You could even buy an Oldsmobile. For workers and the middle class, times were great. Lady Bird Johnson was beautifying America. Lyndon dreamed of going down in history as the greatest American daddy for white workers and poor folk, including blacks. LBJ hated the way Jack Kennedy droned on with his Harvard phrases, but he, LBJ, was delivering mightily. LBJ knew what people really wanted, and he was going to give them the good life.

The American Dream, as seen by America's ex-peasants, was too great to be besmirched by freaks from California. What in their eyes could those privileged California rebels be but commies, kikes, and queers, or their dupes? Why didn't LBJ denounce them as garbage, and let the cops smash them? Who were those California rebels whose madnesses provoked one of the great schisms in America's bicentennial history? In California it started at Berkeley before Vietnam. Several thousand students went into a rage at the spectacle of helmeted fascist cops being called in by the kindly chancellor to control a rebellion. As in China's violent, strange Cultural Revolution, which erupted a year and a half later, the Berkeley students did the only thing they had the power to do: they denied the authority of their elders, especially those exercising power —"Don't trust anyone over thirty!"

In China they put dunce caps on their victims and a necklace of ping-pong balls around the neck of a grand old woman, Wang Guangmei, the wife of Liu Shaochi, disgraced successor to Mao Zedong. She was magnificent facing the students, as was Marie Antoinette facing the guillotine. Was she magnificent before? Defeat, as Richard Nixon noted, has a way of ennobling people. But the authority of those Chinese leaders, on which political power depended even more than on raw power, was gone. Their self-respect was gone. Some of these leaders still rule today. They have power and have done some good things. Their people may need and maybe even like some of them, but do they respect them?

The American students in the 1960s sensed that in a democracy self-respect is vital to one's sense of identity. Deny people self-respect and they will either crumble in destructive self-denigration or erupt in fury. Identity gives you a legitimate place among others, but soul gives you direction. In the 1960s, when workers wanted the American Dream and students wanted to deny them that dream's legitimacy, self-respect was a substitute for soul. Then, only blacks talked about soul.

For a country that prides itself on its pragmatism, it is astonishing that at every turn of America's history spiritual or ideological or religious factors have unleashed enormous energies. The politics of the 1960s were spiritual and ideological, even religious, but definitely not practical.

One can see this phenomenon as a cyclical recurrence of spiritual surges in American history. But one can also look for a more immediate cause. And reflection suggests that it was linked to the assassination of President Kennedy. Many Americans, especially students and the educated, felt robbed by the killing of Jack Kennedy. Kennedy had offered them a vision with direction. He called it the New Frontier. He created a Peace Corps, which sent thousands of enthusiastic pale northern college kids abroad. Others went south to join the civil rights movement. Kennedy talked idealism, spun Irish clouds of sparkling colors in the heavens. He looked young and old at the same time, so setting the stage for the youth who let their beards grow and dressed in farmers' overalls or granny clothes. Kennedy seemed to be saying: it is time for some of you, those who are the best and the brightest, to go beyond the American Dream to something higher. There is a higher plane, beyond even California itself. Maybe it is in some remote Nepali village, like the one to which the elderly expert on international communism, Victor Zorza, repaired in the early 1970s. Kennedy radiated a kind of gnostic aura, which one could sense in his enigmatic smile. By the late 1960s hundreds of thousands of kids— and some not so young—started escaping to that higher plane of existence.

The day Kennedy was killed, the Berkeley campus descended into a profound silence, as did much of the country. Everybody sensed that something important had happened. Those thousand days in which a higher plane had opened up ended, and Camelot vanished, utterly. The barely contained rage was already there a few days after November 22, 1963.

DISCONTENTS AND THE AMERICAN DREAM

When LBJ ordered the bombers over North Vietnam in February 1965, there was much satisfaction among most Americans. Maybe we could win through airpower alone. We could always nuke them, turn all of North Vietnam into a parking lot, as Ronald Reagan suggested. What about the Chinese? They were not a threat. They could not get into Vietnam in any great numbers because of the mountainous terrain of southern China and northern Vietnam, lectured an articulate major in a secret briefing I had been pressed to attend in November 1964 at UC's San Diego campus.

But for the students those bombs confirmed what they had suspected. They saw LBJ as the leader of the forces of the American Dream from which they had rapidly and happily become alienated during the thousand days of Kennedy. The striving, professionalism, and obsession with career of the 1950s were to be replaced by something else—this plane of existence did not count, and somehow a higher plane had to be rediscovered.

It did not take long for the angry antiwar graffiti to appear on walls.

The rebels were challenging the passions of the workers, whose desire to kill them rose to a fever level, restrained only by the trammels of American institutions held together by law. Few groups in America hated the angry students so much as organized labor. Even among the reddish and pinkish unions there was acute embarrassment over these kids who were ruining a good domestic idea—namely, peace. The reds and pinks were overjoyed when I entered their ranks as a dignified gentleman wearing a tie. I smothered the raucous young with scholarly rhetoric, showing that "American policy" was destined to fail in Vietnam.

The sense of evil pervading the country began to spread much faster than anyone had imagined. The very middle class to which the workers so assiduously aspired began to wobble with doubts. Why hadn't the war ended already, as Defense Secretary Robert McNamara had promised? Ministers began to voice concern. Rabbis were worried that once again, as every time radicalism made its appearance, Jews were getting bad press as suspected "communist sympathizers." Priests were beginning to feel uncomfortable in the fascist straitjacket woven by Archbishop Francis Spellman and his ilk. Even within the ranks of government, the doubters began to multiply, to the fury of the military who, like revolutionaries, were determined to prove the validity of their ideologies. While much of the public still hoped that North Vietnam could be bombed into submission, many were not so sure. There was the sense that the freakiness had reached such a scope that it could no longer be dismissed as marginal.

Students on hundreds of campuses began to march, shout, curse. Surely they could not all be dupes of commie professors. What also worried the white middle classes was the stirring of this country's black population. Few whites had any illusions about the terrible human conditions of most blacks, no matter how racist they were. Blacks were caged in ghettoes, and if they started to break out, like any caged person or animal, their fury, energy, and sheer destructive power could be immense. Maybe the radicals did stir up the blacks, and maybe the Kennedys were responsible for opening up a Pandora's box, but the war in Vietnam was only making things worse. What were all those colored men going to do when they came back to Chicago, battle-hardened?

The middle classes came around in ever swelling numbers to question the war. From 1969 on, increasingly strong and numerous voices in Congress began opposing the war. It was seen as a lost cause. But rebels cannot be dismissed as mere catalysts whose radicalism was necessary to get the antiwar movement going. They had become an instrument for hacking pieces out of the American Dream at the very time that big bankers like David Rockefeller were thinking of making immense loans to developing countries to allow them to import the American Dream.

It was no accident that the rebellion originated in California, where it had first been shown that the American Dream could become reality for millions of people. In the San Francisco Bay Area, young people began to shun the suburbs and move into the Haight-Ashbury district of San Francisco and crowd into Berkeley's Telegraph Avenue district. The latter began to look like Paris's Latin Quarter, which has been in existence since the twelfth century. For seven centuries Paris has had students from many nations, disputing, brawling, doing raucous and raunchy things. Many were studying for the priesthood and eventually joined monastic orders. The general hardworking population detested them. Seven centuries of Parisian students remained close to visions. And visions were a main reason why young people came to the Haight or to Telegraph Avenue.

Drugs were the easiest source of visions. They took you right away onto the higher plane. In Berkeley, politics also offered a high, particularly to those who did not believe in a cosmic plane but felt that a higher plane in this world is all there is to reach for. To be clubbed by a cop was to have been tapped by the wand of history. And along with drugs and history came swarms of people, like pilgrims jostling each other in Rome or Mecca or Varanasi. The world was left behind. The American Dream was rejected.

Particularly infuriating to middle- and working-class people was the astonishing filthiness of the new rebels. They did things no self-respecting person would ever dream of doing, like using the American flag as toilet paper. More than fury followed. It was violent, utter incomprehension. How could kids from good families reject everything those families stood for and make a public point of doing so?

Why did the students reject and repel something that seemed so indisputably good that even communists promised that if they took power they would provide it in greater abundance than the capitalists? Why did one radical (who later became an even more famous apostate) say, "America was a mistake from the moment the Pilgrims landed"? He said it because, deep down, the students felt the deep malaise in modern civilization that Freud wrote of in his great essay "The Discontents of Civilization." The original German for "discontent" is *Unbehagen,* which means "discomfort." They felt uncomfortable in American houses, in their parents' suburban spreads. They shunned cars to hunker in their inner-city neighborhoods, or they hitchhiked to India. They refused to grant their parents and the entire American middle class respect, a defiance that appalled those for whom the American Dream had been so good.

Mom and Dad had homes. Hippies had no homes, only *pads.* They moved around endlessly. Any radical soon decided that wherever he or she lived, some major interior decoration had to take place. Big fiery posters had to go up. Beds sometimes vanished because floor space had to be used to accommodate whoever dropped by; homes became like hotels with an endless passage of people. Wherever one lived had to look like the opposite of a suburban house. And that was easily accomplished in a crowded, cockroach-ridden, inner-city apartment.

In Paris, I was once invited to the home of a Maoist radical who had done gunrunning for the Algerians. His home life was that of *la France bourgeoise.* He kissed *maman's* hand, his wife had a supper of *bifteck* and *frites* on the table, the kids were off in another room. When I asked him about how oddly different behavior in the home and on the street seemed to an American, he said you simply don't know the French; what we do on the street and what we do in the home are utterly different. That would have been unthinkable in San Francisco, where only the most accepted radical professor could get away with inviting the radicals to his suburban house for beer and wine.

DISCREDITING AUTHORITY

In the 1950s the car became the true love of the teenager. Kids wanted to drive as soon as they were sixteen. Cars were where your first lovemaking occurred. Cars were where friends gathered. Your house was settled, the car less settled. The car was the great symbol and agent of adolescence, when you were blurredly both child and adult. If you couldn't or didn't drive, you were out of it.

For the hippies and the radicals and the freaks and the rebels, the car meant nothing. As General Curtis LeMay said about the nuclear bomb, "It's just another weapon," so they said of cars. By moving into scruffy inner cities, the rebels were saying that what counts is bunching up with your own, hanging out in coffee shops, doing your shopping with a string-bag, just as they did in Paris. The rebels aped a lot of the old ethnic divisions in which people, years earlier, had been trapped because they did not know enough English and did not have enough money to get out. Bohemians? Yes, but more than that. People were "dropping out" of American society by going into its most squalid parts. It is as if the rebels were making a U-turn on the road of social mobility.

And if they traveled, it was often on strange paths, like the trail that led from Europe to India through Persia and Afghanistan. People hitched rides, took buses, and walked to get to Poona or Goa.

While their parents tried to "keep up with the Joneses," the hippie kids listened to some inner voice. They were indifferent to their bodies; many died young. Some were "A" students, but when they got to the Haight, many could be found babbling incoherently, on some drug trip. All that counted was that inner voice, and their loathing of the American Dream.

Why did the Vietnam War unleash all this, and was it really the war that did it? The rebels attacked the American Dream because they hated it. They also knew that attacking it infuriated those in authority, who happened in good part to be liberals, Democrats, people who in their youth had also often been radical.

To understand the rebellion, one must understand what authority is. In America, when somebody does something wrong, citizens are expected either to call the cops or to report it to the authorities. When you do the former you want the police to use their power to handcuff the offenders. But when you do the latter, you invoke more than power, more than law. You ask the state to come into your affairs and to paralyze the offenders through the awe that results from the sight of an agent of the state staring you sternly in the face. And if the offender is not awed, the authorities can always call the cops.

By ridiculing the authorities, turning their bared backsides to them, the rebels made clear that they were nothing but their pretensions plus the raw power they commanded, which was considerable. Thus they deprived those in authority of their self-respect, the true source of their authority. They left them with only their power, which the gentlemen with soft hands were, fortunately, reluctant to use.

The radicals also clawed away at the self-respect of ordinary Americans, especially white males. They began a process of undermining the self-confidence of white American men that continued through the 1970s and 1980s and continues today, especially in the academy.

The authorities who ran that war, including LBJ, knew that their authority and self-respect depended on success in Vietnam. If they could pound their communist enemy to pieces, littering all of Indochina with a million yellow corpses, the rebels and everyone else would have to hold them in awe again. And if the war were won, the American Dream would be reconfirmed.

Deep down, America's ex-peasants knew that government, not some civics textbook drivel about hard work and getting an education, made the Dream possible. The Dream needed power to be realized, and if the war could be won it would demonstrate, as with every foreign war America has ever fought, that the American state still had power. The road to renewed authority went through power.

SEARCHING FOR NEW VISIONS

The American rebels wanted the United States to be defeated in Vietnam. Withdraw now, they demanded. They hoped to provoke a collapse of government, exactly as would later happen in Argentina, but when LBJ stepped out of the 1968 presidential race, they lost their target. It was as if Louis XVI had made good his escape from Paris and managed to flee to London. They got another chance in January 1973 when an impeachment process against Nixon began, leading to his resignation in August 1974. By that time both the rebels and much of the American political establishment had joined the ranks of those demanding Nixon's ouster. It was as if a revolutionary fire had been started from below and then spread upward and upward until it reached Congress. Clearly there was no revolution, yet those who led the offensive against Nixon believed the potential for revolution was so serious that the system had to be preserved by making use of the revolution—kill the king and then proclaim the revolution ended!

What did the rebels hate more, the American Dream or the American government? It depended on what kind of rebels they were. The Old Left, which was one of the three components of the revolution, did not hate either the Dream or the government. They wanted to become part of the government. The New Left were Jacobins. They hated the government and wanted to see radical change, maybe the writing of a new Constitution. The counterculture, the third component, hated the American Dream. They were part of that current of thinking and feeling among American intellectuals who had long hated the middle class, represented by Sinclair Lewis's Babbitt and H. L. Mencken's booboisie. The intellectuals hated the suburbs, Los Angeles, the enslavement of nature, the parochialism of middle-class Americans, the infuriating pragmatism of their parents, and above all, the absence of any ideals or aspirations to higher planes of existence. Some would not have minded if America had gone up in flames so that a newer and better country could rise from the ashes.

✧

The passions that erupted in America in the 1960s were not so different from those that swirled in the 1970s in Argentina. Save for a few aristocratic generals, the Argentine military was made up of sons of the working class, descendants of Spanish, Italian, German, Irish, and other European immigrants. They had earlier adored Juan Perón, the colonel who linked up with the unions also made up of immigrants' descendants. And Perón used government to give his *descamisados—*"shirtless ones," the near-poor—everything he could of a middle-class Argentinian Dream. But the aristocratic military turned against him when he flirted too much with the left and the bankruptcy of the state became too egregious. It was Argentina's freaks, the *subversivos,* whom Argentina's workers hated with a burning passion. In Argentina too, the radicals came from good families; they were educated, middle-class people, many of them Jews, and they were idealists of the same kind as became prominent and active in the United States.

It was remarkable that young people rose up in wrath in so many different countries at the same time. In America they swarmed from campuses and attacked, being met by brutal and barely restrained police. In Japan, the candle-holding million of the great anti-Eisenhower demonstrations of the summer of 1960 became the infuriated radicals of 1970. I remember marching with them while passing the prime minister's residence as they screamed: *kill him, kill him, kill him,* rhythmically, like a shaman's chant. In West Germany, pale-faced kids screamed, and some kidnapped and killed—like the Baader-Meinhof gang, so many of whose leaders later died mysteriously in jail cells. In France they screamed on the campuses, and finally in May 1968 their screaming gave rise to a vast general strike that toppled General Charles de Gaulle.

In 1848 student revolts erupted in many European cities, leapfrogging from one to the other. In 1871 the Paris Commune took over the city government. In Russia revolt came in 1905 and again in the two big uprisings of 1917. In China, in 1919, student revolts jumped from Peking to Shanghai, eventually leading to communist revolution. All the revolts screamed for the overturn of tyranny and gave forth clouds of visions of a better human order to come. In Italy in the mid-1800s, Giuseppe Mazzini succeeded in riding the clouds of a fabricated nationalism to unify Italy for the first time since the collapse of the western part of the Roman Empire in the fifth century A.D. The Bolsheviks were excellent union organizers, but it wasn't those unions that gave them supreme power. It was the brilliance of their vision and the single-minded tactics of two men, Lenin and Trotsky. In China's Cultural Revolution of the mid-1960s, hatred outweighed love. The rebels lashed out at high party functionaries. When the old man in his apotheosized book-lined study told them to lay off, they went on a rampage, destroying temples, especially in sacred places like Tibet.

The search for wealth and the goad of religion—these have been the two roads of an unfolding imperial America. The workers, their eyes set on the road that would take them fully and finally into the middle class, were traveling the first road. The rebels were traveling the second road. In the 1960s, those roads intersected explosively.

Social science explanations of the events of the 1960s are unsatisfying. Marxists labeled what happened some kind of class struggle, but didn't know what to make of the behavior and attitudes of their prime class, the workers, who, according to Marxist theory, are supposed to be the moving force of the dialectic of history, and whose role was so clearly reactionary during the 1960s. Some sociologists looked at adolescents as a unique social formation whose general behavior was not yet fully understood scientifically, though their revolt against authority was apparent. Youthful rebellion? These are secular explanations that fit into the simple domain of everyday human experience.

But if you admit there is some higher plane beyond this domain, then you are at once aligned with generations of philosophers, of East and West, who have concerned themselves with God and the world. You can be a dualist and believe in this life and then another higher one—life after death. Or you can be a monist, like the ninth-century Indian philosopher Shankara, and hold that this life is only an illusion, *maya*, and that reality is the higher plane, *brahma.* He called that belief *advaita,* nonduality. In either case, once you come to such a belief, the higher plane exerts an immediate gravitational attraction, drawing you to it. The 1960s look complex and confused through the lenses of the social sciences but begin to make sense once you accept that forces of religion and philosophy were at play.

✧

PART II

THE WORLD

In 1945 I was eighteen years old and in the U.S. Army. Early in the year I was sloshing through the north Florida swamps, being trained as cannon fodder. Later in the year I was studying Japanese at the University of Chicago, in uniform. Franklin Roosevelt died in April, and we all felt it to be a cosmic event. In August our side dropped the bomb, the war ended, and not many months later I was in Japan, an occupation soldier, a nineteen-year-old youth overseeing articles in the southern edition of Japan's major newspaper, the *Asahi*.

The whole world opened up before me. Languages, money, chances to travel. Despite occasional money and job worries, the reality was that we young talented Americans were the world's new privileged. We had conquered the world and it was ours. The rebels of the 1960s would later call it hegemony.

The whole world became connected, and anyone could ride the connections to anywhere in the world. I remember taking a flight to Tokyo in the early 1950s. As a recipient of one of the first Ford and Fulbright grants to study in Japan, I was given a first-class plane ticket. On the way we refueled in a blinding snowstorm on the Aleutian island of Shemya and finally landed in Tokyo as a brilliant red sun was setting over the smog-covered city. For the entire trip—some eighteen hours as I remember—I played bridge with two passengers and two stewardesses. Except for the Shemya snowstorm, I noticed almost nothing else about the trip. I even forgot to be scared by the turbulence.

I realize now that an amazing American genius worked hard after that terrible war to knit the world together. GIs smiled at the kids and handed out chewing gum. Immense piles of food came roaring in on plane convoys. Truman seemed stern but fair, a common touch that did not seem parochial. The Germans and Japanese had not known how to preside over conquered peoples and soon descended into savagery. The Americans, however, had not come to conquer or control. GIs just wanted a good time, college graduates were working earnestly and idealistically at military government, a lot of kids like me were just fascinated to see the world, even (or especially) if much of it was in ruins.

The Americans did not go home after setting things right in the world. They proceeded to tie it together even more tightly. Airlines soon flew planes all over the world—and made good money. Americans built roads, dams, and airports everywhere. The dollar became the world currency. Americans taught the world how to develop mass communications, and when television became widespread in the United States in the early 1950s it rapidly spread elsewhere too, aided and abetted by the Americans. It was indeed like the Mediterranean world around the time of Christ. In the first century B.C. Rome had torn itself apart in civil war. Then Julius Caesar began a revolution, seized power, made himself emperor. In 27 B.C. Augustus formally inaugurated the empire. With that also came the *Pax Romana*. Traders and tourists sailed over a Mediterranean that had been unsafe because of war and pirates. Suddenly even distant ports in Spain and Syria were only weeks away from Rome, on regular ship schedules.

In the 1940 presidential election campaign, Republican Wendell Willkie coined the term "one world" and Franklin Roosevelt appropriated it. Roosevelt decided he was history's instrument to bring about one world that would comprise not just Europeans but Russians and Chinese as well and eventually all the world's liberated colonial peoples.

Every person in the world is affected by the legacy of that vision.

HISTORY CHANGES COURSE

By 1968 the vision had dimmed, and the legacy seemed exhausted. Shit had been hurled on it by the rebels. I was one of them. I remember an interview I gave to a Japanese journal called *China*. It was so called because the older Japanese who had started it, like me, had world-encompassing concerns. Maybe once they were sympathetic with Shōwa Tennō (as the Japanese called the one we knew as Emperor Hirohito), but later they looked to communist China for regional and even world redemption. They interviewed me because they thought I shared those sentiments. I spoke academic Japanese during the interview and soon found myself saying that my wish was that America would become a *chiisai kuni,* meaning "small country," that is, a shrunken U.S.A., like Japan humbled by defeat.

In 1972 George McGovern campaigned on the theme: "Come Home, America." One World? Come Home, America?

In the 1960s I yelled: "Get out of Vietnam." I was an internationalist who publicly denounced "American imperialism." At the same time, though, I seemed to admire it in things I wrote, as leftists often pointed out to me.

A friend told me about a political scientist of Czech origin who was furious that Americans were so inept at running the empire they had created. Czechoslovakia was a small country (now the Czech Republic is smaller still). But it has an imperial history. Before the nineteenth century Habsburg Prague was Austria's second capital, more imperial than Vienna. It had a great Renaissance university, Vienna did not. But I did not want America to be imperial because imperialism meant barbarity and cruelties. I was disturbed that the Americans were committing cruelties as the Germans—the Austrians' cousins—had done. I smelled in working-class Americans the same fascism I smelled in my German working-class relatives. Any smell was better than that one.

Wasn't all this "one world" stuff nothing more than American imperialism, and that, at best, a step removed from Nazism? So did it not make sense that my Chinese communist heroes, through their newspapers, were telling their foreign advisers to go back to their home countries?

✧

I was never attracted to consumerism or to life in the public arena or to the self-discovery so common in the 1960s. That alone should have made me unfriendly to the American Dream from which the rebels shrank like the devil's lures. Yet unlike the rebels with whom I consorted during the 1960s I felt an excitement about corporations producing cornucopias of goods and expanding around the world, about this tremendous democracy that saw so many millions move from private homes with their stale smells into the vast open arenas where they could freely live, work, and think, and about a counterculture in which people did crazy and strange and sublime and always innovative and adventurous things. These Americans were not my people, even though I too was an American. But they were part of the context called America in which I lived and in which, in the late 1960s, I was increasingly happy to be.

In 1970 I had a passion about the world even greater than when I traveled, yet I chose the opposite direction for my personal and intellectual life. I suddenly found myself rediscovering the U.S.A. And since many saw me as a "leftist" and, because of my intellectual attainments, did not suspect I was of parochial working-class origins, they naturally assumed I would be sympathetic to workers—as they were, though often for theoretical rather than experiential reasons. They did not know how much I disliked the class from which I came.

I believed that at the time fascists and rednecks, of origins close to my own, were assuming power, rising through the military, the police, and sundry other institutions sympathetic to right-wing ideologies. I knew that fascists and reactionaries had risen to power through militaries, intelligence agencies, and death squads in other countries. I had read about how, in Argentina, Spaniards, Italians, Germans, and Irish had emerged from immigrant working-class origins to become officers in the military and then ordered the torture and murder of *subversivos*.

Later in the 1970s, I added anger against socialists to my hatred of fascists. I did not mind the Jewish socialists, though their Marxist adulation of the working class irked me. I began to feel that the working class was responsible for much of what went wrong in the modern world, not just in the communist countries but in the democratic and socialist countries as well. In Russia and China working-class people had risen to power and were responsible for many of the horrors committed there. Going even farther, I came to believe that the so-called working class adulated by communists and Nazis alike was some bizarre deformation of early industrialization.

I began to see it as a hybrid—half peasant, half middle class. The image I held of that class mirrored that of my own family, of my relatives, of the people of various nationalities who were close to us and some of whose languages my father spoke. We were all strange, unstable mixtures. Memories tied grandparents, especially, to some ancestral turf. But then many husbands and wives had different ancestral turfs, as in my family. And the children became American, sensing that movement was American and that stasis smelled—like rotting food, like the stale exhalations from old people, from the "old country."

The working class, far from being the vanguard of modern industrial civilization, was the incarnation of one of the world's greatest contradictions—to use one of Mao Zedong's favorite terms—that between urban and rural life, between dreams and work, between free city people and bound village people. Everywhere in the world except superurbanized Western Europe and the United States, the vast differences between village and country were destabilizing societies. Their social scientists, realizing that their Western teachers had missed this mountain on the social landscape, wrote about it.

The city, wherever and whenever in history it has appeared, has been free. The village always is bound and bonded. The workers I grew up with could not resolve this contradiction. They wanted order in the family and yet knew that the only way they could make money for the family was through movement, even extensive movement like migration. Because they passionately wanted their sons to move up the ladder of social mobility, they had come to the United States. Their heads were pulled one way and their legs the opposite.

It was hard for them to live that contradiction, and it often was temporarily resolved through violence—violent rhetoric against enemies, violence in the family, violence against self through excessive drink. I heard a lot of the squalor of violence and the talk of it from working-class adults, though not from my parents. My father, who lived so many of those contradictions and hid them behind a timidity that would not even allow him to drive, drank and smoked himself to death in his early fifties.

The yearnings I sensed in the workers around me were for their place, their security, their jobs, their respect, their family, their positions in society. Fascism offered them place. So did socialism. So did communism. Capitalism offered them only the market. But from the 1930s on, American-style liberalism personified by Franklin Roosevelt began to offer them place too, such offers being motivated in good part by the fear of fascism and communism.

When fascism crumbled, graphic pictures of its horrors appeared. Fascism created mass death everywhere. And even before communism crumbled, its horrors were known. The violence of both of these working -class movements was directed against those who did not "belong." They were carried out to fulfill a vision of a place inhabited only by our own. The visions of the two were not that different: German workers in the fatherland and Russian workers in the motherland. Because of their similarities, fascists and communists hated each other like cousins fighting on the two sides of a civil war.

The American leftists I consorted with in the 1960s were not workers, aside from the stray son of a steelworker or two, and these had become as *déclassé* as I. They were overwhelmingly middle class. They all shared my visions of a world. But when my leftist friends looked inward and started talking about socialism, I mumbled some dissent but mostly kept quiet. As I ruminated about American society, I realized that the best cure for fascism and communism was as rapid an absorption as possible of the workers into the middle class. Once they became part of the middle class, the forces of consumer capitalism, personal liberation, and democracy could begin to transform them. They could cease being people half peasant and half middle class, riven by passions they could express only through practicing evil.

Democratic socialist countries, I knew, were not savage like the fascist and communist ones. But in their addiction to place, they exuded the same stale smells I remembered from working-class households in my childhood. They wanted to let the worker keep his village yearnings and used a massive welfare state to make it possible. But when the Thatcher-Reagan revolution began to surge through the world during the 1980s it became evident what a costly pipe-dream socialism was.

During the early 1970s I began to realize that the political left was an unstable hybrid just like the working class. I was strongly drawn by their visions of a just world, their multiracial and multinational character, their intellectual talents, their passionate genius. Their visions were right, I believed. They made me look upward, toward a higher plane.

The political left was never just idealistic. It went upward into politics and downward into the ranks of the oppressed. When they fought for the freedom and rights of the poor, as in the civil rights movement, I felt it to be right, universal, and in the flow of history. But when they pushed the claims of the so-called working class—America's "lower middle class"—then I recoiled from their beloved Marxist visions. I saw the left then as wrong, nationalistic, and the voice of the resentment-filled near-poor. All I could see were images of working-class savages.

The near-poor I hated during the Vietnam War made the victory in World War II, made the world into a world. In the words of General LeMay, they "fried the cities" of Europe and Japan. They killed Japanese soldiers, often already captured, in racist fury. They cared as little about French and Chinese allies as they did about German and Japanese enemies. Spurred on by Franklin Roosevelt's one-world visions, they destroyed the enemies as utterly as Rome destroyed Carthage or Genghis Khan's armies slaughtered thousands. The Americans did not fight a kind and gentle war. They were as ruthless as the Germans and the Japanese who also fought, spurred on by visions, for world dominion.

Hitler believed that the time had come for the Germans to rule the world. Shōwa Tennō also felt the time had come for the Japanese to rule the world, for which reason so many leftist Japanese after the war wanted him deposed and punished. These aspirations recalled Genghis Khan, for whom *Monghol-un chagh bui,* "it was the time of the Mongols."

I felt a dilemma similar to that of historians who have studied the great empires. Great empires were built by visionary leaders who commanded savages. The good could not come without the evil. In the mid-1940s I had been one of those savages. I was too young to have killed or be killed in war. I entered the world after it had been conquered by those a few years older than I. During my two years in the U.S. Army I made the transition from working to middle class. Others would do it by pursuing the American Dream. I did it by becoming an intellectual. Thereafter I rarely returned to visit my family and childhood home. I already sensed then that my vision of the world and my becoming an intellectual were closely related.

When I realized that I had helped bring about America's hegemony in the world and that that hegemony had been good for me, I began to ruminate—and still do—about how my world vision squares with the reality of American empire. All of my loathing of the working class resurfaced when I followed the massive bombing of Iraq during the Gulf War. But only a few weeks later I felt pride when American soldiers went into northern Iraq to protect the Kurds (even though in so doing they were helping advance George Bush's "new world order").

By and large, great empires have been beneficial—to some of its people. They pulled together extensive tracts of land and organized large numbers of diverse peoples. That made large-scale trade possible, and trade was the source of urban prosperity. They kept the peace so that the wealth-laden caravans could move safely over large distances. If they were generally good for core cities, they were bad for marginal rural people, peasant and nomad. Great empires produced "North-South gaps," metaphorically speaking. And often over time the barbarians on the peripheries built up enough strength to conquer the core empires. No empire ever came close to turning into a utopia. And it is unlikely that the United States will ever again attain the comprehensive level of good living it achieved when the American Dream was working.

In 1945 a chasm separated the level of life of the American paradise even from those of the more developed economies of the first world. As the American empire spread over the world, its civilization fanned out with it. Western Europe and Eastern Asia now look much like America. Middle-class modernized and industrialized enclaves are fast spreading in other parts of the world. Historians are not surprised by this. Such spreading of economy and life-style was true of Rome, China, India under its various dynasties, and many other empires.

Now despite a weak dollar and weakening political will, America is still regarded with awe throughout the world. Leftists are chagrined. Even granted that hegemony has brought some good to the world, what about the cost, they ask. To embrace the good also means to accept the evil. Didn't leftists do the same for years when they ran revolutionary countries?

Empires, as historians know, emerge from revolutions, and revolution is an easier concept to understand than empire. Revolution means "turning upside down"—what is at the top comes down, and what is at the bottom comes up. The battering ram of all violent revolutions is the mob, the sansculottes pouring out onto the grand squares of the central cities. In Paris they watched aristocratic heads roll on the guillotine. The conservative Spanish writer José Ortega y Gasset wrote of the "rising of the masses," and it horrified him because they were the savages.

The savagery was inevitable, once the visions were proclaimed. Revolutions are not revolutions without savagery—can one call Vaclav Havel's "velvet revolution" of 1989 a true revolution? Otherwise they are reforms. And maybe reforms are better than revolutions, but revolutions are like great building projects for which, first, the land has to be cleared of everything else.

The 1960s was a revolutionary period that included savagery in Indochina and rebel madness in a dozen countries. Out of it emerged a greater America and a lesser U.S.A. America won. The U.S.A. lost.

Once the war was over, the warriors were no longer needed. The Vietnam vets came home in despair. The rebels denounced them as savages. No honor for them. Around the same time a vast de-industrialization process began. Industrial workers were no longer needed. Blacks, who in the late 1960s finally got their chance to enter the industrial work force and, with new civil rights laws, seemed finally to have the door open to pursue the American Dream, found the industrial floor beneath them vanishing.

Honor came to blacks affirmatively advanced into the middle class. But no honor for poor blacks as more and more of them sank to the level of beggars. And once-honored old white workers now too became redundant, stout figures in bursting trousers sitting in front of the TV.

The lost war marked a turning point for an American militarism that flourished with global hegemony. In the wake of World War II, America's proud legions had been stationed all over the world, and it had seemed they would be there for a long time. Generals and admirals were awesome, even more so the technology their armed services spawned. But in the wake of the lost Vietnam War, voices demanded that the legions be brought home. They too were redundant.

Were the legions rehabilitated by the Persian Gulf War? During that war the ground soldiers mainly watched high-tech weaponry slaughtering some hundred thousand Iraqis. And then when they went into Kuwait and Iraq to do battle, the war was called off. Too many dead American bodies would frighten Americans. In the end battlefield valor was not needed. Later the grand marches made spectators feel good but did nothing to change the fact that America's working-class legions were no longer all that useful militarily.

The Reagan people had decided to shift the U.S. military posture to high-tech—play down the man, play up the gadgetry. Republicans were

never that friendly to the army anyway. The Democrats, who traditionally got the blue collar vote, were. And as the Democrats found it harder
and harder to get their own candidate elected as commander-in-chief, so
the importance of the army has waned. Even under Bill Clinton, it is not
again waxing.

The U.S. Air Force won the Gulf War. Sociologically, it has its roots
in the great American middle class—the descendants of peasants who
came to America and became industrial workers, whose children and
grandchildren finally made it up into the middle class and out into the
suburbs. Like the civilization itself, the Air Force's feats are due mainly
to the technology and the technical prowess of its pilots. Unlike infan-
try savagery, which is direct, air force savagery is abstract, from 30,000
feet up.

Despite the shift of a half million American troops to the Gulf War,
U.S. global military strategy still follows the so-called Nixon Doctrine of
1969: regional allies must provide the ground forces while the United
States furnishes air, naval, and logistical forces. And as America's global
reach has become greater than ever, the U.S. Navy has been the main
beneficiary of America's new imperial role in the world. To this ex-army
person, the navy seems colonial: lots of dark-skinned swabs commanded
by white officers.

Compact professional armed forces, mainly naval and air, armed
with high-tech weapons, form the core of America's military power.
American "grunts" are no longer needed. As in the Roman Empire, barbarian allies can provide the grunt power.

The grunts are also no longer needed on the civilian front. The once-
great midwestern industrial empires with their smokestack factories have
crumbled. The blue-collar workers who were the driving force of the
American Dream have virtually vanished. Their children, even if working
in manufacturing, are middle class. Even while doing hard construction
jobs, they talk like college graduates. And where white workers once
constituted the bulk of America's near-poor, now Hispanic immigrants
doing very different kinds of work have replaced them. The gap between

near-poor and poor, between middle class and poor, between white and "Spanish" is getting wider. Only fading visions of the American Dream link the increasingly foreign and minority "working poor" with the still mainly white mainstream middle class.

The 1960s turned out to be a watershed in American history. As the hard-hats hoped for a touch of fascism to wipe out our own *subversivos,* they did not understand what the more intellectual subversives, those armed with Marxist theories, were saying to them: You are going to be redundant whenever the big bosses decide they no longer need you. When that time comes, you will be discarded like squeezed lemons.

The rebels, in their hatred of America, sensed more than they understood that America was moving into a postnational stage. Did that mean the America of the American Dream was dissolving, its contours crumbling? They did not know and hardly cared that within a few years the nation's once sacrosanct frontiers would come down as millions of illegal immigrants poured across it, or that Miami and Los Angeles would become places where the English language was getting harder to hear on the streets—except from the immigrants' offspring.

ONE ECONOMY, ONE WORLD

During the administration of Richard Nixon the great transition took place, and the United States increasingly became an inextricable part of the global economy. Before then, despite its hegemonic involvements, it had managed to maintain a dual character as a domestic U.S.A. and a global America. When Bruce Springsteen later defiantly sang "Born in the U.S.A.," it was interpreted to mean he wanted the country once again to become the white working-class U.S.A., setting the cultural tone, again a source of power, as it was from the 1930s on, when the unions were able to enforce pro-U.S.A. politics.

The revolts of the 1960s cleared the way for Richard Nixon to come to power. While verbally espousing an American nationalism, he did more to internationalize the American economy than any other American leader. Nixon ended the U.S. independence from the import of foreign oil. Never, America's military strategists had vowed, should the United States become dependent on oil over which it had no control. They kept pointing to Japan's oil vulnerability in the 1930s. More than any other act, Franklin Roosevelt's oil embargo of March 1941 against Japan made Pearl Harbor inevitable. But in 1971 Nixon overrode the military's opposition to major foreign oil imports. Twenty years later, America went to war in the Persian Gulf to ensure control over the world's most important sources of oil, on which it too had become dependent.

Oil powers the automobile, the most representative instrument of American civilization. Not surprisingly, U.S. labor, always eager to show its nationalist patriotism, denounced Nixon's lifting of oil import quotas. Hatred of Nixon was widespread in liberal political circles, but in few was it more intense than in the unions. The then powerful United Automobile Workers (UAW) set labor's anti-Nixon tone. Except for the few left-wing unions that survived the McCarthyite purges of the early 1950s, organized U.S. labor and the military have long been allies in the common defense of the United States. Organized labor could be heard through the voice of Senator Henry Jackson of Washington State, who rose to power through union support and vehemently supported the Vietnam War. Jackson shifted his stance only toward the end, when U.S. defeat had become a fact.

Nixon's moves brought more than foreign oil pouring into America. Toyota became as American as apple pie, as California's Tom Hayden used to like to say of American radicalism. Just as technology was the U.S.A.'s virility, so was the car for the working man. The car was the U.S.A. for every young guy who, before taking a job in the factory, was going to have a ball with the girls and get some daytime hunting done with the gang.

Around the same time, Nixon cut the link between the dollar and gold. In the wake of World War II, hegemonic America had created a monetary system in which all currencies would eventually be pegged to the dollar, and the dollar alone was rigidly pegged to gold, at $35 an ounce.

That not only made the United States the unwobbling pivot of the global financial system, but also kept up a bifurcation of a global America, for foreign policy, and a national U.S.A., for domestic issues, Washington had enormous clout over every other currency in the world, but within the nation's borders Americans were prohibited from dealing in gold. For them the dollar was the only legal tender. And if people yearned for it in distant countries, it was because it reflected the reality that America was all-powerful and that most of the world's above-ground gold was hoarded at Fort Knox, Kentucky.

Like Albert Einstein, who cut physics loose from its earth-based co-ordinate systems, so Richard Nixon cut the dollar loose from gold, let Americans buy and sell gold, and helped create a new global financial system in which everything was relative. Nevertheless, as Einstein real-ized for coordinate systems used to describe physical phenomena, so Nixon well understood that the "preferred" currency in the global finan-cial system was the dollar. America remained central to the new world system, just as the city of Rome was central to its empire.

We—just about everybody in the world—live economically in the mesh of a vast global financial network. Every time we buy food, the network delivers it. No money, no delivery of food! A third of Africa's already decimated population would have died if money to buy Western food were not somehow made available. As a son of the working class, I have often wondered why the rich nations did not just let them starve to death, but then I realized that the new establishments are now so global-ized that they understand the interdependence is absolute. They can't take the risk of letting one unwanted part of the globe deteriorate too much. Contrary to left ideology, it is not the world-spanning multina-tionals but the various national working classes who would gladly let unwanted nations rot, as long as they themselves get "what they deserve."

Nixon had no love for labor and evidently no particular affection for the military. He was attracted to money, business, men of wealth. His decisions to let in foreign oil and to cut the dollar loose from gold were business decisions. Those moves pleased the business community, whose multinationals were just then expanding mightily into the outer world. The multinationals became the big world builders.

Today it is easy to speak of the world in business terms. It is a single financial market, a global technology. Business is money and technology. Money used to be national, with a few select currencies being easily accepted beyond their home countries' boundaries. Now money is global. Automatic teller machines (ATMs) in ever more cities take your card and instantaneously give you local currency.

FREEDOM AND NECESSITY

Technology is global. When you see news shows from Taiwan, the buildings look just like Los Angeles. The same façades, the same cars, the same computers inside the cars, the same office arrangements, even the same people—their "Chinese" features seem blurred as they dress and gesticulate like Americans. The Chinese they speak seems like some translation of American English.

I like to describe myself as one-third European, one-third American, and one-third Chinese. I used to imagine that somehow the three cutlures had gotten into my genetic makeup and that I would transmit them to my sons. I realize now that the three are one, that whatever is European in me is neither Slovenian nor German. My Europeanness is entirely intellectual. No turf smell from Europe remains on me. My Chinese serves the purpose of good conversations and reading interesting books and newspapers, but what comes out is modern, global, turfless. As long as my Chinese friends speak the same way, I understand them, but when they revert to turf-linked language, what they say often escapes me. My American side is as intellectual as my European side, with hardly a trace of my working-class background—except when I get into a rage.

When it is the means of communication of the turf, language consists of terms heavily laden with values, feelings, and memories. Turf language conjures up pictures. If I am not of your turf, the words you use do not conjure up pictures in my mind. Nationalism thrives on turf language. So does fascism. For all their commitment to logical language, in the end communism and socialism too evolved a turf language. Logic is universal. English has become a universal logical language, just as Latin and Greek did in the ancient world. Chinese I have always found to be a very logical language, and it is easy to see why: imperial China needed an imperial language, and imperial languages can only be logical. The "higher form" of most languages, German for example, tends to be logical, while the lower forms, usually heard in dialects, are turf-bound.

So the world now shares not only common money and technology, but a common body of language. A vast logic holds the world together, as logic holds individual computers together. Money, technology, and language are bound to this logic, and the logic is perpetuated through them.

When I started to travel at age eighteen, I sought the world. The world meant other peoples, other lands, other cultures—anything other than what was in America. There was something I did not like about America even though I knew that my destiny was here. The American Dream did not entice me, nor did roots or memories in the small domain of my own family of origin. They were too fragmentary. What did attract me was "out there."

I never imagined that the world would take the form it did. I could not imagine a time when hundreds of millions of tourists would swarm over the world. I never imagined that air travel could take on the scale it has. When I traveled first class to Tokyo I felt like a rich young man, oddly favored for reasons I did not understand.

The world we know today was shaped by American civilization. It has captivated Japan. Neither I nor anyone I consorted with there during the mid-1950s imagined that Japan would one day be the single most powerful and productive stretch of territory on the planet. Or that the Japanese language—the most difficult tongue in the world, filled with so many archaic and illogical features—would become a conduit for the know-how that has created the world's most technologically advanced products. There is no successful modern language in the world that is as nonlinear as Japanese.

Is this language a mix of the old-fashioned and the ultra-mod? No, and that is because there is nothing old-fashioned about things non-linear. Over the years I have tried to figure out what nonlinear mathematics and nonlinear physical effects are. Mathematics books usually say that an equation is nonlinear if it is not linear. In less tautological terms, something is nonlinear if its whole is greater than the sum of its parts. The equation of a circle is nonlinear—since ancient times mathematicians have tried to "square the circle"—that is, to show with rigorous proof that an infinite number of tiny lines laid out along the circle would add up to the circle. They have never succeeded.

Nonlinear equations can be solved, but they offer several solutions. You must choose the solution you need, want, or like. You must choose a particular solution out of the soup of solutions for your own nonlinear equation.

In recent years the word *choice* has become associated with women. In America the term *pro-choice* means that a woman has the right, derived from the inalienable ownership of her own body, to choose whether she wants a pregnancy to come to term or not. There are two solutions to the nonlinear pregnancy equation: either it leads to birth or it does not.

I became a rebel around the time of the Free Speech Movement in Berkeley. The students denounced the way kindly mentors planned every pathway of their careers. They held up thousands of key-punch cards to show what they were rebelling against. They demanded the right of choice for themselves. And when Vietnam came, the rebels called for freedom from the draft; again I found myself supporting choice. By the early 1970s choice had become a vast movement. Every group that was marginal to the white-male-dominated core demanded the right of choice and support from state and society to act on its choice. The disabled demanded that their choice to act like abled citizens be supported. To exercise choice was to act morally.

If something moves from one point to another according to rigorous

laws, it will infallibly arrive at that point. That is determinism or, in Hebrew and Christian terms, necessity. But if something moves toward a
number of points, then the mover has a nonlinear choice as toward which
point it will move. That is freedom in the Judeo-Christian tradition.

Today it is common in English for civilization to be called Judeo-
Christian. When Christianity split from Judaism, the former opted for
freedom from the Mosaic law, while the latter stuck with the necessity of
the law as handed down from God. When Descartes gave mathematics a
rigorous direction, the Judaic spirit of necessity prevailed. But in the
twentieth century, nonlinear mathematics became popular in the field.
Determinism too prevailed in the classical economics of the eighteenth
century. Nowadays the market is indeterminate and consumerism demands enormous numbers of choices every day. But American civilization is also marked by highly complex systems that operate with almost
perfect linear precision. Thus freedom and necessity go together in this
mighty civilization.

Why can't I get excited about a world in which linear and nonlinear
have their respective uses, where there is a powerful system but at the
same time broad freedom and choice? Why isn't such a world an almost
perfect world? In the early 1800s, Hegel suggested that history had come
to an end, and in the 1990s State Department planner Francis Fukuyama
repeated that assertion. All that is left is to finish history's unfinished
tasks, to carry out Western civilization's vision of a better world. What
more is there?

MOVEMENT, REST, AND GROWTH

When I traveled, I yearned for home. What home? Not mama's flat. Not
where I grew up. Not my past. Not what was. Not what could be achieved
with money and a steady job. Home for me was associated with the image
of woman, and with the concept of rest. I knew there was no rest, yet I
also knew that rest is home. And so when I traveled and saw women or
old villages or when I went into churches, heard Buddhist monks chant-
ing, I thought of rest and therefore home. Just before a risky trip to Hanoi

during the heavy bombing of March and April 1968, I saw the cardinal of Paris fidgeting with his robes getting ready for mass at Notre Dame de Paris. The sight of the cardinal as a human and as a man of God made me feel at rest, therefore at home.

When I traveled, I rarely made choices about where I wanted to go. Often I went somewhere because an event made the choice for me. Or I drifted into traveling. Eventually, in my studies of China, I discovered that drifting was what the Taoist philosophy was about. Taoists assume that the drifting or flying or letting oneself go fits in with nature's steady and regular movements. In my drifting, however, I did not have that sense. My own traveling was, I suppose, postlinear and post-nonlinear. I wasn't sure where I was going, or even why. Yet beyond my subjective meandering, objectively speaking I was part of a vast process through which America was bringing about a single linearly connected world. My soul took me in certain directions, and so did a little of my mind and body. But most of my mind and my body served this great historic process. I did what I was supposed to do by the river of history and did it so well I got tenure at a major university.

Women had nothing to do with my traveling, yet I watched them wherever I went. In Japan I got to know some women who worked mainly to entertain men. They were not prostitutes or courtesans or even mistresses. They were part of an old Japanese institution known as *geisha*, a word meaning "person of the arts." Their task was to make Japanese men less stiff, broaden their narrow, goal-oriented minds, relax them, let them understand that the world in which linear success counted was one of women as well as men. I liked these women, one or two a lot. But I never thought of home when I was with them. From my study of history I knew that these women were really quite modern. In the eighteenth-century Japan enjoyed a brilliant urban civilization that was more modern in many ways than that in Europe. Consumerism was the mark of the urban way of life. The arts, especially theater, were highly developed. Men and women consorted freely, as in modern society. There was a lot of pornography. Japan even had a fledgling stock market, and its contemporary word for stock, *kabu,* derives from that period. The Meiji Restoration of 1868 propelled Japan into the Western world. But as newly enfranchised peasants swarmed up to gain power through the military, the cosmopolitan society of the Tokugawa period was quashed. As happened once before, during Japan's thirteenth century, women were shut back in the home.

Now Japanese women are again emerging into the public realm. They want to be educated, consort freely with men, exercise their rights of choice, have the freedom to be both nonlinear and linear. Japanese men may slowly be realizing, as with the special relationships in earlier times between men and *geisha,* that linear men and nonlinear women may fit together quite well in a society in which wealth, ease, consumerist appetites, stunning culture, and great creativity coexist. Japan may have had a head start in modernization because of that remarkable eighteenth-century Tokugawa period.

In the two and a half years I spent in Japan, I never sought home there. But in the years I lived in Hong Kong among the Chinese I often thought of home. When I lived in Japan and then traveled in Afghanistan with a Japanese scholar, I thought of Japan as a country of movement.

China and the Chinese were different. From my earliest contact with that civilization, I sensed there was a kind of gravitational pull toward equilibrium in things Chinese. *Harmony* was the word that reappeared again and again in foreign texts about the spirit of Chinese civilization. Ezra Pound translated that core Confucian concept as "the unwobbling pivot." In the early 1980s, I started reading extensively in physics and mathematics. Rest and movement were core notions in Newtonian physics. Two hundred years after Newton, when Einstein brought out his general theory of relativity, rest lost out to movement. No longer did there have to be a "preferred coordinate system," Einstein argued. He freed physics from that unwobbling pivot, as Galileo freed the earth. We, of course, live in a world of movement. I realized that Japan too was a country of movement, even in its earlier history; in China the importance of rest remained deeply embedded in the fabric of the civilization.

In 1970, my movement, my international traveling, more or less stopped. Two years later my first son was born. I was forty-six years old at the time. When I went out with the baby, I was often thought to be his grandfather. Soon I started walking, going ever longer distances. And then I started traveling by reading, in Arabic and Spanish, and in physics and mathematics. I had found a sort of rest at home, but through walking, thinking, and writing, my movement continued.

I realize now that in reading Arabic I was seeking home, and in reading Spanish, I read about death. Death, rest, and home are related. Physics and mathematics were about the West, America, my own civilization. I was often asked why I didn't read novels and histories about America or Europe. All I could answer was that something in physics and mathematics fascinated me, something cosmological, philosophical, and religious. I looked upward when I thought of physics and mathematics, as I did when I thought of the world.

But in reading physics and mathematics, I also sensed an incompleteness. The great scientific advances of the end of the twentieth century were not in physics or mathematics but in biology. I started to do some reading in biology but soon stopped. It wasn't that I didn't think it important, but rather that there was a cultural atmosphere about academic biology that did not appeal to me. When men beget a child it is a linear act. When women are with child, they experience a process of growth. Usually the embryo grows into a fetus, which grows into a baby and then an infant and then a toddler, and so unto death and beyond. In the biology of everyday life, all is growth.

The idea of growth began to interest me. In economics growth is good. For environmentalists growth is less desirable—they advocate a zero-growth economy. I read a dissertation in mathematics by a friend of mine, Bruce Gardner, who was interested in functions that were "self-reflective." By that he meant that whole numbers, none of which was 1, could be multiplied together to give the product 1, called "unity" by the mathematicians. We all know that $1 \times 1 \times 1 \times 1 = 1$, but how could $2 \times 3 \times 4 \times 5 = 1$? This equation resembles a fully grown organism that keeps eating but no longer grows larger, the food simply ensuring steady-state growth.

A pregnant woman is a vehicle of growth. A woman's body feeds a new person in her belly, while what she eats maintains her own steady state. A man's contribution to the baby's growth is in the instantaneous act of creation, the fertilization by a sperm. Growth is neither linear nor nonlinear. But all growth has a path, more or less predetermined. The genetics of organisms determines that path. Does genetics determine everything about that path? Clearly not. Modern biotechnology has shown how the predetermined genetic path can be changed, and traditionalists warn of the monstrous possibilities that this entails. Nevertheless, all growth involves a path.

Even though the path is neither linear nor nonlinear, it goes somewhere. We grow older on a path. The kind of movement we experience on a growth path is very different from the motion of a particle along a line from one point to another. It involves time. Although Einstein tried to assimilate time to space and was easily able to do so mathematically, people still believe that time is very different from space. And with good reason. Time means aging and aging means death. The notion of death was meaningless in Einstein's world. For him, time was reversible.

In the early 1980s aging men were working to unify Europe. They did not want growth. They wanted Europe, at last at peace, to stay as it was. They wanted to be surrounded by beautiful, elegant women. I shall never get old, they hoped, and a beautiful woman will always be beautiful, and Europe will be just like those stunning medieval and Renaissance inner cities—Nurnberg, Munich, Warsaw's rebuilt Stare Mesto, Budapest, and Paris. The past never grows old.

The symbol 1 means unity, and unity gives such a warm feeling. Oneness is so powerful that it is the core concept of Islam, *tauheed*. For all the repression of women in that faith, its men are fascinated by women (one has the feeling that many would like to do nothing more than endlessly make love to women). I once had a landlord who said he never felt so sexually aroused as in library stacks, where he experienced a tremendous sense of unity from knowledge packed together in such compact, tiny spaces. The sexuality of *tauheed*.

Growth and unity go together. After an organism grows into its adult form, it retains that form even as it ages. A caterpillar undergoes a dramatic change in form, but then retains the butterfly form until it dies. Growth is a path. It should lead to unity.

When economists talk of growth, they think of some eventual unity. They envisage a time when all competition will go from "imperfect" to "perfect." They see a single economic order dominating the entire world. And even if postmodernism's coolness has taken hold of many economists, there is still enough of the idealism of classical economics left to let them hope for an eventual global economic unity, though now they face a growing enemy in the form of a relentless environmentalism. Environmentalists speak endlessly of planetary unity but do not like world unity. And so, like earlier socialists, they are hostile to the free flow of global capital, which is key to global economic unity. Controlling capital flows, in their view, is the only way to rein in rampant development and save the planet.

The product of birth is a unity, an organism with a general shape and direction that it will retain till death. Home is a place where birth, growth, and death take place. And if birth and death are seen as stages of growth, then home and growth go together.

A machine is made—that is, it is fabricated by hands commanded by mind. It has no unity. The machine either works or it does not. It may have nonlinear as well as linear components, but it has no unity and no growth. A house cannot grow. It is a structure one lives in. A nice modern house is one where things are supposed to work linearly, like an electrical switch. And the people who live in it operate in nonlinear fashion, always making choices, which one hopes help to construct a new social reality that will be good for all.

Let there be truth, beauty, and goodness—peace in the world—and that will be a better world. But it will be a world without homes, without rest, with unending motion, like a car driving forever on some unending highway. American civilization is a construct, and a wonderful construct indeed. But it is like a highway that goes on and on, an unending array of wonderful scenery, even beyond death.

Newton showed that motion and rest go together. The biology of everyday life instructs us in growth. Like billions of organisms that for millennia have been but clones of each other, growth without movement is boring. Movement without rest is chaos. Movement without growth is a denial of the future. American civilization at its best is still incomplete. And at its worst it is a denial of the future.

THE INDIVIDUAL

In the late 1980s I often met people who were concerned with "the self." An old friend once gave me parts of a book manuscript to read, a chapter he had written on the "moral self." I did not read it for a long while. Another friend formed a group of people who talked about "aristocracy." They had been close to the Esalen Institute. Esalen—the name comes from a tribe of Indians who used to live on a stunningly beautiful part of the California coast—is famous for the "human potential movement." My friend wrote a book about Esalen. He has acquired calm, perhaps from the influence of Asian thought cultivated at Esalen but also from an awareness of his "self" as well as that of others. Another friend also wrote a book about Esalen. He is into bigger pictures, about the world, about the link between biology (growth) and technology (making things to make other things work). He comes across as a strong individual. These friends are all men.

I also remember an episode in the early days of Pacific News Service, around 1971 or 1972. Several educated and angry young women strode into the office, lashed out in verbal fury at the men, and left a publication, *Women's Page*. It looked like a document that might have been issued by the Moscow State Women's Publishing House. Solid Cyrillic-looking type. The tough-sounding articles, all on abstract subjects, were signed in the Soviet style: S. L. such and such, R. V. such and such. The former wife of a prominent Marxist economist was the editor. I think they were revolting against men—the female collective oppressed vis-à-vis the individual dominant males, outfitted with privileges, ambitions, and vanities. Yet the rebels came across as individuals too, with strong self-identities seeking recognition and power.

In my younger leftist days I was more like the second group than the first. I found it hard to use the word *I*. I was vague about my past. Sometimes I admitted I was born in New York. Other times I denied it. I explained my fluency in various languages by fabricating episodes of travel and residence abroad. I did not really want to lie so much as to deflect attention from my *I*-ness. Even as I became more peculiar and distinct looking, I kept on denying that *I*-ness. I moved more and more in the open, often as a rebel, yet I shunned the higher, democratic arena where the lights shine hard and bright on you. I fled from the private world of my family, yet I yearned to go home. Often I found home in the warmth of a hotel in a distant land.

THE SELF, PUBLIC AND PRIVATE

I did not realize then that the self—the uncomfortable trinity of body, mind, and soul—is at its sharpest, most evident, and salient in the interface of the public and private worlds. Everything in that interface is in motion, oscillating or linear or chaotic. If one is there, hiding is very hard. Lies and subterfuge only tend to make the self stand out more sharply. (It used to be that the selfs of men and occasionally of women were brought into sharp relief only before having their lives snuffed out. Nowadays murderers are executed in a private way, similar to the way that trash collectors remove the garbage in the dark early hours of the morning.)

In those days, I hated America and Americans. Their language grated on my one good ear. The preposterous notion that two "o"s together made the "u" sound was to me to be particularly revolting. I was too young for Betty Boop, but her name seemed to epitomize all that was revolting in America. I did not like people whose names began with "Mc." I was fearful of not having money, yet I did not want to earn my way into the suburbs as my German relatives had done. I wanted to stay on those overlapping margins, ready to step one way or the other and back again.

My expertise in sinology made me a reasonably well known and successful professor. The Vietnam War drew me into the public arena through speech making. When I was in Vientiane, Laos, on my way to

Hanoi in March 1968, I got into a fight with the then American ambassador to Laos. It was reported in *Time*. My leftist friends hailed me as a hero. I was mortified—not by the act but by the publicity. I still regard that ambassador as one of the men who helped commit crimes against humanity by the saturation bombing of the country in which he was posted.

I detested the idea of self-liberation, which was so big with the politically hip and chic people in the sixties and seventies. In America you "liberated" yourself by talking endlessly about yourself, or rather, your self. I know that I do not really appreciate democracy, though I laud it in my writings. In a democracy, people have rights and should want to protect them. But deep down I still am not certain what a "right" is, though I know absolutely what a "duty" is. That should mark me as a conservative. You can claim a right only if you are willing to stand up before a judge and say, "This is my right and I demand remedy for the injustices I have been subjected to."

Yet here I praise the great American civilization; I hail its prosperous life-style, its ability to take people from the herd and make them intelligent, beautiful, and good-doing (fulfilling the ancient Greek ideals of truth, beauty, and goodness), and its tremendous democracy, its ideal of turning all into individuals functioning in the public world.

My leftist tribesmen find it odd, ghastly even, that I sing the praises of a civilization that they see as evil because it alienates people from each other. But those who damn it the most are often those with mighty selfs, who stand out with such sharpness that others fear them, are afraid to approach them. They wonder why they do not feel warmth from others. What many leftists really crave is the warmth that comes when one is an aristocrat, powerful in mind and body, wealthy in pocket, surrounded by fame and privilege, and respected. Aristocrats, or in Lenin's term *vanguards*, have the best of both worlds . . . or so they hoped until the roof fell in in 1989.

I hope that soul is returning to me and replacing some of my self; yet

I am a self-aware, self-contained, and self-motivating person. I am out there in the public arena every time I lecture. America—which, like every other nation-state, wants to make its ideology bear fruit—has done well by me, which may be why I am now reconciled to its language and culture. I am an American and an individual.

I know, however, that the self is an illusion. Body, mind, and soul do not fit together. What makes a person's *I* so powerful in the interface between private and public realms is the discomfort, friction, even conflict between body, mind, and soul, and a powerful *I* wrestles with them in a difficult world. When educated Americans—middle-class Americans who have made it into the public realm—speak about the self, they have already lost soul and are trying to fit body and mind together, hoping that they will manage the task before death. When I say that I am reconciled to America, I realize that means admitting a slipping-away of soul.

AMERICAN CIVILIZATION APPROPRIATES THE SELF

One thing that attracts me in America is its power, the power of a vision spreading mightily throughout the world. *I want it all now.* Self-ish middle-class people in Rawalpindi who sense the power of the *I* move from the tight Indo-Muslim family into the American civilization. The empire is spreading, even as fears arise within America that, someday, Spanish could become the empire's official language. (After all, didn't Greek become the official language of the Latin-speaking Roman Empire after the establishment of Constantinople?) From Rawalpindi they come to America and, when asked, "Do you eat pork?" respond, "Sure, no problem." The empire and the *I* are closely related, and they are impressive. And, in moments when my soul slumbers, I am an impressive *I* also. (But the soul wakes up again and makes me think of going forth on pilgrimages, or even, God forbid, to preach . . . preach what, the American way of life, that half-vision whose light nevertheless remains as intense and bright as that of ancient Rome?).

If I were asked what made me into an American, my answer would be direct: I am the son of immigrants. My father came from Slovenia, then an Austrian province. Close by was Croatia, then a Hungarian province. Both were within the Austro-Hungarian empire. My father's parents and ancestors cultivated grapes to make wine near an ancient Roman hot springs spa. My mother comes from the Ore Mountains on what was the East German–Czech border. Her parents and ancestors were miners, factory workers, foresters. They formed a mixed marriage—a husband who spoke Slovenian but learned German and Italian (but only bad English) and a wife who spoke an obscure German dialect. Immigration was central to life in a family that did not start out as family. There always was a sense of having come from somewhere else and a fear of having to move on. America was the kind of country that pushed you on, as when the factory where the man worked closed down.

As a child my sense of I-ness arose when I refused to speak any language but English. We kids were *I*'s. Our parents were blurry and foreign. The kitchen smelled great, but when the people in the kitchen opened their mouths to speak, I gritted my teeth. All that changed when my father died when I was thirteen. I discovered his languages, pursued them as a lover pursues a beloved, read any book I could find on the Balkans, and painted "Slovenija" on the side of our garage, which my father had clumsily built. I went out a lot but always came back home.

In the process of that back-and-forth between an out-there public and an in-here private, my *I*-ness became stronger and stronger. My sexual development (most Americans pant to hear about everyone's sexual development) was slow. I was attracted to girls but knew nothing about sexual intercourse. I cultivated visions, not sex. I wanted to travel.

I hated God. I now realize that meant I hated my soul, which seemed the enemy to my mind, and, I believed, the enemy to a body that one day would enjoy the sensual pleasures some of my friends were already enjoying. Nevertheless, I was into visions, not mind-honing or body-building. I wanted to travel, but for no particularly elevated reasons—just to smell the tar on a freshly paved road, feel the hot sun on the plains, see mountains, and above all look at the clouds. I still love clouds with passion—they are always going somewhere. (Bertolt Brecht wrote a poem about making love to a woman under a tree and years afterward could remember only the clouds floating above them.)

I don't think there is anything more extraordinary in the contemporary world than the unending movement of people. Once I had to look up the population of Lagos, which the Columbia Encyclopedia gave as one million in 1971. A decade later when I looked again, the population had risen to four million. Now it is more. Many were Ghanaian immigrants. They were all kicked out. Now many of those returnees are busy with enterprises to help revive Ghana's moribund socialist economy. The people's movements are called migration, or tourism. Tourism is the leading source of income in my city, San Francisco. Tourists fill hotels that are fatter and taller than ever. Mixtec strawberry pickers fan out all the way up to Oregon and Washington from villages where their ancestors were until recently among the most place-bound. In Africa, AIDS has spread because there are so many migrants and so many roads and so many prostitutes. People on the move are everywhere: the faithful who are called to prayer in Düsseldorf; Afghans in New Delhi and Uighur youngsters peddling their wares in Canton; Bolivian and Paraguayan campesinos in Buenos Aires; white runaway youngsters on the streets of San Francisco and New York; Jack Kerouac on the road. In Cuba people will not walk two blocks if a car or a bus is available. They aren't lazy; they just think it crazy not to want to move in a piece of technology— that's where it's at in the modern world. A Chinese man, an old friend, was so proud that his daughter has become a New York fashion designer who shuttles between Paris, Florence, and New York. Many love the motion of a city, the fumes pouring into the air, the smell of fresh tar, the crowd at the Moscow McDonald's. They do not like the garbage and filth of modern civilization, but they fully expect that it can be flushed down the toilet, pronto.

Sigmund Freud wanted to live only in Vienna. He hated to travel and died two years after the Nazis forced him out. He did not see what was coming because he did not understand the swirling in Germany that was much more than Oedipal complexes or anti-Semitism. The Nazis brought a revolution to Germany and tore Germans out of a place-bound past. The Americans rode on that revolution to introduce their own revolution, and lo and behold, the Germans have become a wandering people (their tourists are like a vast tide inundating entire countries).

The trouble with so many academics is that they live in ivory towers underwritten by the state, and do not see, let alone live in, the swirl of real modern life: where businesses start with a flash and go belly-up without a groan; where people just get in the car when they feel the urge to see somebody, do something; where thousands of motels have "no vacancy" signs on Wednesday nights.

(But I love to walk the same streets again and again. How un-American! I have become a place-bound person, and I write about movement as the human condition. I have dreams of abandonment, but the abandonment always comes with movements, mine or those of my family. Movement is my nightmare.)

Why this urge to move? Perhaps people who move, deep down, see themselves as something special, not merely some peasant's child. God has given them a calling, a calling forth from the village, from home. Having a calling means pursuing something higher, and that has to involve a moving out. Ancient peoples believed that when we died, a spirit stepped out of our bodies; if others could see it, it would look like two of us, double vision. But the corporeal body is put into a grave, the place of rest, while the spirit body drifts away into the air. Similarly, when somebody migrates, the spiritual self separates itself from his or her social attachments and embarks on a journey. But we who migrate are not dead. We retain our minds and our bodies and, especially, our souls. The three together, in a raggedy way, make up the self, which becomes instantaneously powerful the moment we take our first step on the journey.

Consider what has been happening to Peru. In San Francisco one sees Peruvian Indians with their Inca noses, long and imperial, hawking shirts for Chinese owners who sit back and count the money. They have been flowing from their Andean mountains, like snow or mud slides that keep on coming, or rain that finds its way into rivers and aquifers and keeps traveling downstream. They are the strange peasants José Maria Arguedas wrote about. They speak softly to each other in Quechua. The *costeños* of Spanish descent, and many mestizo who looked Indian but saw themselves as of Spanish descent, were the active ones before the rising of the Indians. They also were the ones everybody knew as *I*'s. The Indians were "theys," always in the plural, the mass. Now they stand defiantly on a Chinatown street and are *I*'s in a neighborhood where the Chinese always look and act like *we*'s. A revolution is going on in Peru, where the Indians are on the move and are becoming powerful individuals, hordes of powerful individuals.

Those Indians stand in a public realm. The Chinese shop owners do not want to do that. Neither do I. In Japan a key part of a management training course is for the young trainee to stand on a sidewalk and shout ludicrous things. People stare, stop, and burst out laughing, not at his funny language but at his funny self. Japan used to be—and in most ways still is—a very private society. But after World War II its leaders understood that they had been defeated by an American enemy that was extraordinarily public. The Japanese were accustomed to going naked into public baths, but they were astounded when Americans bared their souls and their minds. They decided that in order to make their way in this new American world they would have to go naked in mind and soul into the streets. For those who survive the course, high rewards are available, but only if they travel incessantly. The young Indians on a Chinatown street are serving only themselves and their families, but already the power can be sensed in their faces as they make their pitch to the tourists.

Is it economics alone that drags these people out of their villages? Economists talk about push/pull factors—poverty in the villages and jobs elsewhere. Maybe. It is undeniable that what draws these people in is the lure of money. Fifty pieces of green paper marked $100 can, poof, be turned into a shiny car with a motor that purrs like a tiger. Money grants power, and power makes nobodys into *I*'s. They send back money. They have not found a holy grail, but in San Francisco they get paid in magic green paper.

Nomads have always loved money. They festoon their women with gold and silver. They will ride far to steal money. But classical nomads carried their families with them, as the turtle carries his shell. With modern nomads it is different. So many are alone. When I was a child there were many boarding houses around for gentlemen. It was understood that these gentlemen generally had no families and had to travel in order to work at a decent job. Little was said about money. People were as discreet about money as they were about sex. Now we live in a world where too much has been revealed about both. Sex is losing its magnetism as people find out how difficult it can be to have sex without love. But money is losing nothing of its magnetism and power. Money gives an individual power, and nothing else matters.

It used to be that you could get a job in a factory, like my father, work in smoldering silence, shuffle back home, eat, go down to the cellar to tinker. Life was private. (How private the Russians still are, evident in the large but almost invisible Russian community in San Francisco whereas the Chinese are both private and public, but in their own particular way, not the way of "standard" American civilization.) Factories are vanishing. More and more jobs are public. Janitors may find themselves engaged in conversations about the economy or Bosnia when many just want to sweep, dust, and shuffle off to the flats they share with others like them. The powerful American democracy makes everyone go public. Millions of peasants have been torn out of millennial, cyclical, dreamless existences to become individuals, some so strikingly individual that they have become what Americans call "great personalities."

Consider the Jews. Two centuries ago they were keeping a low profile in the *shtetls* of Eastern Europe so the cossack didn't hit them over the head with a rifle butt. Now they appear before everyone as public geniuses and great comedians. Or consider blacks. All blacks know that *black* is commonly equated with evil, violence, infamy, and all sorts of wicked things. And they believe that they were shut up in African darkness while the rest of the world developed great civilizations. Yet they too have emerged onto the American public democratic scene with genius, power, drive, and tremendous individuality. In an American society that prizes individuality, white faces have become bland, blurry, and dull.

When I was a child it was said that only some kinds of people came to the United States. The French, people said, didn't come because they wanted to stay in France, a rich and prosperous country. The Chinese did not come because we did not want them. Now people from every nation come here. Many are drawn by a desire to become individuals. The Japanese, for instance. There is not much economic reason for them to come. The standard of living is high in Japan, and the degree of public safety is greater than it is here. Yet they keep coming. A couple of gay Japanese men told me that it was the attraction of freedom that brought them here—they could live as they pleased without others prying into their private lives.

We are the Free World. Out there is, or rather was, the Communist World. We are individuals. They were the herd. In Russia young people detested the herd so much that they became highly individuated. When the Soviet Union collapsed, that youthful individualism burst into full flower. The United States was founded as the Enlightenment was coming to a close. Its teachings were ready to be exported, and they were—the ideas that fashioned the United States of America and made it into the great experiment for those ideas. The words of the Declaration of Independence that "all Men are endowed with certain inalienable rights, among these are Life, Liberty, and the Pursuit of Happiness" launched an American civilization that still creates individuals everywhere.

Throughout the 1800s, people came to America. Consider the Germans who in 1848 rose up against tyranny. Many came to Texas, which, along with California, became the most individualistic state of the union (in Texas the individualism was expressed by legitimate covetousness but in California by visions). They became ranchers, fencing off great tracts of plain. They voted for crazy Democrats and then for entrepreneurial Republicans. By 1933 they were as different as could be from the still herdlike Germans Hitler faced when first in power. (The Nazi revolution and the destructive wars that followed destroyed those herds and left Germans in the succeeding Federal Republic as American-style individuals.)

Consider the boat people who have ventured forth into the South China Sea by the hundreds of thousands. On the coast of Vietnam they bribed communist officials with gold ingots. On the boat they were attacked by Thai pirates who stole, raped, and killed. Everywhere they landed, they met with hostility. Some were sent back out to sea where they died or were refused aid by passing ships, often American. Yet they all wanted to come here. And when they came, many did well, motivated by their ideas, ambition, individuality. Although fleeing Haitians face being turned back by the U.S. Coast Guard, many make it to Miami or New York where they find each other, maybe open a shop of their own, establish churches, and show rays of individual brilliance one can see in their art back home. The American middle class may be in decline but the spongelike power of the United States to draw in more proto-middle-class people remains as powerful as ever.

AMERICA'S BET ON THE MIDDLE CLASSES

I have read that half of all the world's immigrants (not refugees) come to the United States. In the big cities, you see them everywhere. I see many immigrant Irish in San Francisco (where they seem to go into the home-related contracting business). There used to be a Titograd-Tijuana express—Montenegrins and Bosnians trying to sneak across the border to Los Angeles. Who only a few years ago could have imagined 30,000 Hmongs in Fresno (back in the hills of Thailand and Laos they were called Méo, and in China Miao, laid-back people practicing slash-and-burn agriculture)?

An old friend a long time ago once dismissed the Russian and Chinese revolutions as peasant affairs. At the time I was somewhat miffed by the remark. He was already then a man of the North, and I was drawn by the South. What's wrong with peasants? But he was right. Stalin tried to nail his people down (those who didn't stay put were shot). Mao Zedong favored the peasants. But he kept peasants in the countryside by keeping life in the cities so threadbare that the shrewd peasants just didn't want to come. Deng Xiaoping, Mao's successor, also favored the peasants. Through his rural reforms launched in 1978 he hoped waves of peasants would not inundate the cities. In 1984, when he started favoring city people as well, the peasant waves started coming. That is what happened in the latter part of the western Roman Empire—life in the cities became so horrible that people fled to the rural places to start farming again, this time as Christians and not *pagani.*

But in Latin America they are still pouring out of their Indian villages into the cities. And if the Shining Path had won, a Presidente Gonzalo in Peru would have nailed the peasants to the soil—as Stalin did in Russia, Enver Hoxha did in Albania, and Pol Pot tried to do in Cambodia.

The term "North-South gap" was coined by the late social democratic leader Willy Brandt. He meant it not only as a descriptive term for a poor South facing a rich North, but as a moral mandate for the North to help the South become richer. The North has not accepted that mandate, but American civilization has performed mightily to transform southerners from peasants into movers, and from *we*'s into *I*'s.

So in Kasghar they show American films dubbed into Uighur and Chinese. Deng Xiaoping's former right-hand man, Zhao Ziyang, wanted to rev up the cities so people there could live a little bit like they do in Tokyo and Los Angeles. But arising in China is what some call the "Latin American specter"—too many people flooding into the cities. Inflation, corruption, crime, overcrowding, the massive upsurge of self-ishness appear. Some government officials wonder whether it was not better in Mao Zedong's days when, as in Russia, the movement of the peasants was strictly controlled. And the peasants themselves sometimes wonder whether it is worthwhile heading for the cities, especially since the rural areas are now doing rather well.

American civilization wants to make all people in the world into I's.

The communists wanted to keep them *we*'s but make them affluent in their unmoving homes. Cities have always created *I*'s—to repeat the medieval German cry, "the air of the city makes you free." Villages—even in capitalist countries—want to be *we*'s.

Just a little thought will show that in the everyday lives of every individual in the world life is—and has to be—lived as a mix of *I* and *we*, even if one of the two is so stunted as to be only a wistful longing. We are also both movers and settlers, nomads and peasants, even if one of each pair is stunted. That the two always seek to unite is evident from the fact that the world is coming together faster than it is dividing into a North and a South.

The powerful *I*-ness of American civilization won out over the excessively top-down *we*-ness of the communist systems. But even if its visions blanket the world they can never encompass it all. There just is no way the entire world will turn American—"modern and industrialized" in political science parlance. There is a missing half. Socialism and communism tried to provide it but failed. A communist Peru cut off from Ecuador, as Albania was from Greece, was not what the God of History commanded. And so now Alberto Fujimori leads Peru into the world, and poor Albania has stumbled into it. There cannot be a world if it is divided into a bourgeois and a peasant half. The God of History has decided there shall be a world.

Never, never accept two-ness, the sixth patriarch and Chinese founder of Zen said to his disciples. His favorite metaphor was the clay pot. Without the clay there is no pot. Without the pot the clay is formless substance, empty. Form is emptiness and emptiness is form.

Marx again must be credited with the insight that a true world is coming into being because we must all eat.

The material life of the Roman Empire's citizens depended on trade mixed with some local economies. While it held together, a civilization spread, creating a (Western) world. For geographical reasons it could not reach the Eastern world, centered on China. But from the Straits of Hercules to the Indus River the world was one. Even foreign Parthia did not

ruin that oneness, for to the east of Parthia there were the Hellenic king-
doms of Bactria, Kushan, and the Indus states (Gandhara). That the
world was one was made evident by the spread of Christianity to Syria
and the Nabatean kingdom of northern Arabia. Mithraism and
Buddhism dominated a bit farther to the east, beyond the Syrian and
Arabian deserts, but Buddhism had as its core sociology the acceptance
of the human as an individual, as did Christianity.

The migrations in the world today bypass the great peasant countries:
Russia, China, India (though one cannot overlook the great recent internal migrations in these three empire-sized countries). They flow into
North America, into most of Latin America (from within and from without), and into Western Europe, the oil-producing Gulf states, Australia,
and Africa.

What all this means sociopolitically is enormous strength and creativity. The great strength of America, as in the case of the Romans, has
lain in the production of individuals. Look at the powerful portrayal of
individuality of classical Roman statues! Most were images of men (and
women) of beautiful body (even when old) and brilliant mind (even
when stupid). And they radiated soul because they all seemed to know
what they were doing and where they were going (no matter that in reality
they didn't). Historians lament the decline of classical Rome, yet it took
the work of many individuals to make Roman Christianity the mighty
tree it so quickly became (the same can be said of Arab Islam).

Paul Kennedy, who writes on the decline of America, came from
England. Benoît Mandelbrot came from France and I. M. Pei from China.
T. Y. Lin made pre-stressed concrete, which has transformed entire
cityscapes. All of them speak with accents, are different from the "ordinary" American, are "gifted," as Americans say, and are in that transi-
tional human condition where body, mind, and soul go together in a
raggedy way. The empire needs those *I*'s to keep going. (The world needs
more than the empire, but I turn to that later, when I take up the matter
of rest.) What about educating the gifted?, educators like the University
of Chicago's Mortimer Adler asked in the late 1970s. They were asking

for recruits to the class of *I*'s on which the American empire born of the Enlightenment depends.

As the recruits to the empire keep swarming in, counter-currents are also flowing. Middle-class people in poor countries can't or won't move toward the empire, or they experience the cyclonic movement of worry that makes them crazy. From its founding in 27 B.C., the Roman empire throughout its domains was wracked by madness.

My favorite Arab columnist, Mustafa Amin, who writes in the London-based *Sharq Al-Ausat,* usually bemoans the terrible conditions of life in Egypt while lauding democracy and flailing at dictatorship. His Arabic is concise, simple enough for me to understand. He once wrote: "I do not know how people live in my country these days, be they poor or rich, powerless or powerful; they're all exhausted and overburdened, all complain, not one of them is happy with what they have, all lament how little pay they get—in every house we see it. It used to be they ate a cooked meal once a day; now it's once a week. It used to be that they took a car to work; now they take the tram. It used to be they spent summers in Europe, now they have to make do with Egypt."

Now in the growing turn toward Islamic fundamentalism, the women wear white scarves and the men are in mosque, where earnest, young, black-bearded men preach sermons on the faith. We must recognize that Islam has become the most powerful challenger to American civilization in the world, because Islam challenges the three pillars of that civilization: consumerism, self-liberation, and democracy. It does not accept the notion of a middle class, and it looks with horror at the individuality of the West, where body is one thing, mind another, and soul, Muslims believe, has vanished.

Millions have crowded into Cairo, in a country shaped like a papyrus stem (with just a little bulge at the Nile Delta). When the Firengi were there, there were many social layers. Now the middle classes are vanishing, and the new Muslims are happy as the evil of Westernness (which is still more European than American in origin) too is vanishing. The religion preaches the unity of the person and the community, which means that your body and your mind must be part of the community (the same belief holds in other tight religious groups, such as the American Mennonites, the Jehovah's Witnesses, and the Hassidic Jews).

We Americans want our bodies and our minds. Our profound belief in a humanistic secularism makes us passionate about human rights. We find torture appalling and consider Islamic punitive amputations barbaric. We passionately believe in freedom of speech and welcomed Gorbachev's opening up of the Soviet Union. We are happy when Cuahtémoc Cárdenas in Mexico makes it a pillar of his political movement. The grand historical bet of the American empire is that it can bring middle classes to a good part of the world. In America most of us remain middle class; only a minority are rich or poor. We were the first in the world to seek to realize Marx's grand (and most powerfully prophetic) vision, that poverty could be removed from the world. Many Americans still believe we did it here, and in Western Europe, and can do it in Eastern Europe if free markets, democracy, and human rights take root. Many also believe peace and prosperity can come to the Middle East in the same way. But the counter-currents are flowing faster.

Americans adore body and mind. But when we become successful, soul often vanishes. And when soul vanishes, a settling down of body and/or mind has to occur. Those in counter-currents know that soul has vanished in American civilization. So they flow with a new kind of movement coming from soul that has direction.

LOOKING SOUTH TO REPLACE LOST SOUL

A century ago the socialist countervision arose when warriors were in vogue. Phrases like "survival of the fittest" made it into the common language. Socialism and capitalism seemed to be heading for a grand battle. A two-sided grand battle did come with World War I, though not between socialism and capitalism. In America the Germans were called "Huns," in reference to the undifferentiated hordes crashing out of the East. We were Americans, each one of us individual and possessing God-given rights.

In World War II, the grand battle was different. Again we were the good *I*'s, but this time the Germans were not Huns but Nazis, bad *I*'s. Somehow we Americans sensed there was something not only good about us, but also bad. Maybe in our civilization, the bad was European and the good was American. But then there also were the Russians. There were hordes of them, but they were good hordes, poor people struggling to emerge from backwardness and darkness. And for a short time it did not matter that they were communists.

After the war, the struggle again became two-sided. We were still the good American *I*'s, and the Russians were still the hordes. More hordes joined them as more nations, especially in the third world, became communist. And in the late 1940s Americans split over whether the hordes were the good poor or bad fanatics.

It is hard to say whether a new militant Manichaeanism will arise. Linear men are no longer as firmly in command as they were a century ago. And the visions that men make these days in our civilization are found mainly in films and music. This is no longer a militant age.

But visions exist in the poor countries. The strongest is that of Islam. Some European and Arab writers have seen a reemergence of the medieval split between Christendom and Islam. But the two domains are not so neatly divided. There are splotches of Islam in Europe, and American civilization pervades the Islamic world. And there are other "fundamentalist" visions. In Latin America, evangelicals are reaping great harvests of converts. In some places the left remains strong, as in Chile's poor communities. Liberation theology is spreading in the Caribbean.

In Israel Jews are divided between the secular and the religious. There will not be civil war between them, yet how can the life of the former be fitted together with the visions of the latter?

Then there are the many ethnic conflicts in the world that draw blood. Is the Manichaeanism being decentralized, like economies and administrative structures? In many of these conflicts one side sees itself as an aggregate of *I*'s while the other has a visionary view of itself as *we*'s. And the combatants are not clearly delineated. They live mixed together, like Jews and Palestinians in Israel. Who are the *I*'s and who are the *we*'s?

Former Black Panther Huey P. Newton said in the 1960s that there is only one world with liberated territories within it (such as Russia, China, East Oakland). In his view, nothing in the world is in the end separated from other things. Latin America sloshes over onto the United States as the United States irrigates Latin America with its self-ness. Nicaraguans passionately follow U.S. baseball.

From Teheran and Cairo, from the churches on Ocean Avenue, from the villages of El Salvador and Guatemala and the churches in Brazil and Iquitos, a new vision is arising in which the soul returns and the body and mind's autonomy are questioned, in which to be an individual means to have an everlasting soul; a challenge is being raised to an American civilization in which body and mind are supreme.

In Latin America, the same men who may rape their women also want them chaste, draped, and looking like saints. *La santa y la puta.* In Latin America, bodies get tossed about and few minds have access to even the *New York Times* or *Le Monde*. They have, as the sociologist Nelson Valdes once said, *pensadores,* thinkers, a special kind of people who play with their minds, as *pistoleros* do with their pistols. Both are admired for their skills.

Now the Spanish people—as the kids in California call those officially known as Hispanic—challenge the American Dream more dangerously than any other group in the world. The communists challenged only those in power in our own civilization. Their secularism was just hand-me-down American. The Islamic challenge is fundamental because Muslims see body and mind as knitted in together with a community, and soul for them means that vital link to God. God commands them to go on whatever journeys they do, as Muhammad did, peace be upon him.

Upwardly mobile Mexican-Americans want to become Anglo. They learn English. They look American. Whatever soul they had when they came fades away as they become nice middle-class people. But down there in that vast continent they remain Spanish.

I read the work of Salvadoran poet Roque Dalton, and I was in Havana (in the summer of 1968) when free copies of Che Guevara's diaries were handed out to all takers, including me. Roque Dalton was executed by his own tribe for being a CIA agent. Che had left Cuba to organize revolution in Bolivia. Both, it had seemed to me, were courting death. When young Iranians walked over mine fields, they did so for soul, not caring about mind or body. I remember a beautiful young Salvadoran woman, a member of the FMLN, who came to Pacific News Service in San Francisco. When asked about death squads and the terrible tortures and death they inflicted, she smiled; I was tempted to interpret that response as bravado, but I also sensed something from her that had to do with soul-and-death.

When Spanish people come to San Francisco's Mission district they just seem to want to survive—do a little painting, wash dishes, get the kids to go to school. Few people appear to read newspapers; instead, they seem to love television, and they devour sitcoms. There is none of the bustle you see in newer Chinatowns, where the direction-giving of money is so evident (money can be a substitute for soul). There is a lot of the village in the Mission.

Mexican songs are nostalgic, the kind my father loved about villages back there somewhere. The flowers are bright, primary colors. Aztecs sacrificed humans. Did they do it with stress or joyfully? Life in Indian villages in pre-Columbian times was cyclical, as it was in most peasant societies. But then came the Spaniards, who brought God and made the Indian think of moving. Now the movement has come, and they have moved as far north as Anchorage, Alaska.

I believe that middle classes can never form more than half (more or less) of any nation or regional economic unit or the world. I believe that the Spanish people in America will form the bulk of the lower class that leftists once called the "working class," the lowest, foundation-like level of the industrial system. This new class of the poor will do lower-class work, speak Spanglish, make cities look more and more like Los Angeles and parts of New York. (There are three classes of people in New York: rich [Anglo and yuppie], poor [increasingly Spanish], and foreign [all the other go-getting immigrants, including Cubans and many Mexicans].)

When the slave traders first brought blacks to this country, many plantation owners must have wondered how they could keep them and their descendants peaceful. They hoped that blacks would just accept their lot. (In Europe it was called feudalism.) During the Civil War the slaves were emancipated but then they were pushed back into a new slavery of sharecropping and hereditary domestic service—feudalism again. But then after the turn of the century, blacks began to move north. Many have softly entered the middle class. As they have acquired nice houses in the suburbs, one can sense the same soul-vanishing as in any middle class. Others have returned to the ghetto, their home, no matter how humble. Is there soul in the ghetto or just religion? There remain a lot of *we*'s even in the debris of battle among the *I*'s.

The Spanish are becoming a proletariat, a class of people who work but own nothing. When a people own nothing, their bodies are lumpy and their minds crude. When human beings have pride and a burning sense of their own worth, they reach for their soul. Their love of God can become intense. Their angers can be immense, and their willingness to kill just to show they are somebody can also be intense. They may use their sexual energy to make babies to show that they are somebody, an *I*, not just a particle in a dust heap.

In the Roman Empire the middle classes lost their souls and the intellectuals became deeply pessimistic. Christianity came along and offered soul to everybody. Because people grabbed at the offer, the empire remained around for quite a long time. (The historian Edward Gibbon blamed Christianity, along with the entry of barbarians, for Rome's decay.) Yet the fact is that the Roman Empire and religion (Christianity, Judaism, Mithraism, and many cults) arose at the same time. Each needed the other. Empire too needed the Stoic virtues of higher officials.

When Christianity spread, so did the image of a cross on which the Savior was nailed and tortured until he died. A few days before this writing an elderly man had a heart attack some five houses down from my own. After the rescue unit came, another oldish neighbor said to me, "Pat didn't make it," and a few hours later all was as usual. That's the way we like it—no fuss, no mess, no bother. In El Salvador they looked with fascination at the mutilated bodies stretched out on the streets but then walked by fast so that the informers would not report any unusual interest in a particular corpse. I suppose that is progress toward an American-style way of looking at death. A lot of the Salvadoran death squad commanders were American-trained and inspired.

South and death and life and direction and morality are closely connected. The fundamentalists know it, whether in Teheran or in the Bar Area churches of the Mission and East Oakland. Will the moodiness so common to the Spanish tradition creep into American television with its unending yuk-yuk? No two takes on life could be more different.

These are challenges to the world, and they are challenges to the individual, especially to the great land of the individuals, America. The Americans would like the line dividing us from Mexico to remain (for Mexicans it is a time divider from their future, the land of milk and honey; for us, Mexico is outer space, full of aliens). Let North be North and South be South and never the twain shall meet.

In the rest of this book I say that if you want soul, there is no half-and-half deal. Soul enters only when doors are open, and that means doors of the body and the mind. With soul comes suffering and death, but also direction, maybe some vision, a sense that movement is going somewhere. A hundred or so miles south of Hollywood, in Cañon Zapata, hundreds, thousands of Mexicans wait to come north. One can only have soul as an individual. But in American civilization, you can be an individual just with body and mind. The civilization cannot win its grand historical bet with such an incompatibility.

DEMOCRACY

We live in a world that is becoming a world. Soon the five billion people of the planet will live as individuals. In the meantime we live as citizens of countries, operatives in work places, and members of one sort or another of family. This in-between life is less than life in the world but more than being an individual. In the modern world, a good part of this life involves living in the public realm.

The forces of government we humans have created demand that we move from the shadowy private into the illuminated public world. The automobile made a life of movement possible on a grand scale. Electricity made illumination the sine qua non of modern life—a room should be brightly lit so we can read and see every last wrinkle on a person's face. We were all made to go to school. There we were made to suffer going to a public bathroom (in the military the toilets even have no partitions). We are obliged to do that so we can learn to perform efficiently in the public world. Performing efficiently means, for example, so instilling learning into a Mixtec Indian from a remote mountain village that he can pick strawberries in Oregon in such a way that they are not crushed and are presentable to market.

Moving into the public world is a precondition for becoming a citizen of a country and an operative in a modern job. If your family or community is traditional or poor you may not need to go public to function effectively, but if you are middle class then your family life, whether you want it to be so or not, is within the public realm. If you are unfortunate enough to be in the so-called working class, then you are pulled both ways.

When large numbers of people move into the public arena, the conditions exist for a political order to become democratic. In a democracy the people make decisions. In the modern world people must make decisions every day. In earlier times people didn't need to make so many decisions. One day was pretty much like the previous one. But in the modern world something unexpected happens every day, every minute.

If a modern child is properly pulled into the public world, that child will understand that decisions have to be made every day, hour, minute. When children learn to drive they are faced with urgent decisions, such as what to do if suddenly a car swerves into their path. Such training is difficult, and is sweetened, in Pavlovian fashion, by rewards, such as money, with which all kinds of good things can be acquired (and money always means potential movement). Good public decision makers do well in modern life.

Those with power and influence in the United States thought that people could be so settled down that decision making need not be imposed as a burden on them. It would be enough in a democracy just to vote, to choose between candidates A and B. Similarly, in the former communist countries the rulers thought village life could be brought back under industrial conditions.

But the settling down of the American Dream in the end cannot work in the ever-moving American civilization, and socialism whether "real" or "democratic" is no longer in history's cards. In the 1950s a number of books ridiculed the "organization man," the perfect conformist who was rewarded with a good job and a nice house in the suburbs for himself and his wonderful family. He needed only to be motivated by a vision that was manufactured by those who had power and by the media.

THE SPREADING PUBLIC REALM

The turbulence of the 1960s marked the transition from the modern to the postmodern world. The modern world became postmodern because with so many people in the public realm, things can only function in a nonlinear way; that is, people have to make choices all the time. Market theorists were closer to being able to deal with this new reality than European socialists or American New Dealers.

In the early 1980s radical conservatives fired by revolutionary zeal brought back visions of the market. The market was exciting, they preached, not just because you could make lots of money but because you, as an individual, could step forth from the masses and soar. Ronald Reagan personified the new radical conservatism. Reagan was an old man who looked young.

During the 1980s democracy spread as a political form through many parts of the world. In fact, if anything appeared to have been in history's cards it was that democracy was the only viable political order in a world primarily marked by American civilization, the world economy and the global culture that it spawned. Americans watched as democracy spread through the remnants of the Soviet Union and waited eagerly for the last two redoubts of communism, China and Cuba, to fall.

It is amazing to see how far and fast democracy has spread in lands touched by imperial America. Consider the former West Germany, which was politically unified only with Hitler's *Gleichschaltung,* or "making it all the same," in 1933. But at the same time the Nazis doped up Germans on dreams of the warm home filled with the smells of cooking and grandfather telling stories about elves and gnomes. The homey sentimentality of German Nazism had its analogues in Russian communism. Its shrill internationalist preaching of class struggle was accompanied by sentimental nationalist themes, especially during the war with the Nazis.

Both the Nazi and the communist revolutions were incomplete. Germans and Russians were torn by forces pulling them out of home and others shackling them to the home, the village, the past. Nazism and communism were reflections of the soul-rending contradictions that marked the so-called working class.

Then came the terrible war, mass death, and defeat, followed by the Americans' taking most of Germany. They completed the German revolution. With their swing and jazz bands, they told the ever-obedient Germans to get their asses out of their bombed-out homes and hustle for a living. And the German girls got laid by American soldiers in return for chocolate and cigarettes. From those one-night stands German democracy grew into a mighty political force.

In 1989 the Russians were defeated by a cold rather than a hot war. An Arab newspaper wrote: "This American victory could never have come through World War III, yet America won without bringing the world to the brink of annihilation. The Soviet empire surrendered and its forces left all of Eastern Europe" (*Sharq Al-Ausat*, July 5, 1991). Both the German and the Russian working classes were defeated by American civilization. Now, Russian's too are learning the delights of pornography and hustling. The revolution has been completed in Europe.

I served in Japan in the late 1940s as an occupation soldier. I was a private, first class, ordered to spy on what was being written in the Kyūshū edition of the *Asahi,* the *New York Times* of Japan. In the 1950s I was a student in Kyoto, an old-fashioned city. By then most of the Americans had already left Japan, but the Japanese were pouring into public places, especially schools. Coffee shops were the rage, where you could sip a small cup of expensive coffee with friends, talk intimately the way they did in Hollywood movies, and dream, dream, dream. Going public in a widespread way was Japan's first step toward its spectacular entry into the world economy. The political system, with its elections, open press, fights in the parliament, political anger, ambition, and corruption, was burgeoning. The Japanese were moving ahead.

It would seem that the Germans and the Japanese have had their militarism wrung out of them. They have gone public, taken to democracy, and become nonviolent. Do these three qualities of American civilization go together?

By contrast, the revolutions in Russia and China over the decades were lurching about, leaping here, retreating in disarray, the leaders wondering what the hell was going on. And there was violence, suffering, frustration, anger, and sheer incomprehension that such things could happen in countries that preached the imminent coming of the perfect society.

But as soon as he came to power in 1984 Gorbachev started talking of openness, restructuring, and democracy. I remember around 1988 seeing a T-shirt with the logo in Russian letters, *glasnost* and *perestroika*. An acquaintance showed me a later T-shirt that had added the word *democracy*.

In 1980 the South Korean military made up of the solid sons of the peasant and working classes slaughtered two thousand students calling for democracy in the city of Kwangju. After that they dithered in the face of democratic pounding. When furious students pelted them with everything from spitballs to Molotov cocktails, they fought back defensively with their massive shields, afraid to use their batons and kill a student. Step by step the régime allowed democratic reforms, but more significantly it let the bourgeois spirit triumph, even in the grim halls of government. The same happened as Chile went from Pinochet to Aylwin.

In Taiwan, the stubborn old nationalists are fading away as American-style all-smiles political democracy has come in. Year after year Taiwan has held immense foreign exchange reserves at a level matched only by Japan and Germany. Maybe State Department planner Francis Fukuyama is right—the only political wind blowing in the world is that of democracy, one that began with the bourgeois revolutions at the end of the eighteenth century.

In China, conservative communists struck forcefully against the students on Tiananmen Square. There are very many peasants in China, and the communists always worry that the unity they forged could come apart again. But they cannot keep democracy out, as more and more people move into the public arena. Nudity begins to appear in films.

In East Germany too the grumpy communists tried to hold it together, but what could they do when Gorbachev turned thumbs down on them? They even tried to let the masses have a little democracy, whose strains came in anyway over West German television. But in the end the pressure from the bourgeois bottom and the new top-down reformer was too much. The wall vanished.

These old communists were really very private people, quite feudal.

In Warsaw in 1960 I remember visiting a Polish professor who had visited Berkeley and was a member of the Central Committee. I found where he lived, which was a big complex of comfortable apartments in which other members of the Central Committee and the Politburo also lived. The prime minister was his neighbor. In China the ruling political class lives in a large complex marked by lakes and lawns called Zhongnanhai, "Central South Sea."

In Mexico the ruling Institutional Revolutionary party (PRI) was founded in the early 1930s as a milder version of a Leninist party, somewhat like the Chinese Kuomintang. It has ruled Mexico for more than half a century and pervades the country like Mexico City's smog. Democratic currents in the summer of 1994 flowed faster. Capital and goods are coming to Mexico in great gobs. Carlos Salinas de Gortari has encouraged the bourgeois spirit to supplant the socialist feudalism of the PRI. The Chiapas revolt unleashed a torrent of freedom of media and public expression. Everybody, it seems, is talking about Chiapas, Mexico, and how awful everything is. Mexicans, who have been so private a people, are becoming public now. It is happening, as it happened to the Japanese. Many Japan experts in earlier times considered that unthinkable in Japan's case. Many Mexico experts considered it unthinkable in Mexico's case—until the Chiapas revolt.

In Brazil, peasants have long been moving from the sun-seared rural areas into the cities. Now many live on the streets and beaches. Brazil is, with Mexico, the most industrialized country in Latin America, yet poverty is rampant. Socialists see the poverty as an unmitigated tragedy. Others, however, realize that these ex-peasants are moving, going from passivity to activism, becoming the new working classes. Will they too turn fascist and be pleased as "enemies of the people" are liquidated? Already extrajudicial executions of troublesome street kids are increasing.

Democracy is spreading throughout the poorer countries. Westerners think of Africa as a continent of calamities, but Africans are emerging, rushing, from the bush into the cities. In Nigeria they are so wild and smart that democracy is the only way they can govern themselves. And the country has gone public in a big way—not much bush left there. That is what their seven military regimes feared for so long.

Another favorite Arab commentator of mine, Fahmi Howaidi of Egypt, wrote in the summer of 1991 that he had been surprised to hear Western-style piano music being played in the salon of a Teheran hotel. Many Iranians sat listening. He had later asked the pianist what had changed, since on his last visit the Ayatollah Khomeini maintained rigid control over every last tune played in his realm. He said that for a decade he had had no work and was afraid of being killed. But late in 1990 he got a letter from the hotel manager asking him to play. He wanted the invitation in writing, making him feel secure against the once dreaded questions of the *komités,* and took the job. Howaidi saw five new music schools in Teheran. And others no longer report seeing hanged men and women strung up by cranes mounted on trucks.

Howaidi said that the shift toward moderation has been marked by a crafty centralization of power in the hands of the strongman Hashemi Rafsanjani. He has succeeded in undercutting the power of the working class *komités* and revolutionary guards.

Democracy is a recognition of the irreversible public nature of modern society where everyone makes decisions endlessly and the notion of controlling anyone or any group is absurd. The only way one can "rule" is by cajoling, tricking, bribing (as for jobs), persuading, and just exhausting people by making them wait. Governance in a democratic society is like keeping a family going under modern conditions—no authority, no discipline, no whip, just endless talk, talk, talk in the context of multiple unending decisions.

We are all out in the market. Marx saw that powerful drawing-out-of-dark-corners force of capitalism. He did not like it, and he and his proper wife, Jenny, did not like it that Engels lived with, but did not marry, Mary Burns.

In America we are very public. Our women do not wear veils. Women not only enter conversations but demand to lead them. Men and women walk next to each other in the streets as friends. Imagine that! In the old days Chinese women walked behind their men. I used to see two old Chinese couples walk past my window every day, the men in front talking in a really interesting-seeming way, and the women sweetly smiling behind them (sometimes they looked up at my window and acknowledged my presence).

Of formerly socialist Albania, the late West German journalist Harry Hamm wrote that immense laziness prevailed. The men were in the coffee shop every day. Family ties were very close and many Albanian-American men went there to retire. The mosques and the churches were closed, but nobody cared; the coffee house was more important anyway. They played a lot of backgammon. The country was then tightly closed, and the mountaineers who ran it intended to keep it that way. Socialism with the smell of mama's lamb stew. No democracy was there, clearly.

Elliott Abrams, the assistant secretary of state for Latin American affairs under Reagan, wanted to spread democracy in the world. Abrams wanted badly to overthrow the Sandinista commies, but his avuncular old boss was in the end, despite all the huffing and puffing about an evil empire, a cautious man. That is how he became governor of California and then president of the United States. But in fact Abrams was a rather good man on the subject of democracy and especially human rights. When the State Department's dignified dignitaries were overlooking Idi Amin's horrors, he fought hard to save Ugandan lives. He forced the ever-so-meticulous State Department experts to speak out against tyranny in Argentina and Chile. In Chile, Augusto Pinochet came to hate Elliott Abrams; he loved the People's Republic of China, which stayed on the best terms with him as his police crushed the *subversivos*. Abrams did not understand that commies have human rights as well, and as they get those human rights, they are drawn out into a public world, and the secret to commie success, tyranny over a people kept in a private world by force, begins to crumble, vanishes in the strong rays of a public sun.

THE CHOICE TO BE CIVILIZED

It appeared bizarre to many hard-bitten old communists that human rights became so big a cause in the Western capitalist world. Why should capitalists care about "prisoners of conscience" who often were in prisons because they worked for the revolutionary overthrow of governments that otherwise helped many an international capitalist make fat profits?

Why have elites in so many democratic capitalist countries shown such sympathy for the victims of violence, war, conflict? Why have wealthy and educated people, many of distinguished lineage, become such fervent partisans of peace? And why have many in the middle classes clamored for the imposition of death penalties on the convicted perpetrators of heinous crimes? No one will be surprised that those in the poor and working classes, especially the near-poor, given their old-fashioned values, heartily approve of the proper authorities executing wrongdoers—preferably after the infliction of richly deserved tortures.

Poland's last communist president, Wojciech Jaruzelski, once berated a group of West European parliamentarians for yapping about human rights rather than pushing for greater economic, technological, and cultural exchange between East and West. The West Europeans retorted: it won't happen until you allow human rights and democracy in your country, which he did. During the 1980s a strange political situation prevailed in Poland. The communists dominated the public sector, which squatted like an immense slug on the society. The people dominated the private sector, which had become so public that much of the everyday economy and culture went on there. Heterodox books got published, and women dressed stunningly. Life was lived in streets and meeting places, and while the standard of living was much lower than that in the West, it was higher than in the Soviet Union and far higher than in China. Once a deeply rooted peasant society, Poland went public in a big way. It did so not by defying Soviet tanks but by becoming nonsocialist and making Soviet "real socialism" the laughing-stock of Europe. The in-groupy, highly privatized Polish state, during the summer of 1989, decided, wearily, to officially permit democracy.

The Polish people knew that extricating their society from the trammels of socialism without challenging the Russian-dominated state and joining the West would have been impossible if they had decided to cut communist throats, as the Hungarians did in 1956. Like so many other countries in Europe, Polish history is drenched in blood and violence. As devout Catholics, they believed suffering was their lot, and their German and Russian neighbors gave them plenty of reason to suffer. Yet they have become one of the nations of Europe most passionately committed to nonviolence. During the decade from 1980 to 1989, when Poland was in the process of liberating itself from communist rule, only a handful of Poles died in political action. Hard-nosed police, called *Zomos,* were ready to crush skulls, yet strict instructions went down to them, as they did to the police of many Western countries and to Japanese and South Korean police as well, that no deaths were to occur from seeking to control resistance to the state.

Poland undertook the most daring economic transformation in Europe; every vestige of socialism was expunged from the system to allow the market to reign supreme. Poles, even while they were still being ruled by tiresome socialists, became a nation of hustlers. Thousands streamed into West Berlin every day for deal making. The haughty Bonn government even had to lower the wall it had hastily erected on the German-Polish border to keep this army of hustlers out.

Like Jews who before the Holocaust were Poland's hustlers, these new Polish hustlers are quarrelsome and noisy but nonviolent. How is it that Poles and Koreans, once known for their pugnaciousness, have become so peace loving?

According to the West's cultural standards as set forth in the media, to be Western is to be nonviolent. If you commit murder in the name of Western civilization, you are not Western. You become a right-wing pariah, outside the realm of the empire.

The Argentinian generals made a big mistake when they listened to the assurances of American diplomats, spoken in good Spanish, that their slitting open the bellies of pregnant *subversivas* would be overlooked by their boss's hard-line anticommunist administration. In contrast, the South Korean students were magnificently right-on when they hammered away at the military government and touched not one life, thereby winning the moral support of their own people and of peoples, countries, and governments throughout the world. The main demand of the South Korean students was democracy. (Now, having gotten some democracy, they want reunification, which is a step to their next vision.)

In the Western countries, as opinion polls have consistently shown, great majorities of people favor the death penalty. Nevertheless, parliaments have again and again resisted attempts to reinstate death penalties or to apply the penalty with greater relish. In South Africa many Afrikaaners liked to think of blacks dangling by the neck at the end of a rope. Afrikaaners are a private people, of rural roots, with a strong redneck tradition. Like the majority of people in Western countries, they believed that their own had to be protected from savages, even if that meant liberal application of the noose. Then they wanted blacks to be nonviolent so that they could continue to enjoy their Los Angeles–style swimming pools while blacks got ready to take over the government. But an Afrikaaner prime minister reined in the liberal application of the noose when most of the redneck Afrikaaners had become middle class and the way was being paved for black rule. Not surprisingly, the whites started crying out for nonviolence. Now President Nelson Mandela leads them, they hope, toward a nonviolent future.

Did the Afrikaaners' new loathing of violence only arise because they are afraid of black violence against them? Did the Poles become nonviolent just to forestall a violent Russian move against them? If nonviolence is bourgeois hypocrisy, as Western Marxists have always cynically maintained, then is that kind of wimpy nonviolence just the opposite side of the coin of the strong advocacy of application of the death penalty in Western middle-class countries? Those who advocate the death penalty know full well that for every one or two white middle-class serial killers who are executed, there are hundreds more on death row who come from the poor and the underclass.

Murder rates are high in America. They have been growing in countries marked by immigration. Do poverty and murder go together? It would seem so. Most murders take place between poor people who know each other. A family or gang or group or community or nationality splits, and murder soon follows. Angers peak, and with so many guns and knives around, a fatal thrust all too often ensues. And if it isn't murder then it is another form of violence.

In the United States, people live in clean, middle-class areas and hear, from afar, that there is murder, bloodshed, and mayhem in ghettos and barrios. Many are convinced that the problem goes deeper than individual acts of violence. It is a plague, like cholera. It comes, in the view of middle-class people, from being unclean. It is imperative that the plagues be prevented from coming into the clean communities. If rats have to be killed to contain the plague, then rats must be killed.

More than two millennia ago the Confucian philosopher Mencius enunciated a political precept: those whose behavior is governed by virtue, or as we would say, those who are civilized, need not be ruled with punishment. All others must be ruled with punishment. The Chinese ideogram for punishment has an element that denotes "cutting," suggesting the cutting off of heads or slow flaying of the skin of a condemned criminal, which were common punishments in China till the beginning of this century.

Those who are at the top abhor violence. Among civilized people all behavior must be nonviolent. When tens of thousands of Iraqi soldiers were incinerated on the highways leading out of Kuwait, many elite Americans were appalled. Yet the issue remained largely buried in the American press as victory celebrations resounded. In China, Confucians considered it appropriate that civilized rulers inflict painful punishments on their uncivilized subjects, regardless of whether they were ethnically Chinese or something else. In fact there was no such ethnic category as

Chinese. The only significant social divider was, as it was for the Greeks, civilization.

In the older societies it was always assumed that civilized life was for the few, just as it seemed self-evident that, because of limited food production, the vast majority of people in the world would be poor. And even if all too often the civilized were slaughtered (and it was frequently others in their class who ordered the slaughtering), there was always the sense that different rules applied to them than to the "masses." If the civilized had to be executed, it should be done gently (just before he severed her head, the executioner was said to have whispered to Anne Boleyn that it would not hurt).

The Declaration of the Rights of Man passed by the revolutionary National Assembly in France in December 1789 decreed that such rights are due all men (and presumably women too). That extraordinary statement had already been written into the American Declaration of Independence. We are all entitled to the rights of life, liberty, and the pursuit of happiness. The French said all are entitled to liberty, equality, and fraternity. All humans, no matter how foul smelling and vile they might be, have the potential to become civilized. The French declaration, inspired by Rousseau, stated its vision for the grand community. The American Declaration, inspired by British Bill of Rights of 1688, stated its vision for all humans as individuals.

If people do not choose to be civilized, do they deserve punishment? If the entire world becomes democratic, violence shall no longer prevail. But until that happens, there will be two domains of rule and law, just as Confucians prescribed. Former vice-president Spiro Agnew once justified his support of harsh punishments for criminals on the grounds that "rotten apples" had to be separated from the healthy pile of apples. Those who believe in democracy hold that the vast majority of people are properly democratic and that those who are not should be expunged from the turf of democracy.

Poles have long been desperate to show Westerners that they are European and civilized; the sign of that is their newly cultivated nonviolence. So too the Germans, Japanese, and South Koreans. Americans have no doubt that they are highly civilized. They don't have to prove it. They are also profoundly convinced that below them are layers of barbarism, within the turf of American society. If the barbarians cannot be taught, then they must be held to account, by lethal injection if need be.

YEARNING FOR THE BOTTOM

Body and mind are, in the end, the most prized possessions of middle-class people. In American films more and more older people have joyful sex. Americans realize that they have been missing European-style conversation. Someone said that Gary Cooper, soft-spoken and short of words, was America's greatest actor. Surely he wouldn't be now. Minds grow, develop, shine.

This is all part of a great civilization, of which there have not been that many in the world. Greek civilization spread from Spain in the west to Bactria (in northern Afghanistan) to the east. Rome joined that civilization, and so did the Arabs to a considerable extent—they melded Islam, the world's most powerful religion, to the civilization they inherited in part from the eastern Roman Empire with its capital at Greek Constantinople. Hindu civilization spread over South and Southeast Asia. Chinese civilization spread over East Asia. Civilization spread over Mexico and Central America, and that of Peru spread far beyond what is Peru today.

Great civilizations center on cities, depend on far-flung trade, rule over diversity. The arts and sciences flourish. So too humanism. Rulers begin to fancy themselves enlightened. Frederick the Great, who wanted to make Germany civilized, spoke French and abhorred the German language, which to him smelled of a backward barnyard feudalism. Civilizations tend to worship body and mind. Middle-class people think of peasants as misshapen, stupid, and in more modern times as quaint. They fancy themselves beautiful and brilliant, or hope to be.

Greek civilization featured idealized statues of beautiful people who looked intelligent, gripped by a strong inner life. Roman statues showed individuals with sharply etched faces. The Muslims, like the Hebrews, forbade human representation, but as Hellenistic and Persian influences seeped into the Arab empires, so did poetry and sensuality. Even a cursory glance at an Arabic dictionary reveals a multitude of words dealing with sex. Hindu art was openly erotic, and its philosophy had flights of the mind as daring as those of Greece. A stern Confucianism frowned on sensuality and individualism in China, and only during the highly urbanized Tang and Sung dynasties, from the 600s to the 1200s, did sensuality and individualism become prominent. And now they have again.

In America, evangelicals deplore our civilization as a sink of depravity, Sodom and Gomorrah, life lived only for gluttony, vanity, and exhibitionism. They accuse the media moguls of propagating a secular humanism, which they translate as "the devil's religion." Did not the early Christians regard the Greco-Roman civilization they lived in as froth at best and the devil's work at worst?

All civilizations in the end propagate such humanism. Even the medieval Muslim empires did, and for that were periodically chastised by grim fundamentalists surging up from the desert. Erasmus, the great humanist said, *nihil humanum mihi alienum est,* "nothing human is alien to me." That could be the creed of any great civilization. Yet it also is a sign of a great civilization that, as Freud wrote, there are so many who are uncomfortable in it. Maybe the other side of the coin of a great civilization is its incompleteness, and therefore something surges up, usually from the bottom, to complement it. And that something has turned out in most cases to be religion.

Religions start out as seeds. Of the millions of seeds that fall from a tree, only one or two become trees. When they are saplings, they already are repositories of stories from the past, wisdom for the present, and visions for the future. They are of course more, as Jesus recognized when he separated Himself and God from the domains of Caesar. But when the surge has not yet come or is not recognized, the central actors in the civilization get frustrated at the incompleteness they see around them.

Leftists vituperate about multinationals taking over the world. In fact, what is taking over the world is middle-class civilization. The leftists know they will never be a part of those multinationals unless a parent is a CEO in one of them. But they also know they are a part of middle class civilization. So they hate themselves—a dead-end stance. But others imagine themselves on top, walking on a high mountain and observing the vast space beyond and below. I am afraid of heights, and if I happen to be high, I am always eager to get down. Top and bottom have an affinity for each other. Halfway up steep mountains one often finds pleasant resort hotels.

Throughout history top and bottom have allied against the middle. In Russia, Ivan the Terrible sided with the despised urban merchants against the landed boyars. French kings, too, gained support from the bourgeoisie against landed feudal rivals who despised the money-grubbing burghers. In the sixteenth century Protestant cities rose against the Catholic landed aristocracy. In the eighteenth century the *philosophes* decided to destroy Christianity, feudalism's battered vision. When the bourgeoisie gained power in the nineteenth century, the intellectuals sided with the working class at the bottom. The intellectuals fancied themselves the true heirs of an aristocracy that had lost its place and power. Science became supreme.

Throughout the centuries something has drawn those at the top or aspiring to be there away from the delights of civilization to the bottom. A priest and a nun take the vow of poverty. It can hardly be masochism. A more positive force draws them downward, or sometimes sideways toward death.

Leftists, like all radicals, side either with the future or with the past. They sense an affinity with a higher plane, have visions deriving from either future or past (both are imaginary anyway, like those powerful and highly useful "imaginary numbers" in mathematics). They want to be moved by the forces of visions from past or future. Hegel and then his disciple Marx translated that yearning of young romantic radicals into a theory of history in which an evolving history was identical with God— History = God. The left liked to fancy itself rising while the reigning civilization was dying and a new civilization was growing in a sea of revolutionary discontent. Yet in fact the left has flourished with the flourishing of the civilization. And when, after the Russian Revolution, one chunk of the left branched off to create a new world, that world collapsed seventy years later, and its remnants scrambled to get into American civilization. Reformist socialism and revolutionary communism were both signs of the incompleteness of the civilization. History never destined them to be its heirs.

The incompleteness comes from the fact that the civilization never can encompass everything and everyone. All great civilizations flow down valleys but avoid the hills, or hop from city to city but merely pass over or through the villages. Greek civilization hopped from city to city but only lightly touched peasants and nomads. It only began to touch them, especially in southeastern Europe and western Asia, with the arrival of Christianity.

In the vast expanse of Greek civilization from Central Asia through Egypt, in the end it was Islam that captured both city and country people. Hindu civilization spread as a religion, in fact through Buddhism, a faith that was later repudiated in India during the second half of the first millennium. At that time India ceased being imperial and reverted to village life.

Historians might ask: didn't Chinese civilization spread over the vast expanse of Eastern Asia without religion? Certainly, they would say, Confucianism does not qualify as religion, and neither does Marxism. Yet for centuries Chinese, Koreans, Japanese, and Vietnamese have read the Confucian books the way Muslims read the Holy Qur'an or Jews and Christians the Bible (a word meaning simply "book"). The *Communist Manifesto* and *Capital* never made it as holy books, not even with Peru's *Sendero Luminoso* (though they read some of Mao Zedong's writings as if they were scripture).

Evidently it is empires, created at the top and spreading down, in conjunction with religions, which rise from the bottom, that are able to encompass all. Without religion the civilizations are incomplete.

And as we know from the great art of civilizations, their people manage to become beautiful in body and intelligent in mind. The uncivilized are depicted as ugly and stupid. In the brilliant urban civilization of eighteenth-century Japan, the higher people were shown as tall and beautiful, with long prominent noses, which later Christian missionaries said made them look Jewish. The missionaries thought some of the lost ten tribes may have made it to Japan. The lower people were portrayed as short and squat with pug noses.

During the 1960s American blacks began to speak of their own culture as "soul." The implication was that whites have no soul. Soul is something one senses in humans. Some people have it; others do not. It is a kind of energy and gives off an aura. Or it is a kind of vector that points in a particular direction. When Marx was young, he and his fellow students yearned for soul. They were called romantics. Then he and his sidekick Engels went down to the poor, at least in their minds if not always in their actions. They thought they were creating a new science but in the end created a pseudoreligion, though one that had enormous revolutionary power. Progress, from the Latin *progredior,* to move ahead, the perfectionary vector of evolution. When the religion they engendered faltered, all that was left were some stale socioeconomic theories, which survive mainly on a few college campuses as sterile scholasticism. But the left still yearns for soul and still looks wistfully to the bottom.

In a Buddhist world there would be no violence. In the mid-1980s I visited a monk in Japan whom I had known from my student days. He spent twelve years on a mountain in Japan and then wandered for three years barefoot in India. He founded an extensive meditation center at the foot of Mt. Hiei, not far from Kyoto. In his place of residence lived a woman who was legally his wife. He needed a legal wife to adopt an Indian boy from Nagpur, a new Buddhist center, to be trained as a Buddhist and sent back to India. The "wife" lived in a secluded room within the house where she recited sutras every day. Both had beautiful faces, were intelligent, alert, and effective in their world, but only *in* the world, not *of* this world.

In a thoroughly civilized world we would all be like that monk and his "wife." Did they have sex, some people asked me when I told them about them? I said I thought not, but even if they did, it would have been something remote from the world, not the way peasants frolic in the hay. In eighteenth-century Japan, when there was a great peace, life was affluent but also governed by a Buddhist sense of how fragile everything was—*mono no aware*, "the sadness of things."

Those who yearn for the bottom must realize that they are drawn to violence. Those on the right celebrate their violence. *Viva la muerte*, the Spanish fascists said. On the left I remember a pudgy leftist in the early 1970s getting red in the face as he blurted out: "Twinkies are violent." McDonald's is violent, he added. I wondered then why he was so opposed to Twinkies. Strange, I thought, that something so trivial could conjure up thoughts of violence. Marx too saw violence in all human relations. Was that because of the meaning of Marx's German word *Gewalt*, which basically means "power," but is sometimes translated as "violence"?

One need only consider the fascination with power that still exists among leftist students on so many college campuses: the fascination with Foucault, who thoroughly explored power in human relations; the feminists' preoccupation with rape; the Marxists' insistence on endless exploitation and oppression. They all want peace. They shrilly denounce fascists who delight in incinerating Iraqi soldiers as they flee Kuwait after their defeat. They want peace so no fascists can hurl them into concentration camps and prepare a holocaust for them. Yet at the same time they are drawn to the violence of the poor, the mass executions of enemies of the people. Was there not some reason why Stalin murdered so many people? Of course there was a reason.

The search for peace in the modern world is an attempt to institutionalize an incomplete civilization.

CRACKS IN THE SPREADING CIVILIZATION

When Reagan and Gorbachev had their first summit meeting in Geneva in November 1985, the United States and the Soviet Union joined together to bring about peace in the world. For the first time in history a swath of peace stretched over the northern hemisphere: from Japan through China, the Soviet Union, and Europe to North America.

But the South is not at peace. The Iran-Iraq War or the Gulf War could recur in similar form elsewhere. There is bloody civil conflict. There is monstrous crime and dangerous political unrest. Yet the nations of the North, including the new Russia, want to chill the violence in the South. *Pacem in terris,* "peace on Earth," seems a possibility, even as the open wound of Yugoslavia bleeds in the heart of Europe.

American civilization needs peace, and peace needs the civilization. The civilization needs democracy, because when all are in the public world, then they will act in the fashion of middle-class people, which is peaceful. Thus peace too needs democracy.

If the civilization is truly and eternally incomplete and only half the world's people can enter the lighted arena of democracy, then peace is an illusion. Surges of violence will continue from below, and they will be met by ever greater counterforce from those who have the civilization, like the rain of destruction and fire that came down on Iraq in the spring of 1991.

Since Peter the Great, Russian leaders have looked westward and opened up, or they have pulled back into the Kremlin. Like Peter, Gorbachev looked westward and saw mighty middle-class civilizations in Western Europe. Communist parties and industrial working classes in Western Europe shrank during the 1980s, supplanted by a new class of poor made up in good part by foreign Muslims. Gorbachev was fascinated by Western Europe's extraordinary productivity, the creativity of its people, and the stability of its political systems. He believed that the Soviet Union's long-term future hinged on its adopting middle-class civilization and hoped that a middle class would eventually form a majority in the Soviet Union. And that meant adopting democracy, a word he started using fairly early in his tenure. When Gorbachev fell, the Soviet Union came apart; Russia under Boris Yeltsin came into being. Yeltsin received thunderous applause in the U.S. Congress when he vowed to make Russia free and democratic.

In the new nations of former Soviet Central Asia, the desire for Western-style economic development is universal. But when it comes to Western-style democracy, especially with its drawing out of all people, including women, into the public realm, the desire is far from universal.

Thus demarcation lines are appearing in the former Soviet Union, Eastern Europe, and the world as a whole between the domains of democracy and those of nondemocracy. In the former Soviet Union democracy is most evident in the Baltic states, in the Western Ukraine, in St. Petersburg (the former Leningrad). It is evident in Moscow. It seems less so outside of Moscow. It is far less evident in Central Asia.

In southeastern Europe the line divides Romania from Hungary, Serbia from Croatia. Which side of the line is Greece, the home of democracy, on?

I do not mean that in these nondemocratic regions people do not vote or that there is a penchant for despotism. Rather in those lands people operate predominantly in their private domains. In the Muslim regions women are still not prominently represented in the work force. The Serbians are more old-fashioned than the Croatians, yet democracy flourishes in the city of Belgrade. The Slovaks are more private than the Czechs, a reason why the two halves of the erstwhile Czechoslovakia divorced.

Just as many Poles would like to see the line separating the "West" from "Asia" along their border with the former Soviet Union, so many Russians would prefer to see it as the line separating them from Iran and China. For them the West is *kulturnyi,* and Asia is *ne-kulturnyi.* How could China be uncivilized? That is not the point. The West is the domain of truth, beauty, and goodness. China and the Tatars are something else— not necessarily bad, but something else.

Such dividing lines are not limited to Europe. The Japanese clearly see themselves as different from others, especially from other people living in East Asia. But while they have ambivalent feelings about Koreans and Chinese, they definitely see them as in the domain of civilization. For them the domain of noncivilization begins somewhere in Southeast Asia. In India, I guess, the Aryan north sees a dividing line with the Dravidian south. In the Sudan, the Arab north looks down on the African south.

Does American civilization want to encompass all, or does it want to demarcate itself from "the others"? When the nation-state was in vogue it seemed that those who ruled it wanted to encompass all. In America during the 1960s the descendants of slaves were finally invited to join the national family. Was it revolution from below that made rulers see the urgency of bringing them in?

Not entirely. Since the beginning of the American union, a strong current demanded that the nation complete itself by bringing in its black people. And strong currents opposed it, demanding that segregating lines be drawn, as they were later in the nineteenth century. The American nation did not become complete, but now a new current is flowing; it calls for worldwide respect for human rights and demands that everywhere democracy be supported and furthered.

It is mandated that the rule of law prevail in any country that wants to become democratic. That means, in effect, that few people from the middle and upper classes get arrested or are tortured. Does this mean it is all right to arrest, torture, and kill people on the other side of the demarcation line? Not really, but when this happened in El Salvador, it entered the arena of foreign policy, where decent-minded people lobbied to cut off aid to that country's regime. However, when American nuns were murdered, and then Jesuits, that was a human rights violation, which the many human rights advocacy groups in the United States and the West took up directly.

Human rights have become the ideological spear point with which this new America-led combine of nations is seeking to spread middle-class civilization. Whatever bickering and potential splits there may be within this Western array of nations, they are unified on human rights. For them to survive, the world must become middle class, at least to the degree that the outsiders who are left can be dealt with philanthropically or with police methods.

Few people any longer talk of a first and a second and a third world. The demarcation lines now run right through the second world. Their

Westernizing parts anxiously await the time when they will be drawn fully into the West, like Poland. Their other parts are not certain where they want to be, but in most of them there is a sense that they are different, and not just because they are poor. The Muslims know why they are different.

Can the white men who rule the world spread the civilization to such an extent that only barbarian fringes remain, or in a way that even large numbers of remnants will not make any difference? Not likely. The de facto world government we now have includes the United States and Russia. It also includes the so-called G-7, the world's seven largest "industrialized nations": Britain, Canada, France, Germany, Italy, Japan, and the United States. As a permanent member of the U.N. Security Council, China also is a part of this world government, though on the fringes, and its leaders are still not certain to what extent they want to be involved.

The white members of that government are all strongly committed to American civilization, which, after all, originated in Western Europe and its offshoot, North America. Gorbachev, and now Yeltsin, despite some nods in the direction of conservatism, have made it clear they want Russia to become part of Europe.

A problem currently worrying the Japanese is that their children are vanishing. Their birth rate is down to 1.57, almost half a child below a simple replacement rate. They now know the price they have paid for their wholesale acceptance of American civilization: the loss of the family. Their scientific, technological, literary, and artistic achievements have been daunting. A Westernized soul carried them to those heights. Yet now they are not only without family but also without religion. Others, jealous of their attainments, accuse them of plotting to dominate the world; the accusers are Americans who themselves have long harbored desires to dominate the world, or at any rate to play at it in expensive conferences in posh hotels in various parts of the sun-blest world. But the Japanese know better. They are terrified of their success and of the yawning nothingness that faces them.

Does that make them look wistfully at their Asian neighbors to the South? Maybe not, because their racism has made it hard for them to find in these non-Western others inspiration for themselves.

The Chinese, on the other hand, despite the jolt the leaders received when the world condemned their actions on Tiananmen Square, know that the private world is a cushion on which their society rests. All have the sap of Confucianism running in their veins, and they know that for all its poverty there is something else in those non-Western others that the West lacks. They never were impressed by all the nuclear weapons the West had, though they were stunned by the swift and convincing American victory in the Gulf War. The notion that somehow Western civilization will eventually encompass a good part of the world and succeed in making it rich and stable at the same time is in their view a fantasy.

Japan has changed massively because of the tide of Western civilization it has been swimming in for more than a century. In China today Western classical music is the rage. Even in small towns symphony orchestras play Beethoven to capacity audiences. Yet in both, defenses are going up against the civilization from the West.

American civilization is not only Western; it is also white. When the Soviet Union started to disintegrate, some Russians speculated excitedly about a new world order stretching from Vladivostok westward to San Francisco—a world marked by individuality, democracy, and economic plenty. Now Russians worry they may relapse into some earlier primitiveness. Old and new fault lines are appearing in Europe. America is losing self-confidence. The civilization continues to spread, even mightily, but its limits and incompleteness are becoming ever more evident. Does that mean that democracy, human rights, and the public realm are by necessity also limited?

✧

PART III

CAPITAL

One thing is already clear about the future: there will be no settling down anywhere. The settled order, security, and affluence of the American Dream, or that promised but not delivered by communism, will not occur again. Flux already is the normal condition of humankind and will be more so in the future. Whether in personal, family, work, community, national, world, or cosmic terms, we shall all have more movement in our lives than ever before. The civilization keeps speeding up, and there is nothing to suggest that will change.

As of mid-1994 a swath of peace covers the world's North, stretching from Japan through China, the Soviet Union, Europe, and North America. I believe that peace, shaky as it might become, will be durable. Great power disarmament shuffles ahead. Yet disorder is nibbling furiously at that swath of peace—there are rats in the cellars of its houses.

In the South there is open turbulence. Will the South go through the horrors that marked the modernization and industrialization of the North? The South is different from the North. Children are desired and honored in the South. They are the wealth of the future. Northerners have forgotten that the continuously most wealthy region of the world since the beginning of civilization some five thousand years ago is the three-quarters circle of lands bordering the Indian Ocean. The island of Ceylon was widely regarded in earlier times as the original Garden of Eden.

Much of the South eats rice, and rice is cultivated by people who live in densely packed villages on heavily irrigated fields. Community comes naturally to them.

The North has spurned religion (though religion is gradually returning at the lower levels of society). But religion seems too much a part of
southern life ever to be easily lost. As Melanesians and Polynesians lost
interest in their gods, Christianity came in and swept their souls. They
learned of God when in the West God went into exile.

THE WORLD IS DRENCHED IN MONEY

On Monday, January 23, 1989, the *Wall Street Journal* published the first
of a series of articles by Karen Elliot House on the theme that America is
not in decline, that it in fact leads the pack in world leadership. It's not
that we're the toughest, she wrote, but that we are the only ones qualified,
even if we are not too keen about taking the job.

Does that mean the world will just continue on the course it has been
pursuing since World War II? What kind of future would that be?

An American future will mean, first and foremost, that life for the
world's five or ten billion people will revolve around money. The American empire is a political-economic-cultural fact; the economy links politics and culture and covers them as well. While most people still think of
the production of real things as the essence of an economy, in America
one has to think of money first and production second. The ultimate
contemporary economic reality is money. Like consumer goods, which
are consumed, burned up, production is passing.

Money is order in chaos and chaos in order. Money is movement.
Money grows like a plant, or like a cancer. Money shines with bright light,
which can be seen in the eyes of Reno gamblers. America is money. America is movement. America is order. America is crazy, innovative, strange
beneath its surface blandness. Ask most ordinary people, poor or middle
class, what they hope for their children, after life and health, and they will
say enough money to lead a decent life.

What do young Russians want? Dollars or their allies, yen and
marks, to buy stereos and videos. Money, as that neo-Kantian journalist-
sociologist Georg Simmel understood, means freedom. One of the great
changes that has come over the proud Japanese and Germans is that

they have become people of money. The dollar falls against the mark and the yen, yet it remains the heart and core of the world monetary system. Oil and drug prices are reckoned in dollars. News from any world radio transmitter in any language quotes prices in U.S. dollars. The BBC quotes prices in dollars, not pounds sterling. It is like the calendar. The only one used in the world, even in fervently Muslim countries, is the Christian one.

Think of what you do every day and you will soon realize that money enters into it everywhere. You tank up with gas, pay in dollars (even if you technically pay in pesos or bahts). Chances are that most of the food you buy is or was priced in dollars.

As late as the 1960s, many American economists believed that money would eventually turn into mere units of economic accounting, with cash used for trivial purchases only. Production is what counts, they said, jabbing into the air with a lit cigarette. Such thinking underlay all varieties of socialism. But socialism has failed, and in once-socialist countries the chaos in order and the order in chaos of money is returning. The streets are paved with gold in America, the migrating peasants of the nineteenth century thought. Their settled thinking enabled them to think only of solid gold. They were right, except that the streets are made out of slippery paper dollars, which fly around with incredible speed and reek of gasoline and oil, the physical elements that make this astonishingly immense mobility possible.

MONEY AND TIME

PAST

Money always points us, gets us moving in a direction. Money can point us toward the past, the present, or the future. If we come into possession of money, we can transform it into assets, spend it as cash, or use it as capital.

If we choose the first option, then we decide to transform money into solid wealth. We opt for a past. In many countries, in the old days, peasants buried their gold coins in some deep hole. On his deathbed, the peasant told his sons where the gold was. Did he mean to leave the gold to his sons? Probably, but for a selfish reason: he wanted to live through his descendants. And if someone wants to live through his descendants, to leave his mark on them, he wants to make sure that the past—that is, his ghost—shapes the lives of those who come afterward. Kings who build great palaces have the same thing in mind. They hope that the splendor they have built will forever dazzle posterity (that is, flatter the vanity of the ghost). If the king is a Hammurabi and leaves behind laws, then he wants to do more. He wants to shackle those who come later to the order he has created. He wants the past he has created to shape the lives of future generations.

Money—that elusive but real force—can be turned into wealth, and wealth takes the form of big or small things that become the incarnate past the moment they are built. Ghosts reside in all wealth. When a tourist gazes with awe at the Taj Mahal, alone in the courtyard, in moonlight, he or she is in the spell of Shâh Jahân and Mumtâz Mahal (his name means "ruler of the world" and hers means "the exquisite place" (in many languages the word *place* means "woman," as in the older German *Frauenzimmer,* Turkish *odalik,* and Japanese *okusama*). I have never forgotten my visit to the Taj Mahal on a moonlit night. Not just the beauty of the Taj Mahal, but the seductive thoughts of its immense royal cost reinforces the rooted, conservative, shackled-by-the-past tendencies. Memory of that night makes me feel Muslim.

(In the Islamic religion they speak of "revelation" and "tradition," the Holy Qur'an and the Sunna, which latter is the tradition as handed down from the past. When living in Muslim countries I was astonished by the power of the past to determine the directions into the future for Muslim people.)

We see in this transformation of money into wealth why all ruling classes are, by necessity, conservative. Ruling classes have power, wealth, and privilege. Money links it all together. Even when a rich man swings a blood-red flag and yells, "On with the revolution," his having spent some francs to buy the flag has immediately put a stamp of conservatism on the revolution. The ghosts of the past come in. The revolutionaries who rush forward to kill, burn, and change suddenly see in the rich man what they really think the revolution is all about: that they, the poorer ones, should also have power, wealth, and privilege.

. Ghosts are things shamans know about. And shamans are more active in the poorer countries than in the richer countries. Poor people crave wealth. They dream of the wonderful things the nobles have. As the poor world becomes more and more a part of the rich world, the ghosts of the past will come in with them—Catholics, Muslims, Buddhists, shamanists, animists. So many revolutions have turned conservative, and so can this one. An (unlikely) Americanization of the world could turn it into the American civilization's opposite—a world, as Richard Rodriguez says, not of cheerful comedy but of tragedy and suffering.

PRESENT

Money can also be cash, which is why feudal and socialist governments have hated it. Children are taught to give their money to their parents, put it out of sight in piggy banks, save it like good little children. Money is the devil, the "fiend." To say America is money—dollars in hand—is to say America is the devil. Has not money ruined so many a God-fearing pastor, like Jim Bakker? And what about Tammy Fay, who thought Christ wanted women to be beautiful?

America won the cold war with the Soviet Union—the capitalist world hung together, the socialist world fell apart. American imperialism went from a political-military hegemony to a political-economic nexus. The Soviet economy fell apart. The secret of America's success is money—more specifically, cash. America showed how cash could become the magician's wand, conjuring up one after another wonderful thing. Consumption means to burn up. Things made are burned up so new things can be made. America showed how this amazing process could be kept going, could spread all over the world, and could keep on going, like the magician pulling rabbits out of his hat twenty-four hours every day, seven days a week, fifty-two weeks a year, a hundred years a century (in the great banks they rub their rabbit's feet and hope, hope it will turn out all right).

Cash will do this if all are allowed to consume, if all are personally liberated as individuals, and if all are enticed or forced out onto the public democratic arena where they demand things, take things, and cease killing each other. The rest just requires good cash management: hold inflation in check, do not let debt paralyze the accelerating flow of cash, and provide more and more channels through which cash can flow with accelerating speeds.

This is America's promise to the future. Though glorious, it has one great weak spot. Society (with due respect to Margaret Thatcher, who denies there is such a thing as society) is the body of people who give birth to and raise and groom children to become their successors. A woman once said to me a few days after Ronald Reagan left office that all Ronnie and Nancy thought about was their marriage, so how could they have time for their children? By the same token, how can the head of the Federal Reserve Board have time for anyone's children? A feminist once said to me that the sexual revolution was marked by the separation of sex from procreation. Old people want not just to live and work as long as possible. They want to fuck till they drop dead. (The older I get the stronger my sex drive seems to be.)

America thrives on success and sex. But what about children? Immigrants bring in lots of babies and make even more. Some of these babies are very smart. Most work hard. All want to consume. Their children want personal liberation (their parents already sought freedom in the U.S.A.). And they understand that to succeed they have to step forth into the public arena, speak up, kiss in public, go to college, talk a lot. Money makes America go worldwide, but the sense that others must help where money and success cannot—namely, by producing children—makes America draw in others from other lands.

Thus to reproduce itself America creates even more movement in the world. It stirs up the world. It nomadizes people who have been long settled. It has seduced the settled Chinese to wander far and wide, like

Jews. Do Russians really want to take the risk that America can also nomadize the settled Slavs? The great traumatic Russian fear remains the Tatars, who most likely provided the word *ruble* (probably from Arabic *rub'*, meaning a quarter, and from which also Indian rupee; the Tatars let thousands of merchants in to prowl around the sacred Russian lands with their mystic birch trees). The Russians feared Jews because they were worried that the latter would debauch them with money. Child's play compared with what the Americans are doing to them now. Money will make the bears of Russia move out of their trees—and Alexander Solzhenitsyn fears it. (Would Germans be any less dangerous to the Russians? Hardly. Germans are the Americanized vanguard in Europe.)

The American empire can last only if the present can be indefinitely extended into the future. That means keeping the world economy going and keeping conflict to a minimum. More specifically, it means that the vast house of electronic signals built with American money does not disintegrate into global static, and that wars cease. More trade. More consumption. And while defense forces, like the ancient Roman legions, are important, culture will (and has to) play an increasingly unifying role. More people visiting each other, watching each other's ballets.

The United States is now busily bringing the second world into the empire's fold. The cold war is ended. To keep the empire going—and the American way of life—the poorer countries must be brought in. Consumerism, personal liberation and democracy must spread to "the South." America needs the South's babies.

But down there people are afraid of everything, poor to the point they do not see things getting better. They love babies and are full of nostalgia about the places they have lost (forever). On the left and the right they raised the flags of rebellion and wanted to install revolutionary conservative regimes that would *defiende la soberanía del pueblo,* which meant they would nail down the country and the people. They are scared of the burgeoning nomad in them and remind themselves that the place they have is better than anything the future can bring. Nostalgic American lefties used to come down with their guitars and tell them they were right, that they should obey their revolutionary bureaucracies. (So much weeping and hand-wringing when the Sandinistas retired from power but wanted to keep their perks and property.)

Money can also take the form of credit, but we know that credit is really little more than cash generated from anticipated income. Or it can come from assets, like a home. Turning your assets into cash will mean less money for your kids, which means they have to work harder making cash, and that is good for the American empire. Home equity loans, how sweet they are!

In ordinary American political terms, there is the right, the center, and the left (or conservatives, moderates, and liberals). These are the usual, "meaning-full," bland American terms. The right believes in defending assets with guns and throat-slitting, if necessary. The moderates are our good middle-class people. However much they may prattle about higher culture, in the end what makes their world and heads go around is money. Let's go to Paris for the weekend.

VISIONS AND GROWTH

This leaves the left in some other dimension of time and money. The left has always been eschatological—invoking millennium, Last Judgment, a Shining City on the Hill, final communism, and so on. That is why so many Jews have been attracted to the left, looking for a messiah. And that is why at one time or another millions of people throughout the world have been attracted to revolution—the shining light over the distant mountains heralding a coming from on high. The light after death—the light after death-in-life. Mao walking on high mountain ridges.

Money can also take future forms. That form is capital, the word Marx used to entitle his masterwork. Money becomes capital when it is used to bring about something that does not exist now. Capital is money you use to realize or cultivate a future. A building is realized from an architect's ideas and designs. But a caterpillar grows into a butterfly and a child is raised to become an adult. Capital is needed to make dreams real. Capital is also needed for growth—a farmer often has to borrow money for the growing season.

These are two different kinds of futures. The first is grandiose. It has to be global, in that visions can fill vast spaces in instants, like light. The second has to be much more modest, local, and down-to-earth, since in the end it is biological. Things do not grow on a global scale. Global things can only be manufactured, invented. Things grow only in the intimacy of roots and wombs. Capital is needed to realize visions. But capital also is needed to realize growth, since these days nature's biology alone is often not enough to bring about growth.

An idea is a sketch in your mind. You put it together through your will, or it can just appear. Somewhere pushing it is a spark of genius (from the Arabic, *jinn*, a spirit or demon). What are dreams? For me the most convincing explanation comes from the Chinese: a dream arises when an external spirit takes possession of you. Let us say a spirit or soul or gods, or even, God forbid, God, provides the spark that leads you to the idea.

Dreams have always been big in America. Shining city on the hill. Hollywood was built from dreams. Dreams can also be nightmares; a nightmare gave rise to the atomic bomb. America was created from the ideas of John Locke and of the Founding Fathers, some of whom, like Thomas Jefferson, had visions. In the beginning was the word and then came McDonald's, now all over the world.

The United States is an improbable country. To many Europeans it still makes no sense. Nothing much seems to have roots here except for plants, and even many of them are immigrants, like the great eucalyptus trees that have spread all over California. Everything looks invented.

America is the product of a vast engineering effort arising out of the Enlightenment (the *jinn* that made America possible). The world still needs much engineering (who is going to save Africa?). Immense quantities of capital were needed to create America. Beneath their covetousness, Americans have always been hostile to wealth. America has made the rich man squirm, and he gets out of it by preaching self-sacrificial nobility. America knows it needs wealth, assets, savings to keep money stable, but it also wants to smash assets and turn savings into capital to realize dreams and ideas. Americans have made so much money because, deep down, they hate, fear, and mistrust it. As a conqueror people, they had to show they could conquer their fears before taking on the world.

America's revolution, which still marches (limps?) on, has come from the teachings that dreams are more potent than reality. There is a sign sold in Fisherman's Wharf tourist shops: "Reality is for those who lack imagination." (There has always been a strong dose of mysticism, of reaching for and toward a higher plane, in the American revolutionary process.)

There are two kinds of revolution in the world, revolution being a turning upside down of things. One comes from the top down, the other from the bottom up. The latter is made by the people, poor people, angry people, dissatisfied people. Poor people adore wealth, as nomads always have in history. When they rise from the bottom to take the top, they immediately idolize it, like the johnny-come-lately communists who restored Warsaw's "old town" in the heart of the razed city.

But revolutions from above are made by mystics who believe that they can see into the portals of the higher plane. America was made as a revolution from the top down. So were Japan's Meiji Restoration of 1868 and the German Reich in 1870. The Founding Fathers manufactured a country with bits and pieces of ideas motivated by a vision, one shaped by a heavy dose of classical education and images of the Roman republic. Thomas Jefferson became president through a democratic surge from below. Yet a few years after becoming president he had a dream and acquired the vast Louisiana territories where "Americans could settle." Soon the capital poured in to transform what was. At every point of America's existence vast amounts of money had to be turned into capital to realize dreams.

We remain a nomadic people drenched in money, but with fewer dreams. Too much talk of settling down. Who wants to wander, lonely, from Ramada Inn to Ramada Inn? Who wants another sordid one-night stand? More and more of our money goes into cash and assets, the latter consisting increasingly of debts, which are the assets of somebody else. They are an immense drag on the present, not to mention the future.

We are subject to the pull of an aging left (I hope my pensions can allow me to keep my life-style), which calls for settling down, for the preservation of what is old and venerable, like old wooden toll bridges in Massachusetts. The left, except for a few radicals, has succumbed to the liberals' insistence that conflict is bad, a no-no, and so we are all into peace.

On the right there are crazies, like the followers of Lyndon LaRouche, whose technological fantasies derive from visions of power fueled by hate. They give themselves away as Nazis who just want to get their hands on everything they consider to be social garbage and crush it like some noxious insect. But America cannot remain the heart and core of the world unless there is some crazy divine vision around about saving the world. The nostalgia-driven left wants to see the United States cut down to the size of Massachusetts. The power-driven right has always loathed American mealy-mouthed, messianic-sounding morality. America is in a dream crisis.

But we mustn't underestimate the strength of America's revolutionary mysticism, from which dreams have arisen in the past. The beauty of mysticism is that in the end it is open to all, regardless of race, creed, or color. The world must be saved, and that is not idle dreaming, and as long as the world, the globe, the planet need saving, America will be needed.

But capital also is needed to cultivate growth. Most people are primarily biological, with growing bodies, and mental, with growing minds. Just consider, on the latter point, what loquacious people we moderns have become. (Souls do not grow. They are said to be a gift of God, and can only emerge into the light or recede back into the darkness of what Master Hsüan Hua calls "distorted thinking."

Societies need capital to reproduce themselves. Who is going to pay for the schools? How can one make sure that successor generations will be be on hand with the physical and intellectual equipment needed when it is not at all clear what that equipment should be? It costs money to raise children, even in poor countries.

Growth, as the Taoists long ago recognized, is Nature itself. We live and we die, but the *Tao,* which means *road,* goes on. The *Tao* is a road that itself does not grow but fosters growth in other things. Growing is like multiplication. Something gets bigger and bigger when multiplied, not more and more as with addition. Children cannot grow unless they are fed, raised, and directed, and that happens initially through the free—unpaid—labor of the parents. Soon the parents realize that in feeding, raising, and directing their children—or the children of others—they earn negatively to the point that they themselves must forgo a lot. It becomes apparent that in these enormously complex societies the feeding, raising, and directing of children must be on a scale far above the ability of any parent, even the richest, to provide.

If all people have many kids, a lot of money must take the form of capital to ensure reproduction. And since parents need or want to live through their children, they put aside more money as assets for their descendants. Doing so puts a big dent in the cash available for consumerist consumption. So civilization prefers there be as few children as possible, populations reduced to the minimum needed to keep the golden goose healthily alive. See how the birthrates in America, Europe, and East Asia tumble.

If the world chooses to stick with the revolution that still emanates from American civilization, then dreams—old, current, or new ones—will flourish, and many will be realized. But growth will be stunted. American civilization wants sex but does not want children. Jean-Jacques Rousseau produced seven babies and had them sent to a foundling home because they would have interfered with the great man's cogitations; interruptions made him intensely nervous.

If we had become subject to Albanian-style revolution or, let us say, the sort that comes out of Iran, middle-class Americans would be swamped with babies, and dreams would be punishable by death.

The children of the Enlightenment can be counted in the hundreds of millions, billions perhaps. Yet capitalism finds it difficult to bring children into the world—all that noise, mindless prattle, and pink hair that is not a sign from a higher plane but a sign of madness the adults only barely escaped. In ancient Rome the privileged classes despaired. In modern America the privileged classes despair. And since more children mean more trouble, better that fewer be around. Lenin and his wife and fellow revolutionary, Nadezhda Krupskaya, had no children.

The other, socialist vision failed because in the end it couldn't manufacture and it couldn't grow. It was an engineering vision bereft of the dreams of physics, and it distorted growth into an aspect of "production." Only in a few places like Albania did socialism fill the kitchen with people but, alas, with nothing to eat. The world is hungry for growth, for nature, and so the search for another vision continues. Socialism earlier presented itself as the successor to capitalism. Its own dreams turned out to be only images of what capitalism already was doing magnificently. Now capitalism, with its dreams, reigns more or less unchallenged. But other revolutions are in the offing. Some will come from the top down as the North feels the pain and rot within its resplendent body. Others will come from the bottom up as society is revitalized and seeps into the vast global public realm of the North, a realm brought into being by the onward march of democracy.

FIVE REVOLUTIONS OF VISION

Revolution from the top down is needed to prevent further cataclysms from ravaging the world. The world is our promised land, our Canaan, the land of milk and honey, our Israel. Revolutions are often made not to create better things but to prevent worse.

The eighteenth-century Enlightenment led to the English, American, and French revolutions. They spawned spin-off revolutions over much of the European continent, then in Russia, Japan, China, and even beyond. Out of that revolutionary process has come the present North, the swath of peace stretching over the entire northern tier of the world. That is a remarkable achievement, but it almost destroyed the global economy, the planetary ecosystem, and the world's people. It could yet do so.

Five great cataclysms, all rising out of or linked to American civilization, still threaten our Israel: nuclear holocaust, a collapse of the world monetary system, environmental degradation, AIDS, and civil conflict.

A great step forward for humankind was taken when the United States and the Soviet Union agreed in July 1991 to reduce their nuclear arsenals. That truly is a revolution from the top down, like so many others in the North that have brought about great changes in the lives of individuals, peoples, and the world.

There no longer is much question but that all nuclear weapons must be destroyed. The genie that created the nightmare of atomic bombs must be put back into the bottle. The revolution that would do that began even before the first atomic device was exploded in July 1945. Scientists like Leo Szilard had already brought out the bottle and sought help in putting the then still small genie back into it. In the 1950s the peace movement to "ban the bomb" arose. In the 1980s it became a powerful force—not in the poorest communities where survival and biology were the main concerns of people, but among the educated and civilized—throughout the North.

Likes relate to likes, so it is not surprising that the vibrations from the peace movement went upward and not downward. The American and Soviet elites were captured by those vibrations, and soon they joined the movement. Even Ronald Reagan, as if sensing a good script, joined in. Now, as nuclear arsenals are being cut back in the North, the sights of the northern leaders are focused on the South where unruly new nations are building nuclear arsenals. The North is now determined to do away with those arsenals. The North probably can persuade its semi-northern ally, China, to do away with its nuclear arsenals; the Chinese leaders have much more important concerns than stockpiling nuclear weapons. But the others may pose more of a problem. India is huge, mighty, and arrogant. Who is going to tell India it must relinquish its nuclear capabilities? Or Israel, which sees in its nukes a trump card against the threat of any new holocaust?

The launching of nuclear disarmament in the North and the transformation of the Soviet Union may create that swath of affluence, freedom, and democracy stretching from the Urals to San Francisco that many leftist Russians talked about in the wake of Europe's liberation from communism in 1989. Not surprisingly, there is enthusiasm for that dream within the European and American left. But the "new world order" has to include Japan as well as China. Japan is vital because of its mighty economy. China is vital because of all the members of the northern swath, it alone is both North and South. It is a bridge to the South, indispensable for extending that new world order beyond the Urals-to-San Francisco white man's world.

The second potential cataclysm is the collapse of the world monetary system. Only the most callow campus Marxists still dream of a world without money. If God were to decide, all of a sudden, that all money should vanish from the world, a cataclysm far greater than nuclear war would ensue.

In the so-called developed countries, people are always terrified that the financial system that rules their lives could come crashing down like a house of cards. In America, Japan, or Western Europe hyperinflation would bring chaos. But in the developing countries, people have learned to cope. The poor never had much anyway, and the middle class manage by finding dollars or other hard currency. After all, their middle-class people are our people too, and so, with or without intent, we find ways of helping them out. But the monetary buck cannot be passed upward beyond the dollar. As long as the dollar and its allies, the yen and the mark, remain sound, the global monetary system will stay intact.

The bankers (shorthand for all those up there who are, as the Spanish say, *responsábles*) have to keep the global monetary system going. That requires holding inflation down, yet making enough money available to the people of the globe so that as many as possible can enter the arena of consumption, personal liberation, and democracy. Can capitalism do it?

At the end of the last century, the United States showed how this could be done at the national level. (Now it has to be done globally.) The issue of tight versus easy money had been firing up the American political scene. The left wanted easy money to help poorer folks earn and invest more, and the right wanted tight money to protect assets (the Republicans who held most of the presidencies had gone from being future-looking radicals to past-shackled conservatives). As the second decade of this century began, a revolutionary new institution was formed: the Federal Reserve system. Banks, especially small ones, were made part of a comprehensive national system. If they needed money to deal with a cash shortage, swaps could be arranged. In return for accepting financial discipline, they were assured of help when needed. The result was, eventually, the credit card, an amazingly effective way of generating liquidity. This was a credit revolution, as great as the one that shook Russia only a few years later. It was a revolution from the top down. It came from Washington.

The creation of the Federal Reserve was a forward-looking, positive act, but it also came after long years of bitter class conflict in the United States. Providing people more liquidity while preserving the value of assets was the way to prevent chaos and give hope to people. The way to do that was to prevent inflation even as the size of the money supply grew and grew.

The United States was able to make the Federal Reserve system work because of the strong national government that had emerged during the previous two decades. Inflation can be fairly easily checked if a strong political institution can act to ensure three conditions. First, the prices of the key material inputs into economies—or really the single world economy—must remain stable. Oil prices, above all, must be kept stable, and so they have been since the end of World War II, despite the short price explosion during the October 1973 Yom Kippur War. If, besides energy, the prices of four other basics—food, housing, education, and medical care—can be kept stable, then inflationary tendencies can be contained. Second, wages, too, must be kept stable. In this civilization as many people as possible must benefit from rising wages, but they must rise in a slow and stable way. The "wage explosion" of the early 1970s in most of the advanced industrial countries contributed to an inflationary surge. And, third, as the monetarists long have preached, inflation can be contained by controlling the money supply, and that can be done only through a strong government. Just as a strong national government made the United States Federal Reserve system work, some kind of global political authority is needed to keep the absolutely indispensible globe-spanning monetary system going.

The revolution from the top that now is needed to prevent the collapse of the world monetary system is the creation of some kind of world governance. And indeed a world governance process is going on. It has taken the embryonic form of the Group of Seven industrialized nations whose leaders periodically meet in big symbolic gatherings.

National parliaments are jealous of their powers, but the managers of the American empire know that a "new world order" is needed to keep the world economy and therefore the civilization going. That too requires a revolution from the top down, somewhat like the one American and Soviet leaders pulled off on disarmament.

The North, led by the United States, is organizing itself to govern the world.

✧

A revolution from above is also needed to save the world from the cataclysm of environmental degradation.

Consider a common situation in a vastly overpopulated city in a poor country. The family cooks its meals on a charcoal-burning stove or over a pit in the ground. The wood comes from whatever trees are left not too far from the city. The smoke fills people's lungs. It gets into the atmosphere and creates a pall of smog over the city. Much of that smog also comes from gasoline-burning vehicles whose numbers are expanding at an exponential rate. Then these people create immense quantities of waste: shit, garbage, debris. It is buried in the ground and dumped into rivers.

In the so-called developed world, we make the same kind of waste but get rid of it relatively quickly and odorlessly. We cook with clean gas, which comes from gas and oil fields. We drive many more cars than the poorer people do but congratulate ourselves that the gasoline is lead-free.

When we go to poor countries as tourists, we shun most places in their big, noisy, smelly cities. We prefer to go to the quaint villages, where smells seem historical. Yet those cities are our country cousins suddenly dropping in on our elegant dinner parties.

Archaeology tells us that many a civilization choked on its own waste. Venerable cities were simply proclaimed garbage dumps, and the people moved away. Can nature die from such degradation? I am not sure, but the worry about the greenhouse effect and a pierced ozone layer indicates that many people think so. Their fears already suggest a revolution in the making, one that will in good part, but not entirely, have to come from the top down.

If you regard the civilization, for all its bad things, as basically good, then you want to keep it. This is a civilization of movement, and movement needs immense amounts of energy to keep moving. Coal, oil, and nuclear power have been its main energy sources. All produce toxic wastes that are now widely seen as noxious, even fatal to the civilization.

There are other sources of energy that appear to be less toxic. Water is not toxic, but tapping it for energy can be ruinous to nature. Wind and geothermal energy are promising. And, of course, there is the sun, whose potential energy for the earth seems unlimited and nontoxic. Yet if ever the civilization should become solar powered, an immense revolution from the top will be needed to make it so. It is not conceivable that everybody in the world doing their solar thing with mirrors and collectors will lead to a second paradise.

The world needs immense amounts of fuel, and the only source that will halt environmental degradation and enable the world to keep moving is electricity. If all stoves in the world can be made electric and if all cars in the world move with electricity, then this third cataclysm too can be avoided. Cheap, efficient electric stoves are already widely used. It will only be a matter of time before cheap, efficient, and cost-effective electric cars are available (the Air Quality Control Board of Los Angeles has already called for the banning of all gasoline-powered vehicles from the city by the year 2007). The only question is where the cheap electric fuel will come from.

In 1989 the G-7 acknowledged the world's "debt to nature." That was, in effect, a declaration by the embryonic world government that in addition to protecting the world economy, it would now seek to devise some system of providing sufficient amounts of energy to the world without ravaging nature.

Controversy has already arisen over what kind of energy source will fuel this revolution. On one side are those who argue that the energy needs are so vast that power has to be provided through large-scale infrastructures. These people are said to favor a "hard path." Then there are the advocates of the "soft path," who call for multiple, small-scale, decentralized sources of energy. Most of the advocates of the former are from the already industrialized North, and most of the advocates of the latter are from the developing South.

If there is a breakthrough in nuclear fusion, it will be like the coming of the messiah. The fights among technocrats should cease, and abundant pollution-free power should become available. Political advocates will continue arguing, and those opposed to centralized energy-producing infrastructures will still warn against too much concentrated power and continue to advocate the soft path. But the beneficent payoff from the hard path would then seem indisputable.

If the miracle does not happen, where will enough energy come from to allow the civilization of the North to continue and also allow the South to live at least a semblance of that civilization? There is practically no conceivable way the South, with its new consciousness, ambitions, and arrogance, will accept the preachings of the North about simplified living. The South, with the bulk of the world's population, wants what the North has and will not willingly change course, even if religious fundamentalists come to power in southern countries.

If currents advocating the hard path come more and more shrilly from the South, even as currents advocating the soft path keep coming from the North, then only a third revolution from the top down could create a political superstructure to bring into being organized and globally linked infrastructures that can provide enough energy for both an overdeveloped North and an underdeveloped South. Then, nuclear fission would remain in the game as a major energy source for the world. Can the International Atomic Energy Agency, for example, become the instrument of a new de facto world government and do for the world's energy what the Federal Reserve Board did for money in the United States? The stern, disciplined, highly trained technocrats who increasingly run the world must make certain that no Chernobyls occur ever again. We all live with death and will probably have to live with new Chernobyls as a price we pay for civilization.

What of the waste? Where shall it go? Revolutions from below can empower people to deal with their own waste, but in the meantime the Hobbesian path seems like the likely one—if the sense prevails that only through a top-down revolution can the civilization be saved from destroying itself. After all, revolutionaries from the top down have never been gentle. The most successful among them have, however, been shrewd and often wise.

The electrification of the entire world will require a lot of capital. Vast spreads of solar collectors will cover the earth, and they will have to be guarded from destructive forces. Many windmills will be built. Much geothermal energy will be tapped. Ocean waves offer a usable source of power. And nuclear reactors operating through fission or fusion will dot the landscape. Environmentalists who have a strong autocratic streak in them will rule a good part of the world, and like revolutionary purists before them will realize that in a swirling chaotic world, strong, sometimes brutal hands are needed to rule. We can't expect the grim environmentalists, once in power, to continue acting as if they were utopians.

Why should anyone who is not one of the afflicted consider AIDS a cataclysm that requires a fourth revolution from the top down to eradicate it? Isn't it a matter of "just saying no"? No to promiscuity, no to taking drugs, no to coming into contact with the bodily fluids of people with AIDS? Or maybe one can agree that a revolution from above is needed to segregate AIDS sufferers into stigmatized populations and send them to concentration camps where, like the Jews in Poland during World War II, they can be cared for or disposed of as the Hobbesian authorities decide.

AIDS is spreading fast almost everywhere in the world. And it is spreading by two means that are intimate products of the civilization: sex and drugs. Sex is a personal high point of American civilization. And drugs are technologies used to combat one of its most toxic products: stress. The plague has hit gay men, drug users, Africans, and has spread all over the world. Many people still believe that AIDS is God's punishment for being queer or being black. They segregate the afflicted from us so hermetically that *their* germs do not waft over to *us*, and then let them die.

Diseases hit large numbers of people in different ways. Cholera, malaria, and odd diseases like snail fever usually attack only the poor, the outsiders. Cancer seems to strike people indiscriminately; heart disease is more predictable, being inherited or caused by stress. But by afflicting predominantly gays and Africans, AIDS has struck at two very different population groups. The gays whose obituaries one reads in the papers are white, young, intellectual, artistic—the best and the brightest, it would seem, of the civilization. The Africans are black and far away, or within the United States, at the bottom, hunkering on city streets asking for handouts.

Jesus called for a revolution from the bottom to bring all the poor and the suffering and the outcast together so they could lead others in the march into the Kingdom of God. But in the alleys of San Francisco's Castro district and in Africa, where the "slim" disease rages, men and women are looking upward to government and science, hoping for money to help scientists find a cure for AIDS.

AIDS and cancer are two diseases that have so far stymied the West's medical genius. During his presidency, Richard Nixon launched a war against cancer. But it failed, fizzling out like some ill-advised venture. Nevertheless, it appears that progress has been made in the area of cancer therapy. An enormous spread and democratization of medical research has taken place in the world, and new cancer therapies have increased the survival rate of victims. People know that we all must face dying, and that while it would be nice to live to the life expectancy of 85 years for human life (many scientists now see age 85 as a "natural" life expectancy for population groups, though not for individuals), many will die before that limit, and many will die of cancer.

The expectations about AIDS are different. Many religious fundamentalists believe that afflictions come from sin. They see defeating the HIV enemy as akin to defeating the challenge of Nazism, communism, or Muslim fundamentalism—but they see no need for a revolution. Let the disease ravage the sinners, and so will it become evident that a wrathful God is punishing those who transgress against His moral law. Then the kingdom will come and those who are pure will enter it.

Maybe no revolution from above is needed to speed up AIDS research. What is needed is more money, more researchers, more tests. But a revolution is needed to deal with an AIDS epidemic that has now spread far beyond Africa. Thailand, which has become a major site of global capitalism's sex industry, now has close to half a million AIDS sufferers of both sexes; a decade ago it had almost none.

AIDS, because it spreads over both North and South, could be attacked by a global war launched by the North. It would be a revolution from the top down, carried out in recognition of the oneness of the world, as were the wars against Nazism and communism and the former socialist world's war against imperialism. If relatively few in the North would enlist in any army to save homosexuals from AIDS, a missionary urge still strong in many Americans might find more volunteers if the aim of the war were to rescue the poor of Africa, Asia, and Latin America from its scourge.

Successful wars are driven by moral imperatives that move millions. As long as AIDS is seen mainly as a cataclysm afflicting white, gay, Western men, no revolution from the top down can significantly speed up the pace of scientific research for a therapy. If it is stigmatized as the result of evil behavior, then every society in the civilization will polarize, just as they have over abortion. But if it is seen as what it is—a plague afflicting the entire world—then there is a chance that the globe's power elites will consider the need for a revolution from the top down.

A fifth top-down revolution is needed to save the world from the cataclysm of civil conflict.

Civil conflict seems like a social disease that has been spreading faster since the end of the cold war. Charles Manson so hated America that he wanted to destroy it; he tried to foment a race war by committing a massacre that he hoped would be blamed on blacks, who would be killed by whites in revenge.

But God has been good to America, and a race war has not broken out; yet ethnic wars have erupted in so many countries. In Yugoslavia, the hatreds, feeding on a long and bloody history, erupted in terrible bloodshed. So too in the former Soviet Union, Liberia, Rwanda, earlier in Sri Lanka. And if the causes of civil conflict are not ethnic, then they are religious or ideological or tribal. Two groups bound together by strong ties of solidarity square off with white-hot anger. It doesn't take much to get a war going, especially when power-hungry politicians sense the chance of power gains in those conflicts.

People kill each other, their neighbors, when they see in such killing an importance transcending personal hatred. It is God's or history's will that I kill or even be killed. That is why the death toll is so high in wars of religion or ideology. We read a lot in the papers nowadays about casual killing—a flick of the trigger finger and someone falls into a pool of blood. Murder is an awesome act, and the killer knows, when killing, that he (and increasingly she) is important and that the person he kills is important as well. (Good hunters respect their game, even when they make it die in agony.)

The more civilized people become, the more they kill. No "primitive" society has ever seen wars on the scale of destructiveness of that of Europe's two world wars. The killing in those wars was so extensive that only the name "world war" seemed apt.

Of all the ways sociologists divide human society, only one division makes sense to me: that between state and society. There is the public world and the private world. The public world exists when doors and windows are open. When the shades are drawn and large walls with few openings enclose a living area, then we know a private world exists.

But I would add a third element to that sociological mix: God. As the ancient Greeks already knew, God is the prime mover. And as the Hebrews and then the Muslims also knew, God is unity. God is "0" and God is "1." Hegel saw a continuum from the individual through the state to God. By equating God with history, Hegel made God a part of the world. Rabbis, priests, and imams should rightly be appalled at such a view.

When the Enlightenment began, toward the end of the seventeenth century, God saw He was no longer welcome in places like Paris, where the lights got more and more brilliant. He went into exile, but pointed His wand at the state. The state, He decreed, is important, and society is less so. Not unexpectedly, the state began to take on aspects of God. The sun-king wondered whether he himself might be the sun. God is loving, judging, and wrathful. When the state assumes those qualities, its members, especially its power-obsessed politicians at the top and power-seeking outsiders at the bottom, become loving, judging, and wrathful. When the latter two qualities take on disproportionate dimensions by a state or political movement, terrible and even massive killing can soon follow.

The people of the South are now the children of the North. American civilization has drawn them by the hundreds of millions out of their villages, mountains, and deserts. As with children, we cut them loose. Will they cut themselves off from us to leave us alone in our retirement? Even if the North no longer wants or needs the products of the South, the North is in the South as much as the South is in the North. The bonds cannot be sundered. In the end we all live in one home.

The strategy of the North until now has been "development"—turn them into northerners. Give them the means to become consumers, press them toward personal liberation, take them out of community, and make them into naked individuals who seek to adorn themselves with finery to clothe their aloneness. Just as in the North the people sought community (by creating nations, for example), even as the vision of the civilization pulled people ahead, so in the South there is a similar quest for national or religious or communal belongingness. In both instances people killed and are willing to be killed in that quest.

Suppose eight hundred million Hindus decide they want a final solution to the presence of one hundred million Muslims on their land. In the Holy Land Palestinians are convinced the Israelis want to drive them all into Jordan. In the Soviet Union, a nationality wants independence from the Russians but then squashes smaller nationalities within its borders. In Africa the civil hatreds are in good part responsible for the economic and environmental horrors that have occurred. In Rwanda the Hutu militias envisage a "final solution" against the Tutsis. Even if we in the North cared, wept, tore out our hair to find some way to bring *pacem in terris,* how could we?

It is conceivable that the North could find a way of putting all the nuclear genies let loose on the world back into their bottles. It is likely that the powers-that-be can keep the world's monetary system going so we all do not die from a massive breakdown of the distribution system. It is conceivable that strong efforts can succeed in rolling back the tide of environmental degradation. Given earlier successes of medicine, it is conceivable that once again we can triumph over a deadly disease, and that would indeed be seen as a gift of God. But how can any revolution from the top stop the kind of suicidal killing that is proliferating in the South? This seems even less likely now that the North's earlier hope for bringing progress to the South, "development," has withered; the global fiscal crisis has not left even enough money in national coffers to keep the civilization's main class, the middle class, from drowning in a sea of debt.

In the summer of 1991 stories about the Soviet Union presented a picture of fissiparous wrangling. The idea that this was an empire suddenly seemed ludicrous. Today its remnants seem like a run-down city neighborhood where the head man is desperately trying to get some outside money to make life just a little better and mitigate some of the local rancor. On the other hand the United States, despite Clinton's fumblings, seems more than ever like an empire. With its smashing victory in the Gulf War, the United States was seen as an empire as it never had been before (though in 1945 the Russians and British were still reluctant to concede the United States that status). The emergence of the United States as an empire has given the United Nations astonishing new force. It now ventures into regions it earlier did not even think of looking at. In region after region, the leaders and even the quarreling peoples are looking to the United States or the United Nations or the North in general for a new *Pax Americana* or *Pax Universalis.*

In the Middle East people are still convinced that real peace can never come about between the Israelis and the Arabs unless the United States forces it. The Israelis will keep their ultimate deterrent, nuclear weapons, and the Arabs will keep on arming themselves, throwing themselves into suicidal missions, maintaining their societies in a state of frustration, suffering, and wild dreams.

Even in proud, arrogant India, there is a similar fatalistic sense that sooner or later the final battle must be fought with Pakistan; the result could be a Hindu-Muslim holocaust. In the eighteenth century the British moved into India and for more than a century brought peace to the subcontinent. Now Indians hope that the United States, acting with fairness to India, will muster the moral force to prevent that holocaust. These thoughts derive from unspoken Indian memories of the positive side of British imperialism.

Great and grand China every once in a while fell apart into bitterly quarreling entities. But unity was always restored from within. In the ancient world, only Rome and China had linguistic expressions for world peace.

The only hope for the South to avoid the holocausts that accompanied the North's industrialization and modernization is for the "great powers" (China, Japan, Russia, the United States, Western Europe) and modernizing powers (Brazil, India, Nigeria) to assume their imperial responsibility for the South and for the South to accept it. And since all the other great powers can be only lesser partners to the one imperial power, the United States—the reincarnation of Rome—must take the lead in a truly global peace process. The United States must make it clear that it and the other great powers will not tolerate civil conflict, and if such erupts on a serious scale they will act forcefully to maintain the *Pax Universalis.*

One part of the world that is being shredded by civil conflict can be rescued by a revolution from the top down: Africa. After millennia of darkness, shut off, except for a few fringes, from the world's civilizations, Africa is moving onto the stage of history with explosive force. The yearning for consumption, liberation, democracy is tremendous. At the same time Islam, Christianity, even animism are moving Africans to visions and aspirations, and also to conflict. Millions have left the land for swollen cities. Immense numbers of babies are born. Trees die. Water vanishes. Charcoal smoke covers the cities with choking fumes. AIDS proliferates. Hatreds fester. If any part of the world wants to move out of its millennial isolation it is Africa. Some Africans fear renewed domination by the North, but there is as much chance that Africa will again become subject to direct foreign imperial control as that America's blacks will again acquiesce to slavery.

Both the Romans and the Chinese saw empire and the keeping of the peace as a moral good. Yet while many were strong, the Roman emperors of the first century were among their vilest, and three of the greatest imperial figures of China (the first emperor, who in the third century B.C. unified China; Liu Bāng, who only a short time later founded the Han dynasty, Rome's equivalent in the East; and Zhu Yuanzhang, founder of the great Ming dynasty) were all killers on a vast scale.

In my lectures on China's history I have said that good and evil are two sides of the same indivisible coin and that this duality becomes especially evident in the formation and life of great empires. I opposed America's entry into the Vietnam War because I saw it as doing evil in Vietnam. But I saw it as doing great good in World War II—one world came out of that war, although with the cold war the unity cracked. I saw both good and evil in the Gulf War. I have seen both in every empire I have studied. But I also believe that empires survive over long periods for two reasons: they must manage the necessary human diversity of empire and they must manage trade beyond their imperial boundaries. To achieve these two necessities, they need peace.

They can achieve peace either in a positive way (through negotiation and conflict resolution) or in an evil way (through bloody war or oppression). To entrust some new imperial world order with peacemaking is a risk, but better than nothing.

COMPLETING WORLD CIVILIZATION

All five of these revolutions have to do with realizing dreams, not cultivating growth. Their grandest dream is peace. And for years peace has been the grandest cause of the aging left.

Yet Marx despised peace and called for revolutionary violence. Martin Luther called for the bloody suppression of rebellious peasants defying the God-given authority of princes. Muhammad, peace be upon him, took the sword. Jesus said, "I came not to send peace, but a sword" (Matthew 10:34).

Peace has always been the dream of those who already have the power, wealth, and privilege. Today it is the dream of the whites, the

North, the rich. Those who in earlier times denounced evil at the top and preached righteousness at the bottom spoke not of peace but of the sword.

An emperor, a dynasty, a creed rises from below and supplants what is at the top. Socialism rose from the bottom in an effort to supplant capitalism. It did not succeed. And when it assumed power in some countries, it ruined people's hopes to gain the civilization they saw, out there somewhere, beyond the wall, where millions of points of light gleamed and movement was dizzying.

The revolutions from the top down cannot bring about growth. Their dreams are more in the realm of physics, which soars into vast space or bores into minute space, than in the realm of biology, which goes inward into bodies and leads to growth, to birth and becoming, and again to birth and becoming.

Capitalism and biology never got along that well, just as nomads and peasants do not. Nomads have few children, and the open breeziness of tents is not conducive to the intimacies that make it possible for peasants to bring forth so many children. In our civilization, sex substitutes for procreation and growth. (The Catholic Church knows this and wants the faithful to grow while the elect priests shuffle near and around death so that they alone can gain a look at the higher plane.)

The capitalist order depends on consumption. Consumption destroys wealth, but gives pleasure. Pleasure is the chief positive emotion of capitalism, as fear is its chief negative one. The want for more pleasure creates a demand for more wealth. The fear that one's moment of existence in the present might be lost also creates a demand for wealth, because wealth is what fills the emptiness of that moment.

Over the past two millennia no civilization has been so successful as that of China. Except for a few centuries, China retained a remarkably stable political unity, during which time it developed, changed, and spread; by the eighteenth century China had the highest general standard of living of any nation in the world. The core political principle on which China's success rested was enunciated by Mencius, who taught that only a realm in which the peasants were the foundation could be stable, and only if the peasants could prosper from generation to generation could that foundation last. In short, China's millennially successful political philosophy was focused on the future, the "road ahead" as the Chinese say. The continuing growth of life-death-life was the optimal condition.

American civilization can complete itself only if a sense of future and past can be joined with the pervasive sense of the present that reigns in modern capitalism. In short, a society must arise to complement the state, that vast public realm of affluent, middle-class civilization.

In the western part of the Roman Empire society reappeared, but the great public realm declined. The cities lost population, and people migrated to the countryside, where they founded villages, called *vici,* which had never before existed in Italy. Eventually the emperors removed to Byzantium. And so Italy became rural, and largely remained so, though in the Renaissance cities once again appeared. But in the eastern part of the Roman Empire society had remained stronger and was strengthened even more with the new religion, Christianity. Byzantium survived, not brilliantly but in a way later to provide the conquering Arabs with a model of a strong state and an even stronger society.

CONNECTING PAST TO FUTURE AND PRESENT

Before the coming of Western imperialism, society was the strength of the South. Conquerors came and sometimes created great states, but they vanished while the society continued. That has been the history of India. Buddhism became the state creed during the reign of the great state builder Ashoka (269?–232? B.C.). Monasteries sprang up everywhere. The monks and nuns left behind splendid art depicting the higher life they lived. But then Hinduism returned with a vengeance. It was anti-state and pro-village and preached a pantheon of gods who lived in a society of the higher plane, not like Buddhism's transcendent state where individuals merged into a cosmos.

In Russia too, Russians lived in society while foreigners ruled the state. The *muzhiks* were shapeless and ugly. The men and women of the state were resplendent. But then in the nineteenth century people rose up demanding a state. And now they demand democracy.

The South is seeking state as the North realizes how ravaged both its environment and its society have become. When a southern country gains the state, its new rulers milk it of its resources to pay for the state. Capital goes to realizing dreams, all too often (as University of California Professor Percy Hintzen points out) for the dreamers' own self-aggrandizement. These *nouveaux riches* and *nouveaux puissants* simply assume that the capital needed to train successor generations for the future will come from the labor of the poor, cheaply or even freely provided to rear the children of the *nouveaux priviligiés.* That's how it was under feudalism. And feudalism can flourish under capitalism, under socialism, and maybe even in paradise.

The yearning for consumerism, personal liberation, and democracy proves to be the Achilles' heel of the South. Eventually that yearning reaches everyone, and soon enough resentment and then white-hot anger build up against the new middle-class tyrants. The *nouveaux nouveaux* want what the *vieux nouveaux* have, and so war breaks out.

When the poor yearn to crash into middle-class society, then they are revolutionary. By revolution I do not mean they are eager for violence. Rather it is that they are eager to change everything including their bodies—to look handsome or beautiful rather than ugly—minds—to speak well, not in jerked sentences—soul—to give themselves direction until, having arrived in the middle class, they no longer need it. Many, however, still want their children just to survive or stay around the old home. They sense that to become middle class means sacrificing society, the bonds that hold them together.

Progressives still like to talk of "empowering the poor." Once empowered the near-poor acquire income and a little wealth and often a little more power. They will defend it with a vengeance, especially against the poor who nip at their heels.

What about the rich? Do they fit anywhere in this landscape of social class? I have not known many rich people, although a long time ago I did see the Vanderbilt castle in Asheville, North Carolina, at night some miles away in a dense forest. The castle was massive and dark. The only light was from one tiny upper corner window. "There is where Mrs. Vanderbilt lives, all alone," a friend said.

Despite all their wealth, parties, and the awe others still show them, I think of the rich as "alones." They have few social bonds except through prosperity. They often lack the markings of individuality. In America the only aristocracy are "celebrities" who have money, glitz, and enormous vanity. The really rich have been made to feel ashamed of themselves. The rich everywhere have the world's wealth. The middle class has substantial income but little wealth. That is why, despite their addiction to freedom and choice, they depend on the state to assure that income through entitlements. The poor have neither wealth nor income and so become revolutionary. What is more revolutionary (in a personal sense) than migrating, often alone, thousands of miles for an uncertain job? Socialists would take away the wealth of the rich to help the poor. But taking this redistributive route only makes the realm of the state stronger and leads to the further triumph of market capitalism.

Rich people are often poor in soul. Many are poor in mind. Some are poor in body. Why is it that since biblical times the rich have often been miserly and fearful or philanthropic and compassionate? The histories of religions and revolutions are replete with rich men and women passionately devoted to serving the higher and lower planes. The poverty around them can give them compassionate insights. By their wealth they are linked to the past. By their liquidity they are sought after by operators in the present. But their poverty and aloneness give them a vision for the future.

Rich people helped bridge the lethal cold war hostility of two mighty states. They can help bridge the gap between North and South. But most of all they can help bridge the gap between state and society, between the great public realm of American civilization and the restive and dangerous diversity of the rapidly growing half-private and half-public worlds of ethnic groups, communities, and religious faiths.

COMMUNITY

During the Protestant Reformation there was a widely accepted political device called, in Latin, *cuius regio, eius religio,* "a person will take whatever religion his lord adopts." The device reflected the timely fact that society is shaped in whatever direction the authority from above wills it to be, even on as intimate a matter as religion.

Will the sheep follow wherever the shepherd leads them? Are their eyes and thoughts focused only on their leader? Can television shape an entire society, an entire world? Can American civilization become so global that even among the poor, discontented, oppressed, and unfulfilled their only images are those of our civilization? As they starve, do they think sadly of the lights of New York they have seen on videotapes?

Ever since the Enlightenment began, Europe has sensed that powerful currents well up periodically from deep in the oceans of human society—and that rulers cannot control them. José Ortega y Gasset called such currents the "rising of the masses." They could wash away the state's grand boats and even crash onto the shores of magnificent cities. They could be terribly destructive, but they also could infuse tired old states with new energy and direction.

COMMUNITY, RELIGION, AND SOCIETY

The popularity of the word *revolution*—"to turn things upside down"— implied that political rule could not be based on the simplistic assumption that whatever the lord did and thought, so would his subjects do and think.

Whenever the politics and ideology flow only from the top down, sooner or later a countercurrent will appear from the bottom. This has been so in Europe since the Reformation. It was so in ancient Rome in both republican and imperial times. China's rulers from earliest imperial times developed a fear-filled respect for such periodic eruptions from the bowels of society.

When, at the end of the eighteenth century, the French Revolution triumphed, its leaders believed that the ideas and actions of the revolutionary state could shape society, from the top down. The slogan of that revolution—*liberty, equality, fraternity*—was seen as providing direction for society. It was assumed that as the "people" (later to be called "the masses") became enlightened, they would practice liberty, equality, and fraternity.

The French Revolution left behind a legacy of transformative visions in the nineteenth century. Liberalism heralded an era when all would be free, affluent, and individual. It envisages a society freely chosen by people, as in a marriage where each freely loves the other and contracts to live in a state of matrimony with the other. And if the contract be freely terminated, then so be it.

Political scientists often point out how different American liberalism is from its European counterparts. Influenced by socialism, it took a more benign view of government than European liberalism. It sees government not as an impediment to affluence but as a necessary instrument to bring it about. American liberalism, like classical European liberalism, has always seen personal liberation as its supreme social goal. And the popularity of the word *liberation* attached to one or another political movement—women's liberation, gay liberation, even animal liberation —indicates how strong that Lockean tradition remains.

If liberalism latched on to the French Revolution's slogan of "liberty," socialism latched on to "equality." Socialism denounced all societies marked by class divisions. And classes were ranked from higher to lower in terms of power, wealth, and privilege. But a road marked "revolution" pointed toward a shining future. And when the final destination was reached, all would live in a state of equality.

Nationalism, in contrast, held that all peoples were bound together culturally and linguistically as social entities. Nationalism is a tribal concept applied to modern social conditions. Whatever the differences in power, wealth, and privilege within the nation, nationalists hold, all its people are linked by an essential racial or ethnic bond—"We are all Americans, Germans, Russians . . ." Nationalism thus latched on to the third slogan of the French Revolution, "fraternity."

Since medieval times, Europeans have been familiar with the social concept of class. Feudalism divided people into clearly defined classes: nobles, serfs, burghers. They also were well familiar with the concept of nation. For example, since early in this millennium, students at the University of Paris were grouped together by "nation," that is, people who spoke the same language or dialect.

Europeans were also familiar with the idea of individual freedom; in their cities, which blossomed during the Renaissance, individual liberty was legally sanctioned. As a German law applicable to fugitive serfs who found refuge for one year in a city put it, *Stadtluft macht frei,* "the air of the city shall make you free."

The French Revolution took the abstract concepts—*liberté, égalité, fraternité*—and filled them with a content familiar to people. They turned ideas from the past into chariots for driving into the future. But already during the nineteenth century, all three—liberalism, socialism, and nationalism—were recognized to be incomplete as ideologies. Liberalism proclaimed freedom but also promised a society shaped through a social contract freely entered into by free individuals. Socialism promised not just equality but a society that would be better because of equality, as French utopians argued. Marx predicted an eventual communist human condition in which all would be free and equal and live in brotherhood.

After the Russian Revolution, socialism split with communism over the issue of freedom. The former and its largely Western adherents strongly advocated freedom, while the latter, with its powerful following in the non-Western world, focused on equality and community. Nationalism too was ambivalent on freedom. The milder nationalisms accepted bourgeois freedoms, while fascism, like communism, opted for equality and community. Nazism went further and chose a mystic Aryan community, injecting a pagan element into its ideology.

But throughout the nineteenth century liberalism, socialism, and nationalism were dogged by a hoary ghost they all disliked, even loathed: religion. Religion offered no shining vision for the future. It only kept on sniping at those secular visions, prophesying their ultimate failure.

Religion had its radical days in the sixteenth century, and the lakes of blood that formed in the wars of religion had made religious people cautious and conservative. In the seventeenth century religious dissidents fled to America, Russia, and other countries. In the eighteenth century religious turbulence subsided. In the nineteenth century people of religion were alarmed by the revolution sweeping Europe but were unable to mount a counterrevolution like the counterreformation they had mounted in the sixteenth century. They had no future other than patient plodding along the road to death and beyond.

But religion had one social concept to offer that neither liberalism, nor socialism, nor nationalism could convincingly deliver: community. All great religions began as communities of believers. And those communities were unities of different kinds of people held together mainly by their faith. They had faith in some especially blessed leader or body of doctrine and also felt a link to a higher plane. No matter how small their numbers, all the original disciples and apostles of the various religions knew that they were part of a divine force that gave them strength and promise far beyond their numbers.

Religions reached beyond the state into the heavens, but they also reached down, sometimes even below society into the domain of the dregs. Think of Salvation Army bands playing in the filthy parts of cities in different countries, with beggars and hookers as audience.

In the nineteenth century most of the world's religions had turned into tired institutions, often endowed with great wealth. The sense of a link to the higher plane was wiped away by a worldliness that widely satirized religion. Nevertheless the old tree cast down seeds, which carried in them the same elements that had been there when the religion was founded. The other three ideologies just assumed the tree had become barren.

As the twentieth century and the second millennium come to an end, the three great ideologies of the Enlightenment and the French Revolution are in trouble. But religion is returning, like a deep current rising to the top of the oceans.

Liberalism remains the strongest of the three. The visions of American liberalism—consumerism, personal liberation, and democracy—still radiate a powerful magnetic force all over the world. Liberalism is the creed of American civilization. Yet, just as in the nineteenth century when liberalism in Europe already was losing its ideological force, so today people are again beginning to sense its limitations as a vision. Doesn't consumerism quickly lead to gluttony, one of the seven cardinal sins? Doesn't personal liberation lead to Janice Joplin—"Freedom's just another word for nothing left to lose"? Why are the young, the poor, and the dark-skinned not voting?

Nationalism became a powerful force in the nineteenth century and has remained so throughout much of this century. Nation-states have arisen all over the world, some 150 of which have seats in the United Nations. Yet the Soviet Union, which tried to become a nation-state (as it thought America had done), fell apart. The would-be tribal confederations are not holding, not even in Europe. And when tribes form smaller nation-states, invariably even smaller nations want their freedom. No sooner did the Romanian-speaking Moldavians proclaim their autonomy from Russia than their small Turkish-speaking but Christian Gagauz minority demanded its own autonomy. Throughout the world nation-states are cracking as rapidly as they once were built—just like the shoddy buildings of socialist countries.

Why did socialism crash so spectacularly in Eastern Europe and the Soviet Union? Unlike liberalism, but like nationalism, it had something of a communal promise. While it preached class struggle against external enemies, it encouraged solidarity within society's institutions: factories, offices, schools, military units, the professions. In China the social unit that all are part of is called the *danwei* (unit). The *danwei* is supposed to be your home. A university professor once said to me, "After all, Franz, the university is your home." (She was wrong.)

In the Soviet Union restaurants were done away with. People were supposed to live close to where they worked and to eat in the canteens there. Isn't that sort of the way it was in the village? A village in the city? Greenwich Village? Village Fair? When Mao Zedong decreed a Great Leap Forward, all peasants were supposed to eat in a common canteen. Why didn't it work? In the Tang dynasty the emperor awarded a prize to a gentleman who had 500 family members. They all ate together, and none would commence eating until the 500th arrived at the table. He also had 500 dogs; and no dog would start eating at the common trough until the 500th dog arrived. If it worked for the nobleman, why not for socialist commoners?

Of course we know what happened in the authoritarian socialist countries. The state crushed all freedom. And so the people retreated from a public realm of slavery into a private realm of individual freedom. Out of that latter realm arose a black market of stupendous proportions, which in good part kept the Soviet economy going when the state system collapsed.

The lesson is obvious. Community can exist in society, but not in the state. When it is forced on the people by the state, it is the community of a prison.

But what about the democratic socialist countries in which the state did not deprive people of freedom? There the doctrines of liberalism remained alive and strong. People in those largely northern European countries opted for consumerism, personal liberation, and democracy, leaving it to the state to provide welfare or to help in production and distribution. No community arose there, only an individualism as strong, widespread, and eminently individual as in the United States. Maybe a little more nostalgia for old farms, forests, and villages, but no community. Democracy took hold because most people were in the public realm.

Do they like their lives in those northern European countries, or do the high suicide and alcoholism rates indicate a citizenry that is uncomfortable in its civilization? Although I cannot answer that question, few in the world any longer look for inspiration to the examples of democratic socialism. Socialism's vision has faded for good, but some memory remains that it saw community as an ideal.

Unlike the other three, religion is reviving rapidly almost all over the world. Its revitalization has been most spectacular in the Islamic world, which stretches from the southern Philippines and Indonesia westward to the shores of the Atlantic, southward deep into Africa, and northward into the Slavic lands and Europe. Hinduism has become a scarily powerful political movement. It cannot be dismissed as nationalism because, like veil-wearing and beard-growing in Islamic regions, Hindu revivalism includes all Hindus, from those in city neighborhoods and rural villages to the political elites. Almost half of South Korea will soon be Christian. There too the faith in Jesus goes from neighborhoods right into the headquarters of the once opposing and now ruling political movements. There are Christian churches in Orwellian North Korea. Christianity is spreading in China much faster than church attendance indicates. Underground churches proliferate. I have heard young to middle-aged Chinese speak with great knowledge about different Christian denominations, although they do not often go to church. Middle-class Jews in America are vanishing through intermarriage and cultural assimilation, but at the bottom Hassidic and other Orthodox communities are growing rapidly. In fact, community is the salvation of the children of Israel. *Santería,* or what Americans call "voodoo," is reviving from the Caribbean northward, southward throughout Brazil, and among whites and mulattoes as much as among blacks. New cults are taking hold among young people in Western Europe, and a revitalized Catholicism is spreading out of Italy.

The concept of community is central to all these religious revivals.

THE TWO WORLDS OF RELIGION

In secular civilization it is simply assumed that we consist of body and mind. These are both visible and measurable. Life is the result of a union between the two and can be destroyed when either or both vanish or when vital components of one or both fail. Then we die, and mind vanishes and body rots.

But all religions assume we live in two worlds. We live in a secular world in which body and mind are what count, but we also live on a higher plane to which we are bound only by soul. Soul is neither visible nor measurable. It exists only if you believe in a higher plane. Then soul becomes the force that moves you toward that higher plane. So religions that believe in soul also believe that after dying, the soul alone, liberated or cut loose from body and mind, seeks "paradise." The Chinese, taking their cue from Buddhism, called paradise "the pure land in the west" (did the ancient Chinese Buddhists already have California in mind?).

One can take the secular view that a higher plane and the soul are illusions that waste valuable time. Or one can take the opposite view, that the living body is incipient rot and the mind is a supreme vanity, and, like St. Augustine, live only for the soul and God. Or one can decide that life is made up of all three—the soul, the mind, and the body—and that all three have weight and value.

If you accept the notion that we are made up of body, mind, and soul, even if unevenly developed, then we might consider how the three are related to each other. Body seeks place, a home, where the bones can rest. Bodies in the end find final resting places. Minds move, extremely fast, like telephone calls from thousands of miles away that arrive in a split second. Minds are movement. Souls are the creation of God, and God is the direction-giver of the cosmos. Soul is direction.

Time is also direction. Time is not reversible. Body, mind, and time intersect now, in the present. Body and mind remember the past and can project a future. Only soul knows where we have come from and where we are going, because only soul can intuit time, birth, death, and the journey beyond. Body, mind, and soul can never be comfortable with each other (perhaps body and mind alone can, as expressed in an ideal of Roman and American civilizations—*mens sana in corpore sano,* "a healthy mind in a healthy body").

Religions are communal. They have to be. If you want religion's comforts without other people around to bother you, then you become a philosopher, like Boethius, who wrote *The Consolation of Philosophy* as he was awaiting execution alone in a prison cell. If you believe in and practice religion, then you live, work, and think with other people. I am a philosophically oriented writer, for however much I may believe in God and fancy myself a Catholic, in fact I am just me, pecking away at a computer with a view of the Pacific—somewhat like the one on the cover of this book—to my left. (To my right are various easts from where I came and where there once were whatever communities I was restlessly a member of.)

We are all born somewhere from someone. The somewhere gives us place; the someone enables us to be raised. Those who raise us push us ahead in whatever direction they are moving. If the movement is cyclical, as it was in old peasant societies, then the somewhere just rotates around a fixed axis, like the earth around the sun. Community gives us place and it links the movements of our lives to that place.

Nationalism told peasants who spoke an obscure dialect that they were Italian. So when they went from the Abruzzi to Turin, they were, miracle of miracles, Italian, at home, in *their* nation. *Paesano* but also *Italiano.* But socialism found it hard to give its members much movement beyond the cyclical movement of village life. In China you were stuck with your *danwei,* so you did little more than diddle or dawdle in it for your entire working life.

Religion is different. God is always with you, even at the hour of death. And when in Christianity you take communion for the last time, you are part of the body and blood of Christ, which is the church, which is all the faithful in Jesus. Jesus was crucified and buried and on the third day rose from the dead to wander among the people for forty days before ascending to Heaven. All religions have pilgrimages of one sort or another. The pilgrimage is the journey into death and beyond. Yet pilgrims return home, and there, in the community, is the place of worship, often with a cemetery around it.

Nationalisms and socialisms arose in the nineteenth century. Religion is coming back in the twentieth. American civilization driven by liberalism has visions of movement, of great leaps forward. But people also want a home.

FROM STATE TO SOCIETY

In a home you do not own your own body and you do not own your own mind. You own only your own soul. In older, settled societies, bodies were tortured into ugliness so everyone would have a home. Every peasant had a home. "He's living in his home like Adam in paradise," goes a Russian saying. In those societies minds were crude, and peasants rarely spoke. But they had a home. And as to soul, too much soul was dangerous. Who knows, the peasants might cease being cyclical and turn linear; and so the pope (which is what the Russians call their priests) inundated the peasants with incense (a sort of opium, as Marx spat out on the subject of religion) so that soul would be blunted and they would wearily sink back into angular rotation like the tired old earth around the sun. (When the sun rotated around the earth, even the peasant marveled at that wondrous orb that was so logical in its movements and gave light, but also was God and could be capricious, could engage in strange doings that aroused dreams and, of course, was the agent of all growth. After Galileo, peasants became "village idiots," Marx's contemptuous term for them.)

It is not surprising that the revolutions of nationalism and socialism were meant to liberate bodies and minds and, yes, even souls from the deathlike darkness of homes. A peasant home stank with every person's and every animal's smells. It resounded of obscene noises, including those that came from the mouth (especially those). God seemed far away; only saints or holy men with their ridiculous images were close by. But the intellectuals who made those revolutions hated priests, the earthly agents of God who they believed shackled the people in homes while feeding their own clerical bodies with pleasures and engaging in wonderful intellectual play. In the intellectuals' view those priests were the true anti-God, anti-Christ because their souls were dead; they worshipped at the temples of body and mind.

When nations came into being and social states brought social justice and capitalism created consumerism, personal liberation, and democracy, all the homes vanished. Where are all the people's homes? The nation was not a home. The work place was not a home. And capitalism is just good at building houses that it calls homes but that are just houses, in the end a combination of a pad and an asset to be handed down to the kids.

Nationalism and socialism never produced anything but revolutions from the top down. Yet their leaders portrayed them as revolutions from the bottom up that were creating new homes for people who had lost them. They would create abundant economies for all the people. The word *economics* derives from Greek *oikos* (home) and *nomos* (manager). (Was the *oikos* a home in ancient Greece?)

At the same time nationalist and socialist revolutionaries doused their preachings with a perfume hinting at a higher plane. Communism turned into a kind of religion, one that was not all that deep as it turned out. Yet few rose to the higher plane, unless by that one means bureaucratic sinecures. So these top-down visions generated few dreams beyond such wild schemes as Mao's Great Leap Forward or Castro's ten million tons of sugar. No Hollywoods. No comic books. But they did respond to what seemed like an immense, despairing, angry, demand by people for a home. The people yearned to go home.

Nationalisms and socialisms created vast states, and so too do religious revolutions. Society means nothing to them. For Hitler, society was a breeding ground for soldiers. For Stalin it was just serf peasants and serf workers. For the Ayatollah Khomeini, society didn't exist; there were just believers in God and the enemies of God. None of these autocrats ever looked at the people and said, "Your communities are good, you should have homes, there is a place for everyone and not just in the enormous card files of the police." (Maybe they were all just agents of the industrialization and modernization process, as political scientists might say.)

All nationalisms, socialisms, and religions have understood that in the end the greatest human force comes from the bottom. Nationalist revolutionaries knew they had to organize armies made up of peasant boys. Socialists knew they needed the disciplined power of organized workers. Religion, of course, is nothing without communities of believers. What lies did they tell their followers to motivate them to such stupendous sacrifice?

In one fashion or another they all spoke in honeyed words about love, work, and justice. But these were not phony words. They reflected values held by common people that, if cultivated in their communities, would ensure their survival. Although dying and death cannot be avoided, there will never be extinction.

People of society want the love of others and want the growth of their own capacity to love. Love arises when an *I* sees its own body and mind as the servant of the beloved. Love is the force that creates community, the loving *I* that serves the "we." People of society want to work because work does more than create value for the public domain. It also binds people to others. In work, bodies and minds become interwoven. As members of the community work together, the products of work go from being individual products to community creations.

American civilization is made up of many societies. Ideally they are peopled by individuals held together through some social compact and set of overarching institutions. If the institutions work as they are supposed to according to the best values of the civilization, the people should have no worries about justice. But if communities rise up to counteract the isolation and alienation common in the civilization, then the communities may be satisfying to their individual members but cause enmity toward other communities. Then justice becomes an issue. If you gain a home, can it really be a home as long as others still do not live in a just environment, a just world?

The people have so yearned for revolution, and all they have gotten is the state, a higher plane on earth inhabited by demons. Their capacities to love were debauched and their work subverted for the goals of the state. Things have definitely been better in liberal than in nationalist and communist states, but there too love has been replaced by desire, and work has been distorted into a job.

Nationalism was the furthest removed of the three modern revolutions from the people's yearning for home. Nationalism created states that nailed down boundaries with armies and police and then teased the people with romantic fantasies about wonderful old villages. Socialism came closer. Socialism thought the work place could become the home. Where you lived and where you worked could be brought together. But while socialist homes could be cozy, there was too much vodka around to make them real. They lacked the wonderful smell of black village earth.

Religion comes even closer. The Muslims speak of *umma* (community)—the root of the word is *um* (mother). The mosque is close to people's houses, and on Friday the men gather to hear the sermon. The women are at home taking care of the children. Modernization may be transforming the world along American lines, but it is also leading to a religious reaction. Revolutions produce reactions. Movement hurls people into the future and reaction draws them back into the past. But religion is closer to home than either nationalism or socialism. Religion is down there among the people, not up there in the state (socialism thought it was among the people but ended up very far away from them). Nationalism and socialism have created public states, but as a reaction people have created their own strong private societies. In capitalism, societies have crumbled, with so much of the private going public, like the private parts of people. Here religion, with its promise of home, has an entry.

In America, Christian fundamentalism is a reaction against capitalism, against its secularism, its liberalism, its vast public arenas, its Enlightenment ideals, and its revolutionary pretensions that have transformed societies, such as those in East Asia, more thoroughly than have the socialist revolutions. Christians believe in private communities, not in public arenas. In the latter they do badly. They love the intimacy of churches.

In the end, I am most interested in soul. Because soul is linked to God and both are linked to direction, what concerns me, in a sociopolitical way, is whether there is more soul in state or society, or whether my own soul is healthier when I function in the state, which I do as a teacher, or in society, which I do as a parent, lover, and journalist. Every time I cross the Bay Bridge to go to the public university fully funded by the state, I feel my soul shrivel up, tremble, hide, as my mind and body come to the fore. When I come back I know my body and my mind do not belong entirely to me, but I rediscover my soul, and I rejoice as the ancient Israelites did when they once again came upon the face of God after erring in the darkness for so long.

God has shifted His wand from the state, where it went with the Enlightenment, back to society. When, around the time of Johann Sebastian Bach and Isaac Newton, God shifted His wand to the state, He must have felt how sordid society—stupid peasants and greedy burghers—was, though in His infinite compassion He still loved it and them. Now, those peasants who once were so benighted have come forth into the light by the millions to become people with bodies and minds. He wants them to rediscover their souls, for their souls are their link with Him (or Her).

History is the interaction of God, souls, and humans. History is change, flows, the strange and wonderful ways people have broken loose from set ways and found new directions. God has ever been ready to guide people even as He guided Adam and Eve when they left paradise. But that guidance is given only when souls reach out for God. History is the story of ever new directions, ever new reachings out of souls to God.

The real revolutions from below are just beginning. In the state the ultimate values are power, wealth, and privilege, or a variant: power, wealth, and knowledge. The state confers power on any who serve in it, as any policeman knows. The state may pay you well or poorly but any credential conferred by the state, like a university diploma, along with private help from other members of the state structure, will get you good earnings and maybe even some real wealth. The privilege is evident in the respect granted you and in the finery you wear, which makes you stand out just as a uniform does. In the era of the triumph of the will (Marx, like Darwin, was a man of overpowering will), the revolutions zeroed in on building states that some believed might eventually encompass or replace all society. Building states cannot reflect the values of society and thus cannot be thought-forces (turn-of-the-century French psychologist Alfred Fouillée's term) driving the revolutions to come, those that will bring community as once they brought state.

Society is the roots, and the state should be no more than the branches. The state gets the sun, and the leaves are the body in which the seeds are nurtured. But the living, thinking, flowing, sensing foundation is society—people as individuals, groups, and communities. God has pointed His wand at them. And the dynamic forces bringing about the revolution are the search for love, work, and justice.

Society is below the state, and God is above the state, just as the sun is above the leaves. The state is the grand middle, like the great global middle class it has engendered. The revolution completes the civilization by restoring a foundation that disappeared when we all became shopping mall consumers. And it welcomes God with prayer and praise back into the world He left when the Enlightenment began.

Postmodernism is a cloud of windswept foam that will soon vanish, and we shall see then whether a revolution arises from below for society. If it does, life, especially everyday life, will get better, as it in fact has for much of the five thousand years of civilization. If not, the cataclysms will come.

LOVE, WORK, AND JUSTICE

What could a revolution for love, work, and justice be?

Love is a reaching out to another so that the other will grow. A mother reaches out for an infant so that it will flourish and turn into a she or a he. A mother, it is said, will die so that her child can live. Is it vanity? If it is, it is not love, only attachment of the sort that Lord Buddha taught was the source of evil thoughts. Love is an affirmation of biology and has no interest in physics.

Love can come only to those who surrender their bodies and minds to others. I will give you my arm to eat so that, in this lifeboat adrift on the stormy seas, you may live. In Holy Communion we eat Christ because He has asked us to as a sign that we accept His love for us. There can be little love in American civilization because there only are bodies and minds, and the only "love" is one that emanates from the self, is a self-made picture that fastens onto another, thereby creating an attachment, or if reciprocated, two attachments, which in the end relate mostly to the pictures each has of the other. Those pictures can become dreams to be realized, but growth is another matter. When the reality of one or both pictures changes, then they become blurred, and mind and body get confused, divorce soon follows, or mercifully, death. In America what the pop songs call love flourishes only when everything is hunky-dory. The German Green Party has said that we must go from the politics of production to the politics of reproduction. From physics to biology. But there is no biology without love, because for the seed to grow it must first eat the food that surrounds it in the pod or in the womb.

The ancient Chinese philosopher Mo-tzu said that you must first have love for all before there can be any decent human order. Lao-tzu never talked about kids but said to go straight to nature and live-die, which is growth and its inescapable death. Confucius said to love your own kin first, and he would say look after your own kids first before worrying about the world's kids. Lao-tzu said that anything except getting right back into biology is an illusion and that going into nature will bring you onto the Tao, or the correct path. The opening lines of the Holy Qur'an plead with God to be brought onto the correct path.

Mo-tzu's prescription for a revolution that would lead to universal love was imperialist. Create an overarching imperial structure and the rivalries and jealousies of the nobles will be crushed; so the field will be clear for all to love each other. Lao-tzu's prescription was to do nothing: don't fight, don't love, don't even learn. In practice it was a recipe for radical individuation. The Buddhists took this insight a step further and said that love is an attachment and if one can get rid of all attachments there will be enlightenment, peace, and salvation. Confucius's recipe was to build a realm from a foundation made up of many loving families. Gradually, love coming from the bottom would gain control over power coming from the top.

Mo-tzu's prescription is the most contemporary: by creating a just, vast, and effective public realm, we can achieve universal love and peace. Postmodernism. Lao-tzu's too is contemporary, flowing along the same current as environmentalism and ecology. Once nature's primacy and health are restored through self-sacrificial human action, then harmony will come; whether that means love or not is irrelevant. Confucius and especially his disciple Mencius—both of whom recognized the essential individuality of all humans, their capacity to make choices—called for a strong familial, communal, and social foundation. Both lauded enlightened lords, but both also had little respect for most other rulers. A central concept was loyalty, which was written with a two-part character: one part a verb meaning "to hit the target at the center," the other a noun meaning "heart."

A revolution for capital, community, and cosmology could be understood as a return to hoary ancient things. Old teachings always stressed having and raising many children, having harmonious families, and praying to whatever god one happened to have around the house. But a revolution for capital, community, and cosmology also looks into a future, one beyond high mountains covered with dark clouds.

Nationalism preached love for one's community. Nationalists all too quickly equated community and state. But this time a real revolution for community would mean that love and loyalties go first and foremost to the community that is in society and only in secondary ways in the realm of the state. Jehovah's Witnesses have been practicing such ideas for a long time, often suffering persecution as a result.

Socialists preached equality. They meant equality of wealth and of privilege (or knowledge). But when it came to power, they balked, preferring to believe that those who held power did it in the best interests of the people.

A communal revolution that preaches equality would no longer tolerate any special power. Within the community all are equal. Are not men and women equal? Are not adults and children equal? How can they be equal? Of course they can be equal. All, whatever their age, can sit at round tables, as they do in Chinese homes and restaurants, where no one is at the head or the foot of the table. Socialism started going downhill when the party bosses ate at their special "clubs."

Religions preach devotion to God and love of one's own kind. Love of God and love of one's fellow Jew, Christian, or Muslim are central tenets of the faith. Hinduism believes in caste and Confucianism in family where something between attachment and love is to prevail. The idea of bonding is central to all religions except Buddhism.

In earlier times, nationalist, socialist, and religious movements masked their hunger for power in the realm of the state with communalistic camouflage. Now those movements have to reckon with the hunger for real community—that is, community without the state. People want to belong, to bond with each other.

Yet that bonding can sometimes become a source of violence. In the former Yugoslavia being a Serb, a Muslim, or a Croat is both a religious and a national matter. When the nationalist urge, with its yen for power and its leanings toward a strong state, remains firm, so does hatred—love's opposite—toward "the other." But when communities let their religious character come to the fore, love and bonding prevail. Nevertheless, just as love and hatred can be two sides of the same coin, so can peace and violence. I am willing to die for my community, but I shall also kill for it.

Whether or not there will be community-based revolutions is no longer an issue. The process has already begun in many parts of the world, in the revival and spread of religions. It is only those in American civilization who do not want to see it. Even when the revolutions kill, they are revolutions not just for society and community but also for love and bonding. Love can kill, as we should know, and that is why Buddhism has so vehemently rejected love because it sees love as leading to attachment, then to vanity, and finally to violence. Buddhism has always been insistent on nonviolence.

Work! *Dolce far niente,* "oh how sweet it is to do nothing." My friend Stuart Miller envisions aristocracies that do not work; they live in leisure so that they can see truth, bring forth beauty, and do good. Mencius said that while 90 percent of the people worked, 10 percent would be leisured so they could cultivate the higher virtues. But Stuart is thinking within the framework of American civilization. The rub is that to be an elite these days means having power (and how much labor that requires!) and wealth (how much worry it takes to keep and manage it!) and privilege (how insecure and flaky a thing it is). Having all three adds up to exhaustion, the opposite of repose and leisure.

Work is not labor, Hannah Arendt wrote. Labor is only expenditure of energy, as she saw it. Work is making and shaping things, like what artists do. *Homo laborans* and *homo faber.* But with her end-of-the-nineteenth-century disposition she did not go far enough. Work, Pope John Paul II said, is what binds people into communities. People once signed letters, "I am your obedient servant." The statement implied, "I am bonded to you. When I serve you, I bond myself to you (whether you like it or not!)." In earlier times peasants worked not just to create value for their lord but to remain bonded to him. They were his peasants. He was their lord if he worked to protect them. But if he was a *roi fainéant,* a do-nothing king, then his peasants were just useful pests for him, whose smells and sounds he could not stand.

The revolution of work comes when those at the top become the servants of the bottom. Until now the realm of the state has always lorded it above the realm of society. When the state truly becomes the servant of society, we shall be close to the millennium. The Pope washes the feet of working people at Easter time. When the revolution of work comes, the Pope will put in regular hours at a Rome soup kitchen. Will those who eat together at that soup kitchen be his community for the hours he spends working there? Will some of them call him John Paul, Giovanni Paolo? I heard that China's ruler, Deng Xiaoping, when he was purged during the Cultural Revolution, went to some remote area where he cleaned toilets. Did they call him Xiaoping, a name that in Chinese sounds as if it means "little bottle"?

In the heyday of nationalism, socialism, and the American Dream, fraternity—as preached in the French Revolution—meant the collegiality of people in the public realm. It was good to be a successful individual. It was even better to be part of a group—network as they now say—in the state, like a group of physicists excitedly coming up with a new scientific or technological process, or like a bunch of police beginning their inquisition of a lone prisoner. Society was debris, corruption, pathos. Only in the state was there nobility. Real work went on in the public realm. Anything else was at best fooling around, tinkering, leisure.

Once the revolution of work occurs, real work will cultivate growth, bring forth capital, use that capital for growth, spend it on children, hold communities together, and glorify God the way people did during the Middle Ages (like the poor juggler of Notre Dame who, ashamed of his trade, juggled for the Holy Mother in the dark hours of early Christmas morning and was rewarded by a kiss from Her).

Once there is such a revolution, the public realm will consist, as it should, of small numbers of monks, loners, learned priests, and experts, people who know that their lonely task is to serve those at the bottom, to wash their feet, heal their sores, stand guard hours on end with little reward to make certain that those whom they serve remain secure and healthy. They will labor, as proletariats do.

Some, maybe many, of the gifted and lucky—and gifts can come only from God or gods—will have dreams that they will be paid to realize. Realizing dreams requires effort different from both work and labor. Work is hard but is pushed along by soul. Labor is hard but is pushed along by the carrot (paycheck) and stick (time clock) of the boss. Realizing dreams is fun, self-fulfilling. The mind and the body get taxed, but the people get drunk on power, and they can and should get drunk on realizing dreams. Realizing dreams is like skating over clouds.

The Amish have lived and farmed together over the generations. Today they are an oddity, but why should their practices not be the norm? Why should wife and husband not work together? Why should children not do work that keeps them bound to the community? Why can't the rhythms of farm work, which of course are not those of nine-to-five, be transplanted to cities?

Japan has shown that you can have community and people living in or near that community and producing value that feeds positively into the world market. You have a small but highly productive state sector peopled by individuals. Great captains of industry like lonely samurai in battle. Buddhist monks working hard in modern research laboratories. The Japanese romanticize the "old village" (*furusato*) where they live in their little homes with their gardens and kids, tending their shops.

The revolution in work comes when people begin to demand that they live, work, and love together. They want jobs that are work and work that furthers the community. The Hassidim in New York's Crown Heights are such a community. How the Hassidim live, work, and love together is a positive model even for people who want to make it into the grand public domain of democracy, consumerism, and personal liberation. Others will eventually realize that the Hassidim can teach them good things just as they can teach the Hassidim that they must not stifle the universalistic vectors in their own faith just to keep their own community hermetically sealed.

A revolution for society that changes the way people work could transform a city into a collection of villages. That is the way Tokyo used to be. Beehives everywhere, close together. People want to *live* in communities so they want to *work* in communities, like farmers, people in villages. The liberal, nationalist, and socialist revolutions created cities.

Cities were the opposite of villages. Cities had division of labor. Villages had undifferentiated work, hard work in the fields and the cow sheds. Now as God shifts His wand back to society, the village will come back, but this time right in the city.

Justice is the rightness of the human order around you. To love means you are part of, attached to, an "other" or other individuals. Work binds you with others, a community. Seeking justice binds you to the world. God is just because He loves those whom He has created. Because there are many individuals and many communities, justice is that through which the world becomes worthy of His name. The world will only move in a right direction, will have a Tao, when it is just. In Chinese the idea is rendered as "universal equity."

Justice can prevail only when the relations between and among individuals, communities, and states are universally fair and equitable. And justice can come only when the old Roman principle of *suum cuique* (to each his own) prevails. It means that each of us has a place in society as well as rights in and claims on the state. In this modern world of movement it also means that the roads and the borders are open.

If we lived in a vast tyrannical empire, the roads and borders would be open because the tyrant would want the trade routes functioning to bring in the wealth. The tyrant would also bloodily suppress all conflicts between communities. By simply decapitating some communal leaders, he could make it clear to all that fighting is verboten. But the tyrant could never ensure justice within the community and among individuals.

Democracy can ensure justice among individuals if it can encompass the entire world. If American civilization becomes universal and we all become individuals, then justice for all is conceivable. Everyone will have claims and rights in the public realm. If the economy is prosperous enough then why should not all claims be fulfilled with checks ample enough to make life sweet for all?

We shall all be individuals, alones; who needs society and communities if there are so many Ramada Inns around that we shall never be lonely? Could we not all become Buddhist monks, shedding ourselves of attachments and preparing to rise, lighter than air, to the higher plane and then meld into the cosmos? We shall have gone from biology through physics to enlightenment, and with light glowing from our auras we shall ascend. The higher we rise, the less the need for justice, because we shall all be both "0" and "1," nothing and unity.

Justice is a need that must be met as long as we have a world, the World. If we accept the idea of the World then there is no escaping the challenge for justice. Either we have cataclysms that will eventually destroy and devour the World or we shall have to create an order that will make the biology of growth, the dreams of physics, and the light of the higher plane a part of human existence and the directions it moves over time.

Communities must have place. Their people must live in a particular somewhere, just as people lived in villages. All communities must have land, and such land soon becomes a sacred place. In the United States gangs fight over turf. Having a legitimate turf is the first step in the long march toward universal justice.

What happens when two communities demand the same land, like Jews and Arabs in Israel, or Indians and whites in America? No rights in the state or claims on it can decide who gets the land. And open roads that lead down into the soul or outward into the world or upward into a higher plane will not have any weight in deciding the issue of turf.

To gain justice, there is only one way. The two tribes must deal with each other face to face. A Jew and an Arab meet in the middle of the field to begin a process that can lead to bloodshed or to healing. But whatever happens, justice will finally emerge because it will have happened just as Hollywood would have portrayed it—in a field with the setting sun, the two sides ranged against each other, and two great samurai striding out into the field. Even when the film is terrible, one senses God in the heavens ready to let the spirit of justice flow down while blood is spilled and many weep over their fallen sons and fathers.

If the revolutions for love, work, and justice come, there will be a vast public realm, maybe many of them, throughout the world. Those realms

192 ✧   *Community*

will be linked to the management of the world economy, which must continue if American civilization is to continue. Political covenants will confer rights and wealth, which will go to pay those who labor and create in the state system, or to satisfy other claims from the people. The basic constitution will guarantee all their place somewhere in the vast complex of the world. Everyone has a place. Everyone has rest. No one does not belong. And blessed be they who are alone and belong only to God.

COMMUNITY AND COSMOLOGY

Environmentalism has fractured American civilization's elites. The movement has swept over the Western world. It has converted many and has become common ideology in the media. Its adherents preach the impending demise of nature and call for a halt to the civilization's destructive behavior. Radical environmentalists—the extreme on a scale that reaches out from a timid center—want an end to consumerism; they have even preached "nature first and people last"; and like socialists and populists, they want to demolish the vast corporate structures of the capitalist world.

Environmentalism challenges liberalism, the creed of American civilization. It has taken the place of socialism and of nationalism in the first world. It has made great inroads into the former second world, where socialism wreaked hideous environmental destruction. And it is asserting itself in third world enclaves, among the middle classes of those modernizing and industrializing countries.

It burst forth as a new ideology in the late 1960s. By 1972 the U.S. Congress had enacted major environmental legislation, the Clean Air and Clean Water acts. Why did such an ideology, which challenges the idea of "economic development,"—so fundamental to the civilization, to socialism, to nationalism, and to capitalism—come to the forefront at this time? An answer can be found only if one remembers how great an upheaval the Western world went through during the 1960s.

The radicals wanted unrestricted personal liberation. The elites were not interested in this issue. The radicals wanted more democracy. The elites directed their messages to governments. But both agreed that consumption had to change.

In northern Europe personal liberation is far advanced. Everybody is an *I*. In many respects, women are at a greater level of equality with men than anywhere else in the world. Socialism has left welfare state structures that work very well. The environment is protected, yet private business and industry produce enough wealth to allow those countries to maintain high standards of living. The few children that are born are well treated so that these precious few can maintain the continuity of the present. There are few immigrants, and the ones there longest, the Finns in Sweden, are still made to feel unwelcome. Scandinavians think globally and act locally. They act to keep their forested lands from the contagions of the world. They go out with their backpacks but do not like too many others to come in. They keep the streets of their pretty cities squeaky clean.

Environmentalist values have now seeped deep into America's middle classes as well. People with little houses resent seeing another house go up across the way. These older northern middle classes are now ready for a new revolution from the top down, which they feel will protect them, give them security. Environmentalism fits the bill because its values sound progressive, its intents seem moral, and its message seems to make so much sense. Isn't it obvious that unless we stop using so many wood products the forests all over the world are going to vanish?

If such a revolution from the top down should triumph in the world, it will be a northern triumph. The revolution will serve to protect the North from the prospect of joining a world with the South in it. Western Europe and the United States will be the core of this new world, the negation of the idea of the World. Russia could become a member if it adopts the new ideology. And certainly Japan, despite its current obsession with technology and consumerism, would be welcome, since its exclusionary policies fit in with the exclusionary thrusts in environmentalism: cut off immigration to protect nature and preserve the wholesomeness of the environment in which northern people live. China, much of which is geographically in the North, is much more questionable since it is huge, populous, poor, so much like India or Brazil, and so unpredictable.

With an environmental revolution, the North, like Scandinavia, could feel in its mind and body that it is progressive, all the while surviving nicely in its well-protected countries. But there is another revolution going on in the world, this one in the South and in the South within the North—at the bottom, below the civilization's political classes.

I recently read that Confucius, the descendant of an impoverished but noble northern family, was drawn to the South where people grew rice and lived in large, tight families. It was not consumerism that drew Confucius to the South. He was actually a man who believed in God (he called it Heaven) and the moral power of the individual, but he also looked down to the earth, not only up to heaven. As he looked down to the earth, which was more barren than bountiful, he was drawn to the South, the kingdom of Chu in the central Yangtze valley, which then was inhabited by a southern people who did not speak Chinese.

It seems to me that the religious revolutions began around the same time as environmentalism soared forth in the North. In Libya the quixotic Moammar Qadhafi held up the Holy Qur'an even as he was preaching a moral mix of nationalism, socialism, and tribalism. Every once in a while, he hanged people on the steps of the university in Tripoli.

In the mid-1970s, I began to hear of hordes of evangelical missionaries who were descending on Latin America. Then came the Brazilian "base communities," Catholic believers at the grass roots. The liberation theology of elite priests seemed in part to mirror stirrings of religion from below. I became interested in Islam and decided to study Arabic. I heard about Christian missionaries proselytizing in Africa; Islamic missionaries were doing so even faster. The popes began to travel in the poorer countries, seeing them, and not the decadent West, as the source of new religious strength. Then came Khomeini. And even the Shining Path in Peru took on religious traits, as had the Chinese communists in Yenan, traits they surely must have acquired in part from fundamentalist Christian missionaries on China's streets earlier this century. A movie theater near where I live has turned into a Pentecostal church, which year after year looks better, more lively, and stronger; some cosmic current is pushing it along.

I sensed in those religious movements capital, community, and cosmology. All were oriented toward the future, even those who believed the world would soon end and the rapture of all saved souls to heaven would soon occur. All of them, however, have practical attitudes toward the economies they live in, which are parts of the world economy. Some like to live well and have succumbed to consumerism. Others live in simpler ways. Some of the liberation theologians, too much influenced by Marxism, still show an agonized preoccupation with "the economy," as if the economy were God and must be reverentially understood. But in the end the people are wiser than the pundits, and so these grass-roots religious movements get cash where and however they can, but always use a good part of it for capital—that is, for the growth of children.

I was also struck by how communal these movements are. I like to see Orthodox Jews wander on Sabbath, children in hand, dressed in their finery. I am in awe of the Amish. I am also in awe of the poor people in Iran who found a home in and around the mosque, like the poor people in East Oakland who too have found a home in and around the mosque.

All these religious movements have cosmologies. Ridiculous cosmologies, a member of civilization snorts. But then what kind of cosmology can he show them except a slick article from *Scientific American* on the latest controversial studies of the receding universe?

The religious movements are spreading and reaching upward into the middle classes at the same time that environmentalism is reaching downward into them. While civilization's elites are arguing over the uses of *capital,* at the lower reaches of civilization and throughout the poorer countries, revolutions of *community* and *cosmology* are spreading. National, religious, and even cultural communities are fast arising. And the spread of religions mirrors a yearning for a new sense of the cosmos, with direct implications for moral direction.

At the top, visions of still unfulfilled consumerism clash with environmental visions of coming doom. At the bottom, the visions come out of religions; those at the top come out of a secularism that grew out of the Enlightenment.

The class struggle between top and bottom that Marx described does not exist. Those at the bottom have few economic demands except for survival. Those at the top argue economics because they are the stewards of the world economy. But at the bottom, where they want love, work, and justice, conflict and violence are increasing. As communities consolidate and different cosmologies take hold, angers surface. People are killed in hideous ways.

Chaos is spreading at the bottom even as communities and the belief in a direction-giving God become stronger. The realm of death is natural at the bottom. There is no realm of death at the top, only a gleaming realm of life, which started somehow with the pressing of a button that brought electric light to a room, and then the exhaustion of the bulb. Someone else may come with a new bulb, but the room just darkens when death comes.

The civilization has a world government that meets periodically in grand summits to give guidelines for world governance. It has been preaching a "new world order" over the globe and the planet. The need for such governance has arisen because modernizing liberalism and an industrializing capitalism have spread complex networks not only over the rich countries but also over a good part of the poorer countries.

The rise of an official "new world order," the continuing spread of modernization and liberalism, and the rise of revolutions of community and cosmology are the chief features of the world landscape as the century and millennium end. All three are revolutions.

The first revolution from the top down has gained the adherence of the world's seven leading industrial nations, the "G-7." They have become committed both to liberal and to environmental values. They are terrified of the revolutionary thrusts from below, just as conservatives have always been; but like earlier conservatives who knew sooner or later that they had to accommodate the socialists and nationalists making trouble from below, they now know that they have to "deal."

What is magnificent about the liberal and capitalist revolutions— coming neither from the rich top nor the poor bottom but from the middle!—is that they go their merry way, cheerily romping throughout the world telling people how they can make a buck or two. They are providing the cash that trickles down and ripples out and makes survival and even a little hope possible to so many people. Socialism once was an alternative economic idea. Now there are no economic alternatives.

Yet the civilization of alones seems hollower and hollower. No direction except flying from one Ramada Inn to another interspersed with some good meals and satisfying sex. Truth, beauty, and goodness get boring at best and at worst begin to look frightening. Shakyamuni the Buddha understood that even before Socrates was born.

Down there something else is growing in blood, sweat, tears, death, pain, humiliation, suffering. It is growing, just as the faith that rippled out from Jesus of Nazareth did two thousand years ago. That faith spread a new cosmology and a new sense of community, and was indifferent to economics and politics. It came from the Palestinian backwater and during the Romans' bloody counterinsurgency campaigns.

History never repeats itself, but rivers downstream can sometimes look somewhat like they did upstream. In the financially unsure middle classes of American civilization a search for direction is growing. People are getting weary of consumerism and personal liberation, and they are getting tired of democracy, despite the continuing agitation of the civilization's political propagandists. They want community, and they want cosmology even more. They want to cultivate their souls as well as their bodies and minds. The poor are ahead of them in the search for soul and God. The rich, more alone than people of the middle and bottom suspect, too yearn for love, work, and justice. If all these three socioeconomic currents should converge even only in part, then the next millennium could see a change in the world as significant as that which occurred in the first century A.D. when Christianity grew. Or even as dramatic and convulsive as the spreading of American civilization over the world after World War II.

THE WORLD
AND THE ROAD TO GOD

I remember being afraid of dying when I was very young. Every twitch in my chest was to me an almost sure sign that I would be struck down. When I was thirteen my father died; I stopped thinking about my own imminent death.

Now in my sixties I do not think of dying very often. I do think of death, but rarely with dread. I do not wonder what life is all about, nor do I think much about the past. I also do not think much about the future except in whimsical ways: a century from now, will we have the power of individual levitation so that we can float past second-story windows on crowded downtown streets? I think about death because it seems like a way station on a journey.

When I felt chest pangs as a child I would get up and start walking. For many years we lived next to a cemetery. I was terrified of that dark swath beyond the backyard. But during the day I enjoyed climbing the fence, going through the cemetery to reach a woods that stretched quite far. I liked walking through the woods.

Since then I have walked thousands of miles and traveled through the world many more. To me, being outside meant moving in the world; being inside a house meant being stuck with myself, my thoughts, my fears. Over the years I have come to feel that somehow my own life and the life of the world are intertwined.

Most people know their own lives, the paths they have taken to get from then to now. Most people have a rough sense of how the world got from, say, the Roman Empire or ancient China, to now. Young people all over the world are said to be afraid of dying in a nuclear holocaust, but I think the world will continue in its rutted tracks . . . and get more interesting.

But the world bogs down, and so do I. When that happens I know that I or the world have lost direction, and despair settles in. When I have no direction, I feel an emptiness. In earlier years, and even now, thoughts of dying have come at such times. I used to tell my students that worrying was a form of boredom: when the mind is empty and the body is going nowhere, tormenting thoughts enter it. "No way out," the Chinese say.

A PERSONAL VISION

In the 1980s these thoughts led me to begin writing this book. I would go on long walks in and around San Francisco and in other cities. On those walks I had thoughts of the world and of me and of others, sometimes pleasant, even erotic, thoughts. I was always astonished that the sense of despair, emptiness, banality wafted away the more I walked, especially up hills. Even more astonishing, I found spiritual and religious thoughts creeping into my mind, as if they were themselves spirits. When I began my walks, the word *God* usually made me think of a devoutly Catholic Goan friend who loved to remark that God spelled backward is doG. Now *God* has become as important a direction-giving word to me, as earlier the words *revolution* and *love* were. Not to recognize all the ironies in life and the real world is foolish. The Chinese have always seen the fool and the wise man as two sides of the same coin.

Over the years roads and directions became important to me. Life became a road. The Chinese like to talk about the "road of life," and their word for the future is "the road ahead." Roads never end, like mountain trails you follow up to the watershed, until, just over the crest, another stream bed begins and soon another trail. The Taoists use life-death as a single word. Souls are what give us direction on roads that go from life-death through life-death and so on, maybe infinitely, maybe with some final resting point.

I realize now that in my life I have gone back and forth between the world and a soul I knew only by a continuing quest for direction. My spiritual life in fact has consisted of that back-and-forth. If I now bring God into the back-and-forth, this is a new discovery, something I did not expect to find in earlier years.

At the same time I feel a curious distance from life as mind and as body. People live with each other as shared minds and shared bodies. They make their livings using their minds and bodies—leftists love to use the word "exploit," as in exploiting resources or exploiting labor. We see each other as minds and bodies. How can we see each other as souls?

The life of the soul is solitary, and yet I do not feel all alone. I feel less alone now that I have discovered God, who is after all an "other" in the cosmos. My abstract writings risk removal from the life of the mind if the abstractions strike no common chord in others. They also risk removal from the life of the body because aloneness always comes from writing in abstractions. When all alone, what you're left with is soul or nothing.

At the same time, life in the world brought my mind and body closer to others. When I was young I was more alone and more a loner than at any time since. I had no God, was not aware of any soul in me. I felt fat and ugly, potent only when animal sexual urges arose in me. I was not bound by my body to any other bodies. My mind life was a vast indulgence, a game I played all by myself, which others watched, amused, but apparently did not want to join.

As I traveled and learned languages, I came closer to others. As the world revealed others to me, I understood that in life one shares one's body and mind. The Latin root of the word society is *socius* (ally). In life one needs allies. Even as I gained more allies, I still had the yearning to travel, walk, move in body and mind. When I was able to move in body and mind, I realized I still sought something more. I sought a series of lamps lighting a road that moved away from me into the distance.

Human beings have, since ancient times, been moved by visions. Visions are pictures in your mind's eye; they make your body move toward them, even if only your arms reach out. I have always had visions, mostly small ones; even the most trite visions, though, got me to move in some direction.

When I lose my visions, I have little recourse but to get on the road—almost any road—and get moving somewhere, anywhere. But now, in the common way of putting it, I "believe in God." Even when there is no light and I am sitting in a place, the thought of God creates a picture in my mind of roads leading somewhere and of others traveling that road as well as I.

So now I believe in God, the "prime mover," who makes me go in straight lines, heading somewhere, when I have been forever going around in circles. And as I move along, the visions come. Trivial and transient as they so often are, they feed my soul, which gives direction to my mind and to my body.

I was never drawn to move by visions of beauty, truth, and goodness. I realize now that what moved me were visions that said, in big neon lights: "Do the right thing." When I did the right thing, or thought I did, then I found myself moving in straight lines, going somewhere. Without direction, I found myself going in circles or doing nothing, a condition that does not suit my temperament.

I usually feel good when life is routine and cyclical. All things, all people, are in the right place. All my bills are carefully stacked, and at the end of the month, I write out the checks in orderly fashion—and then suddenly sink into despair, even panic, as I realize no money is left. I feel a void, more than fear, an aloneness that is almost absolute, until I start moving again.

Such movement can be illusory, like a narcotic, because the movement becomes routine and therefore circular. Life lived this way is movement indeed, but it goes nowhere. (Buddhism offers a way beyond the unending circularity of life, death, and once again life; it is the "path of enlightenment," a road shaped by the soul-light of the knowing self so strong that it can move free of recurring mind and body.)

When life is cyclical there is not much need for soul or for visions. The mind is restless, and the body senses the need for physical exertion.

So mind and body begin to move. But without soul or vision—and I would now say God—there is no direction other than the circular.

As an observer of politics and a student of history, I have found that all governments mightily hope the people they rule will settle down to cyclical life, through which they produce wealth, bear and raise children, and make no trouble. But if life is only cyclical movement, without true direction, then the periods of despair, of sensing a void, will become more frequent. Eventually people feel acute pain in mind and body, yearn, search. Under such conditions visions arise to offer them a direction.

(Peace is a wonderful word, but it so often results only in circular motion that relieves the worries of government treasurers but can make people crazy. War always offers directions in the short run but as the body count mounts and signs appear that the war ends up more or less where it began people sense the linkage between killing and circularity.)

If God exists, and people have souls, then visions will arise that give people direction. When life becomes circular, despair and evil soon follow. Unless all the world and all people shall burn up in a vast fire, survival instincts will make people either "turn to God" or sense that within themselves there is an entity other than mind and body, or respond to some vision that others conjure up before them. I have come to believe that these three things—God, soul, and visions—are closely connected. Latch onto one and the others will follow.

All visions offer hope, yet death lies at the point where one touches them. As an older child I felt hunger for visions and grabbed snippets of them from books and from the words of older people. Suddenly someone, often plain or even repulsive in ordinary life, would say something wise, and those words shone with a light that affected me.

What had the greatest glow for me was something my youthful companions called *revolution*. I was moved by revolution and its wars and heroism and bloodshed and the tears it evoked, which I knew came from silly fables; yet even now, on occasion, I find myself drawn in by them.

Now I know that what drew me in was in part revolution's inseparable companion, death. Dying is a passage we must all go through, but death is a trajectory beyond, and therefore, as I now realize, a direction, a road leading there.

When young I had little patience with the common religions. I saw Christianity as childish, and I did not want to be a child. The cross on which Jesus writhed was nothing more to me than a weird and transparent symbol. Religion was for "other people," and I was special—the loner's ultimate cop-out. Revolution was a vision that pulled me along. As a child and later, Jewish friends drew me out of a place-boundedness, an addiction to routine, a circularity that I ascribed to my remoter peasant origins. They were attracted to revolution like moths to a candle. Did they know that death lies at the ground over which that vision hovers? I think they did, and so did I, though I was too cautious to actively seek that trajectory beyond. Jews, more than any of my formal teachers, also taught me learning and scholarship.

Farther down my life's road, revolution became an academic subject, and then a career. The vision paid off. So, my academic paycheck is linked to a vision of revolution, radical transformation, with death as its central element. And like real-world revolution, the vision eventually, maybe inevitably, brought routine, circularity, place-boundedness.

I have always felt that I lived in an exciting civilization. The story of American civilization is in the end that of millions of individuals. Each and every American has an individual story, but not a collective one. That our civilization has accomplished the mighty feat of binding the entire planet together has not given rise to any great story, any single American epic. The stories are those of individuals, and we watch and hear and even feel them every night on television. The civilization is incarnate in each of us, as individuals.

Of the collective stories that made the rounds when I was young, those of nationalism were not about individuals. They were vision-generating stories of the origins, heroic growth, and death of a nation as tribe. Even though no stories from my several tribes ever moved me, I can see that they indeed did and do move people, millions of them.

Though socialism was too abstract and bloodless for me, it too has stories, "scientific" ones, about humans evolving from dark primitive to brilliant modern and beyond-modern stages of development. The visions of socialism were those of the Greek heritage, the incarnation of truth, goodness, and beauty, the humanism that energized the Renaissance and that energizes so many Westerners today.

Religious stories for centuries have moved people in linear, not cyclical directions, through the power of death, martyrdom. As socialist visions vanish, religious visions are returning; their old stories again move many toward God and death and beyond.

The humanistic healing visions are giving way to religious healing visions. In a civilization of individuals, individuals want to be healed, and the religious visions of healing tell them of higher planes, beyond everyday consciousness, even beyond life. I have not been taken by such visions, but I sense that the people who have are going from body and mind to soul and moving closer to God.

In Judaism, the world is the backdrop for the drama of humans and their relationship with God. In Christianity, St. Augustine dismissed the world as the city of man and called on Christians to move toward the city of God. In Islam, the world is man's slave given to him by God. Buddhism reaches for the higher plane, seeing the world as illusion. In the end most religions do not regard the world as central.

In the stories I read as a child I looked for visions of the world. I collected maps and hung them over my entire room until they they glowed as a world when I closed the door.

The world I live in has given me visions that have moved me forward. I believe that God and the world are linked, and that the souls of human beings keep the two from drifting apart.

Only recently have I started learning how to pray. Even as my place-bound life leads me in a Buddhist direction, I am also, reluctantly, drawn in a Christian, Catholic direction. Christ suffered and died outside, in the cold. Jesus said to God with his last breaths: *Eli, Eli, la ma sabachtani?* (God, God, why hast Thou forsaken me?) I do not want to be outside unless I am going somewhere, to a definite place, even if I have no idea where I'll stay. Walking toward a goal brings me closer to God, and as my sense of abandonment grows, the image of Jesus on the cross grows sharper.

When I am outside, moving, I become conscious of God, and more and more find myself mumbling to Him. And as the pace of physical and electromagnetic motion has massively increased in the world, I have come to believe that God has returned to the world after a two-century exile. The tidal wave of religious talk one hears on the electromagnetic media suggests that many others have also found God. They have gone toward Him or He has come toward them.

Jews and Christians and Muslims believe that God created us and then let us fly off on our own like a bird leaving the nest—of our own free will. When the despairing Jews left Egypt and wandered for forty years without a compass, God became distant from them. In the eighteenth century God went again into exile as He watched to see how Europeans would master the world, his creation. In recent years people have been seeking community, huddling together as they did in earlier times, and God is now once again not so distant.

VISIONS FOR THE FUTURE

The story of the world begins with the fact that we are alone in the universe. There only is an earth with people, animals, plants, rocks (and as I believe), spirits on it. There is no sign whatsoever of cognitive life anywhere else and only the faintest signs of organic matter.

Yet as the evolutionists know, an astonishing story has been unfolding about the world. Evolution is the story of the world moving in directions. Religious people who are not defensively angered by the theory of evolution should see it as the revelation of God's plan for the world.

Some biological species go in cyclical directions. They have not changed in hundreds of millions of years. On Ocean Beach in San Francisco I see sand dollars whose form has not changed in what may be a billion years. Other species appear to go in linear directions—from amoebas to humans. And dinosaurs evolved in forms that a few hundred million years later were replicated by mammals. Linearity and circularity together!

The stories of biological evolution feature animals and plants with rocks as backdrop. The stories of the world's many religions feature people and spirits (for some including the Great Spirit). In these, people move, around or ahead, under some higher plane, while spirits have directions of their own. The stories of the current civilization's visual and print media feature people as well as animals, plants, and rocks as victims. Their directions seem to be downward or, if made into comedies, circular.

People, animals, plants, rocks, and spirits make up the world, and the world is going somewhere. Those who say it is heading for doom, as the creationists do, envisage a finality so terrible that the only way out is through God. But the vast majority of people know the world has a story, like those that emanate from television screens. Television tells stories, and all stories have direction. Most "ordinary" people believe in the world if for no other reason than that they want it for their successors.

The teachings of the great religions instruct that we can move linearly from earth to heaven, or from a lower plane through the universe and then finally to the highest plane, God's abode. While the Chinese have long known all kinds of esoteric religious teachings, their main philosophical thinking is circular, spherical; it concerns things recurring. "Things recurring" are what Lao-tzu and Chuang-tzu wrote about: growth and death, stuff of the earth. Confucianism saw the history of life as endlessly cyclical but degenerating in the long run; Taoism saw nature as eternally recurring.

Another class of religions that is linked to the earth is what we now call shamanism. The word makes me think of a voodoo statue in a *Yóruba botánica* of a stooped black man munching on a huge cigar. It makes me think of Mongol shamans who advised Genghis Khan (what could they have told him that made him sally forth to conquer the world?). It makes me think of Japanese Shinto, with its sense that everything in nature harbors a spirit, a nice *kami* (a spirit that never had a body) and a bad *oni* (a spirit that once had a body, or ghost). *Kami* is also used by Japanese Christians for "God," though with the honorific suffix *sama*.

Christians and Confucians do not like shamanism. The shamanist view is that the world is peopled by billions of spirits that have power over you. Shamanists believe your will is far from being free, while Christians believe the soul is entirely under your own control. Confucians hate shamans because shamans see the darkness as more real than the light. Yet in both West and East people have long believed that spirits come into your consciousness through dreams and can take control of your body and mind.

I suppose the shamanist view is that you do best in the world when you come to terms with the world. For the Taoists one does best in the world when one "does nothing." Doing nothing means surrendering to nature, allowing its rhythms, which the Taoists consider benign, to take control of you. I consider nature and God benign, for I cannot believe that the circular, cyclical motions of nature and the linear ones that God gives humans (and other creatures) can be malign. We are born, grow, live, expand our consciousness, and die in such a way that the process is good, not bad; right, not wrong.

American civilization, while it does not know exactly what to make of the world, has embraced the world. It has created an operational globe linked by communication and transportation. It also understands the world as planet, as the environmentalists have been teaching us.

World, however, means people (as in the French for "everybody," *tout le monde*, "all the world"). People whose grander identities are still largely shaped by ethnic nationalisms are uneasy about "one world" of people. They prefer a globe of things and a planet with cosmic dimensions (so far away you don't have to touch people at all!) to a world where some

Paraguayan Indian may turn out to be your cousin and be invited into your home.

American civilization has not turned circular. Modern capitalism must keep plunging ahead on a straight road toward more and more growth—a billion cars; otherwise it will implode and vanish. It was socialism that produced circularity and made people despairing, suicidal, and cut off from all hope, except that of finding capitalism and latching on to the great visions of Western civilization. (Socialism could not even attain nature's circularity, evident in the hideous ravaging of nature it has brought about.)

American civilization has created far more truth, beauty, and goodness than its discontented socialist and environmentalist detractors would admit. It is an astonishingly successful civilization. But God has left it. It has no soul. And because it has no soul, it does not really have direction. It moves, but it moves toward nowhere, a mix of circularity and directedness, directed by visions that hang on walls like great masterpieces of art.

This civilization has drawn us to move with breathtaking visions, grand TV commercials that reveal to us a paradise on earth, to be attained without God or soul. Only our will moves us in some direction, to work hard, to confidently hold forth our credit card, and to take immediate delivery.

Soul is the potential, in the physicists' sense, that leads to movement, not just with a speed but with a direction. God and soul are linked. If we seek soul, God shall return to us. As soul returns, so will direction, and direction will lead to God even as God finds us as He returns to the world. God and soul are linked, as are God, soul, and the one world in which we all live.

Isaac Newton came up with the idea of inertial movement: things will move in the same way forever unless deflected. Many people, and not just conservatives, are convinced that new visions will just produce more catastrophes. The best the world can hope for, as they see it, is to stick to an inertial course. No more visions and no more revolutions! Yet new visions keep coming.

In the late 1970s and early 1980s, when socialist visions were fading, capitalism came up with some new visions. The market, many were convinced, would eventually sweep both the communist and the developing countries, and the twenty-first century would witness unprecedented global prosperity. But these visions too have faded even as capitalists rake in bigger and bigger profits from the global economy.

Grim visions have become more common and convincing. Environmentalists warn that the planet is being ravaged so fast that it will soon perish. The late B. F. Skinner, however, believed cataclysms could be avoided if governments, working together, limited population, conserved resources, and curbed wars. His vision in a sense echoes that of technocracy, which appeared on the scene a hundred years earlier preaching that general affluence could come if experts were given the power to bring it about.

Economists like to use the word *global* while the environmentally minded speak about *the planet*. The word *global* has a manufacturing ring to it, like a desktop sphere with a map of the earth. *Planet* implies the holistic look of the earth from outer space, an orb with cloud-covered features. Both words have an elite connotation: anything can be done by a few leaders turned on by the right visions and advised by the right experts.

Because things have become so immense, hopeful global and planetary visions are becoming fewer. Visionaries are discouraged by the world's huge population. There are too many people. The world has become ungovernable, it is widely believed.

When hopeful visions fail, pessimism becomes rampant, as it has among the world's elites. But there is an alternative to their pessimism. And it requires, first, seeing the world as world—a very big community— and not just as globe or planet, and second, deciding whether people need a future in their lives. If so, then they will need visions, lights to lead them to a road on which they can travel.

If you feel you are a member of a community, you want it to survive after you die. Survival has long been the name of the game for humans, animals, plants—and rocks and spirits as well. Survival requires growth that is biological. The world is the planet's oldest survivor.

During the past millions of years there have occasionally been cataclysms, but only very few. The dinosaurs died out, maybe in some giant catastrophe, but they survived for hundreds of millions of years. During that time they experienced life-death-life and evolved in spectacularly different ways.

Do rocks survive? Physicists are struck by how unchanging physical laws keep the bulk matter of the universe so finely balanced. One slight change in any one of these laws could cause the universe to vanish instantly. Yet as the big bang theory indicates, the universe has also been changing and shows irregularities after evolving from symmetrical and uniform tiny beginnings.

Do spirits survive? When humans first started to talk, symbolic memory began: they remembered language as well as things. Spirits were created: ghosts from the past and angels to help out here and now, but also gods to show ways into the future, past dying into the domain of death.

From this arose stories of memory (past trajectories) and imagination (future trajectories). Then these stories became songs, poems, holy books, novels, and now TV. Even when it is wordless, music—which pervades the airwaves—tells of memories and arouses imagination. The secular preachers of American civilizaton speak of this as "entertainment," and many seem to believe that what they hear from their radios and see on their TV screens is not real. But those who believe in a higher as well as a lower plane might see these images reflected on their TV screens in ways not intended by the show makers. Such viewers might see real angels—divine beings which never had bodies—or ghosts—the spirits of the earthly dead—not just "actors."

Throughout history, visions have arisen out of cosmologies. Since the remotest times people have looked up to the heavens, and they have always looked down into tombs. Death has appeared to all of them as a future, a passage to another domain. Cosmology and death have traditionally been linked, professional priests dealing with both.

Cosmologies are views of the entire heavens, of the origins of their constituent parts, how they move, and where they are going. The first great Chinese historian, Ssu-ma Chi'en of the third century B.C., was an astrologer. He turned astrology upside down. He believed that the patterns of heaven could be found in the patterns of the human world. The German historians viewed history as cosmology during the eighteenth-century Enlightenment. That inspired Hegel to equate God and history, a view that achieved monumental and cataclysmic proportions in the twentieth century.

The biological is down here and the cosmological is up there. Religious visions have grappled with both. Socialism used history to make the state seem like a caring God who would give the people growth and security. Capitalism scorns history with its smell of the past and rejects futuristic visions. It is impressed by what rationality—money and technology—can offer in the present. It is awed by physics and takes the biological for granted, or squeezes it through laboratory tubes, or turns it into "sex." Like its great middle classes, capitalism is in the middle, neither up there nor down here.

But the new and old religions are again raising issues of earth and heaven (bottom and top), the biological and the cosmological. More people throughout the world are seeking religious visions. Yet at the same time they want the good life of American civilization. The civilization promises them wonderful rewards: affluence, fulfillment, pleasures. But the more alone they become in their success, the more they want to belong. They flourish in the movement modern life offers, but they also want place, rest. Even as they worry about the biological—that is, survival—they also want a sense of a future, a link to something beyond the dying of individuals. A hunger for the future requires visions, because the future is the trajectory of death.

Survival in American civilization depends on movement, on an ability to function in a world in which you have to move a lot to earn the money you need to live. Place is ephemeral, including the security of human relations, and especially, home.

Religious visions offer the promise of place in paradise. But that is often not the main reason people turn to religion. Religion offers a road into the darkness of the future and illuminates it—a future that will be inhabited by your children and those who are not your children.

Isaac Newton thought about ideas of rest and motion—the sun is at rest and the planets move. He used mathematics to show how they go together and thereby laid out a path for modern science and civilization. The reviving religions seek to do the same. If visions are to lead people into the future, they must combine rest and movement, physics and biology, cosmology and life.

HEALING THE INCOMPLETENESS

Taoism and Hinduism accept notions of circularity as ways to survive. Taoism teaches melding into nature. Hinduism teaches living with people, animals, plants, rocks, and spirits, and especially with oneself. Its teachings are effective for survival and indicate that life in reincarnation can be lived in a better way.

Buddhism teaches escape from circularity, not into the world but out of it onto a higher plane. One strain of Mahayana Buddhism in China preached that the compassionate Maitreya Buddha would return when the world fell into extreme depravity. It gave rise to some revolutionary movements.

All three of these religions have aroused interest in the West among people seeking a road from movement to rest.

But the God-seeking religions—Judaism, Christianity, Islam—abhor paganism, a faith that preaches living in harmony with people, animals, plants, rocks, and spirits. Jews and Muslims must break with all paganism and submit to God. Christians must die spiritually and be born again, like Saul who became Paul when he gained faith in the risen Jesus. Christianity especially envisages a break in the life of individuals, communities, and the world so that darkness can give way to light. The idea of revolution in the West came from Christianity.

Revolution and death go together, not the peaceful dying of circular life, but the hideous deaths states have for millennia inflicted on those they particularly loathed, like the crucifixion of Jesus or of rebellious wretches in Japan before modernization. Yet revolution and hope also go together. And hope gives direction, which circularity never does.

The God-seeking religions believe that direction—the straight path leading toward the face of God—must be chosen even if it means undergoing the torments that Jesus did. But a Godless ethos, like the ideology of American civilization, would hold that the despair that arises when life becomes circular is inevitable. There are no ways out except choices that are individual, different from person to person. Buddhism, a Godless religion, uses the triad of life, circularity, and despair as a springboard for jumping onto a trajectory toward supreme enlightenment, where one becomes lighter than a feather and floats upward to the higher plane.

If we live in a civilization that has no visions, has lost its direction, runs on accumulated assets and energy, then what alternatives are there but *either* returning to circularity, trying as many technical fixes as possible and hoping it will turn out okay for the greatest number, *or* looking for some new visions to give direction, knowing surely that those visions will walk hand in hand with death, as the old ones did?

Radicals used to talk about revolutions coming "from the masses." In earlier times, socialist ideas did arouse response among millions of peasants and workers. But socialism and communism—what's left of them—have become elite ideologies.

There is, however, a revolutionary current flowing through the world's "masses," flowing much deeper than the earlier ideas of socialism. Those currents are almost all religious: Islam and evangelical Christianity in Asia, Africa, and Latin America as well as in many bourgeois democratic countries. Popular revival is also evident in Catholicism and Judaism. There is a tremendous Hindu revival in India.

So far there is no mass revival of Taoism or Buddhism, though there are signs of revitalized animist faiths. The new religious forces are largely from the God-religions. Except for Hinduism, there is little saint worship in these revivals (maybe the Hindu revival has something to do with India's becoming a world power faster than most people expected; so something of Europe's bane, history = God, is afflicting India). Prayer is directed toward God or Jesus, who is, in Christian belief, a member of the divine trinity.

This current's missionaries are not preaching the good life. Their views of the world vary from hostile to accepting. Their souls and minds are concentrated on God, and their bodies are disciplined, as all religions, great and small, require.

Is this a revolution? If by revolution we mean institutional transformation, then no. But if it means that people are changing in some fundamental way, then yes. The changes are evident among new Muslims, Christians, and Jews. Among them, communal life takes precedence over individual choice, a core value of American civilization. In them, children are valued as bridges to the future, whereas in American civilization they come through "family planning." And in them, prayer to God is central, whereas in this civilization, religion, like philosophy or sex, is a matter of individual preference.

Revolution means turning upside down, and the tenets of the new faiths are the opposite of those of this civilization, which evangelicals call secular humanist, meaning that humans, not God, are the source of all values. No one doubts any longer that if radical Muslims come to power in Islamic countries, things will change drastically. There is a lot of fear in secular Israel of the "blacks," the growing black-clad religious. Many in the West fear the same if evangelicals ever should come to power here.

Every lesson of history suggests that if these new revolutionaries from below come into power, blood will again flow. The God-religions have a long history of violent intolerance.

TOWARD ONE WORLD

The trajectory of world history is toward one world. No one should doubt this assertion. Ten thousand years ago the world's entire population probably numbered in the low millions. There were maybe ten thousand distinct languages. Today more than half of the world's five billion people speak only a handful of languages.

The force propelling that trajectory has been and continues to be revolution. A revolution is a radical change in the way people live, work, and think. Historical trajectories can suddenly change—for individuals, families, communities, nations, the world. Why they may do so is not always clear. For example, after World War I aggressive jazz suddenly appeared on the mainstream American entertainment scene. It pushed aside the gentler popular music of earlier decades, driving American culture into radically different directions.

Revolutionary changes signify a big increase in movement of all kinds: personal, social, economic, political, cultural. But, as Lao-tzu observed, whenever there is sudden change a restoring force pulls change back to inertia or equilibrium. Isaac Newton taught the same: action equals reaction. Movement is always followed by rest. Lao-tzu also held the reverse to be true, that rest can suddenly turn into movement.

The Enlightenment produced many revolutions. The three biggest are the Industrial Revolution in England, the American Revolution, and the French Revolution. American civilization then gave rise to even more revolutions, such as the transformation of popular music.

Other European revolutions went nowhere, movement producing only more movement. But as American revolution led to American civilization a yearning for rest joined the revolutionary urge to move. That led to the the rise of the American Dream, an ideal of rest to be achieved by a lot of intense movement. On a much larger scale—moving on both higher and lower planes—American civilization gave rise to a successor stage to revolution. I find no other name for it except *empire.*

I believe the American Dream has ended. It was something that arose during America's nationalistic period, when the American *we* was more U.S.A. than America. Now with globalization, America is more America than U.S.A.—it has become a global empire.

Empire is a bad word in this country. American children are taught in grade school that Americans, a freedom-loving people, overthrew a bad king to gain independence. Then we set up a democracy. We help other people gain their own freedom and build their own democracy, but we seek only thanks in return. Having done the good deed we go home to our own shores. But of course it is not so. Anybody who reads American newspapers sees editorials, analyses, and even news reports asking questions like, "What should we [that is, Americans] do about Rwanda, Bosnia, Mexico, Yemen, Russia, China, Japan, skinheads in Germany, terrorists in Egypt, endangered species in Brazil . . ." I haven't finished reading today's newspaper yet.

Empires create fairly lasting order over large numbers of diverse people and great tracts of land. Most have been marked by prosperity and by tolerance of diversity, many by the rise of impressive civilizations. They come into being through revolutions of state, society, or religion. Empires that last are often associated with a great historical figure: Hammurabi, Ashoka, Qin Shihoangdi, Caesar. All of these figures changed political orders, transformed the way people lived their everyday lives, and brought in new religions or ideologies with the force of religion.

The greatest of such figures must be reckoned the Prophet Muhammad, peace be upon him. Through the revelations granted him from God, he changed everything, first in Mecca and then a few decades after his death in a vast swath of land going from the borders of China to Spain and West Africa. The early Arab empires created a civilization of stability, wealth, progress in learning, science, and culture. Muhammad launched one of the most comprehensive revolutions in world history, and with astonishing speed revolution turned into a lasting empire (even though individual states often broke up).

Numerous other historical figures made great attempts to create empires but failed: Charlemagne, Tamerlane, Napoleon, Hitler, Stalin. It is too early to judge whether Mao Zedong succeeded or failed.

I would rank Thomas Jefferson with the successful empire builders.

He was a great revolutionary in his younger years, and in the Declaration of Independence he wrote the revolutionary words, "All men are created equal . . . endowed by their Creator with certain unalienable rights, that among these are Life, Liberty and the Pursuit of Happiness." And he launched America's transition from revolution to empire with the Louisiana Purchase of 1803. Abraham Lincoln successfully defended that empire against southern parochials. Franklin Roosevelt extended the empire over the entire world. And God did say at this point, "It was *very* good" (Gen. 1:31).

Some writers have said recently that America is in decline. If that is so, then we should now be seeing revolutionary movements arising from below to overthrow the old order. The Enlightenment from the late 1600s to the late 1700s spawned revolution. The French revolutionaries then destroyed an *ancien régime* and founded a *nouveau régime.* There have been many warm-ups to revolution in America, the most recent being the 1960s. Its baby boomers are now in power, and its songs are all over popular radio. I can't think of much that has been changed, let alone transformed.

An earlier mortal threat to America came in the middle of the past century: the Civil War. The South was not prepared to fit into the emerging imperial order, resisted, and was crushed. The United States became a mighty nation identical to a continental empire. U.S.A. = America.

Ever since the Civil War, Americans have tried to understand what this bloodiest war in the Western world during the nineteenth century was about. It was a civil war between whites, two kinds of people as similar and dissimilar as Croats and Serbs—so alike linguistically, so different culturally. In the American case the issue was culture versus civilization. Empires produce civilizations while nations produce only cultures. The American North was already an empire with a burgeoning civilization. The American South saw itself as a kind of special nation with a special culture; to make the North grasp this fact it seceded and started a war.

The southern white way of life was abhorrent to the North. But once the North won, its foreign concerns then started mainly to go along an East-West axis. During the war with Spain the United States went south but also west, taking Hawaii and the Philippines. In World War I the United States went eastward against Germany, in World War II east against Germany and west against Japan, in the cold war both east and west against the Soviet Union and China.

A major stage in America's empire building came in 1947 when, acting according to the trajectory of Roosevelt's universalism, President Truman established a doctrine that held that the United States was justified in intervening anywhere it felt its national security threatened. That doctrine came into being when the cold war was beginning. To many Americans, it seemed the Soviet Union was a new empire seeking to take over the Eastern Hemisphere. Resistance was seen as justified, as it was when Germany and Japan, in 1941, between them sought to do the same to America. Victory in World War II ended the latter threat, and when America "won the cold war" so too ended the former threat.

The East-West conflicts were all wars between states. Spain was a rickety old empire that the United States decided finally to liquidate at the turn of the century. Imperial Germany was an awesome new empire determined to supplant Britain. Hitler's new order was a revolutionary version of the earlier imperial Germany. Japan's greater East Asia co-prosperity sphere was, like Napoleon's domains, a vast but fleeting empire. The Soviet Union was seen as an evil red empire. The U.S.A. fought them all in the name of democracy. Yet in fact it was America that then arose to spread its aquiline wings over the entire world.

These were more than wars between states. They were fury-filled wars between political classes and public sectors with devoutly held ideologies. These classes and sectors have become very big in this age of modernization and industrialization. In enemy countries political classes took the form of ideological political parties: Nazis, fascists, and communists. In the democracies we don't have some single imperially ideological party, only "activists," who now must number in the low millions. One can see them in any city on street corners collecting signatures for this or that cause. They used to be called public-spirited citizens, but "activist" is more appropriate now.

In these East-West wars the activists on all sides were impelled by revolutionary fervor. Each side believed its cause was in harmony with the trajectory of history. Only one could be right, and so the outcome was usually either/or: either we won or they did. This can be considered a Manichaean strain, one that has long been latent in Western civilization.

Manichaeanism was an offshoot of the ancient Persian Zoroastrian religion. Mani (third century), its prophet, held that life and the world were marked by an uncompromising struggle between good and evil, God and Devil. Manichaeanism spread like wildfire in the late Roman Empire, especially among the military. It had a powerful hold on St. Augustine until he tore loose from it. For almost seventeen centuries it has been a living ghost, an alter ego of Christianity whence it made its way into modern secular revolutionary ideologies. Kids in America used to innocently play "good guys against bad guys." Now they play to kill, not knowing that in so doing they have been captured by the Manichaean ghost.

In the Manichaean view God (light) and Devil (darkness) are eternally intermingled forces. Only when a tremendous conflagration destroys the world will the two be finally separated. The saved will then be gathered together with God (light) for all eternity. The ethics that flow from this view call for eternal struggle by every human for God and against Devil so as to move closer to light and away from darkness.

In 1789 the Manichaean ghost gained a hold on the French revolutionaries; through Marxism, it spread to all the revolutions Marx's ideas spawned. The concept of class struggle justified a war to the death against the bourgeoisie. The counterrevolutionaries, quite naturally, saw the revolutionaries as evil to be extirpated from the world. The German Nazis slaughtered Russian Bolsheviks as evil incarnate. The West got its own pleasure in killing evil Germans and Japanese during World War II by launching massive air bombardments of Germany and Japan and finally dropping an atomic bomb on Hiroshima.

Manichaeanism was a revolutionary creed. It arose in a Persian Empire that could never stop fighting or expanding and ended up breaking apart again and again. As Parthia, it was a kind of Soviet Union, but even under its final classical dynasty, the Sassanians, it never could become an empire of order. It was only to be under the new religion of Islam that Persians finally learned what an empire really is—one tolerant of diversity and deeply respectful of society as well as in awe of the state.

In contrast, the Christianity that emerged from all the early doctrinal struggles became an imperial creed. If you doubt this assertion, go into any older Catholic church and you will see an architecture that goes directly back to imperial Rome. When the Pope addresses his messages to *Urbi et Orbi,* "the City and the World," he expresses the Catholic dream of a universal empire that will hail the risen Lord when He returns. Protestant evangelicals see this stage of history as the reign of the Antichrist from which believers will be saved by the Lord in a great rapture, the scooping up of all saved souls to be taken to heaven.

Evangelicals would, of course, not put it in these terms but their determination to serve God in unrelenting battle with the devil is a manifestation of a latent Manichaeanism in the Christian tradition. To die in battle against evil is to come closer to witnessing the greater glory of God. In the Catholic faith, with its many memories of Rome, ancient and modern, that phrase used to be said in Latin: *ad Maioram Dei Gloriam.*

With the end of the cold war it would seem that East-West revolutionary tensions should vanish. They have, not because there are no longer tensions between countries facing each other along this axis but because the issues are no longer revolutionary. The issues mostly boil down to winning or losing something, and that is a far cry from winning or losing everything. The Manichaean ghost reappears with those seeing a danger from Islam or China. The ghost is there, but the human energy for doing the ghost's work is not.

The attention-catching new juxtaposition is the "North-South gap." The term was coined by the German social-democratic leader Willy Brandt. It implies there is some permanent gap between the rich and superior North and the poor and inferior South. Willy Brandt called on the rich and superior people to help our poor, and by implication inferior, cousins to "develop."

222   ◆   *The World and the Road to God*

The "South" is a much more complex and interesting thing than the image implied by Brandt's term. For one thing, historically it was neither poor nor inferior. If you put one point of a compass on a large map showing New Delhi and rotate the other point in a circle crossing Manila to the east and Cairo to the west, the area circumscribed covers the single most prosperous and stable part of the world over the past five thousand years. The central swath of the region is the Indian Ocean. When Columbus sailed westward and Vasco da Gama first southward and then eastward, both were looking to reach the fabled Indies and steal the wealth of the countries bordering that ocean.

For five thousand years this region was wealthy and stable because, first, its soil and climate were so good that all kinds of wonderful and useful things could be grown; second, its people had tightly textured social structures where their we-ness was strong; and third, an extensive network of trade, pilgrimage, and exchange of ideas had the same developmental effect then that the world economy has now: to stimulate growth. To trade, to pray, to think requires strong *I*'s. As a result great civilizations grew up in these southern regions.

Consider Egypt. Its civilization began in its south and then spread northward down the Nile. Or Mesopotamia. Its earliest cities were strung out along the southern and middle reaches of the two great rivers. So too in the case of the early Indus valley civilizations. A Bronze Age civilization of quite early date flourished in Thailand. In China civilization had one center in the north in the Yellow River valley and another in the south along the Yangtze. They eventually merged to form Chinese civilization of the past three thousand years. In North America civilization developed in the south—by the Mayas and then the peoples of the Mexican highlands. In South America civilization developed in the north—in Peru, closer to the equator.

When I began writing this book, I had not much sense of the South. All of my intellectual life till then was shaped by East-West history and dramas. But as I came to realize that so much of that life was lived in and about "state"—something I considered the higher plane in those days—I then started to wonder what "society" was. Having a family with children helped push my thoughts even further in this direction, as did working for the Pacific News Service, where so many "people of color" work and pass through, and something like a village atmosphere developed. Slowly I understood that the South was much more complex and interesting than a sandy beach surrounded by palms somewhere in the South Pacific.

Until around 1968 I regarded the South as the lower plane and, like my state-obsessed Marxist confrères, I looked down on it—"benignly," of course. With its settled villages community is a mark of the South. But I then realized how deeply, if not fundamentally, southern all the world's great religions are: Judaism, Christianity, Hinduism, Buddhism, Confucianism, Taoism, and most of the world's major forms of animism. Thus I realized that the South, during most of the last five thousand years was not only materially but spiritually richer than the generally poor North. Its economies, cultures, and religions were more complete than those of the North. And that is why the North has been invading the South for five thousand years.

The North invaded the South to steal, pillage, dominate, get slaves for an easy life and other wicked reasons. But all these northern invaders also yearned to merge with the South, to become one with them. Out of these mergings all the great civilizations, save one, have evolved. Greek, Roman, Egyptian, Mesopotamian, Indian, Persian, Islamic, Chinese, Japanese arose in the East-West interface of South and North. Those civilizations were *both* southern and northern. The one exception is American civilization which, while more tolerant than modern European attempts at forming civilizations, nevertheless is, in form and essence, northern. Yet American civilization's yearning to merge with the South clearly exists. If it can learn to move on a southern trajectory, then American civilization can become a truly world-spanning empire that can bring peace and prosperity—a *tauheed* of rest and movement to the world.

The empires are in the North, and the population is in the South. The South is poor and weak, but that is changing. Historically, the South was often rich but weak, while the North was poor but powerful. For centuries northerners have invaded the South, seeking its wealth and good life. In India, the northern Aryan invaders with their superior lethal technology and cosmological visions mixed with indigenous Dravidians who, more than three thousand years ago, had created wealthy and productive civilizations. Their ancient waterworks rival those that exist in today's India. Today, Aryan and Dravidian in India are both separated and mixed, bound together by history and modern democratic India, which holds together despite all the centrifugal forces within its body politic.

North and South are locked together, as they have been since civilization began in the South. Southern wealth and learning pulled in the North. New civilizations arose which then spread.

The first and second worlds are coming together; it is likely that North and South will eventually come together as well. Will it take the form of an American empire that spreads its power and way of life through the South? That is already happening. Will it take the form of a revolution from the southern masses that will transform the North, as Christianity transformed Roman society? That is conceivable.

Revolution and empire go together. Revolutions are produced by visions. With the waning of visions like socialism, which promised revolutions from the top, new visions are arising from the bottom, and they are almost entirely religious. And those visions are spreading primarily in the South: Africa, Asia, Latin America. The North is transforming the South, but the South could also transform the North.

In the *I Ching*, a student told me, if the hexagram for shade/woman is on the bottom and that for light/man is on the top, the two will fly apart from each other. But if they are reversed, then they will come together and fruitful things will transpire. Am I suggesting that the *I Ching* predicted three thousand years ago that the South would someday emerge on top of the North? In a way, yes. If current birthrates in these two worlds

continue, then darker-skinned people will come to numerically dominate the world.

Physics has made the globe and wants to save the planet, but biology
will make the world. The good rises to the top. The bad sinks to the
bottom.

Is not what is true, beautiful, and good, and rises like fine cream to
the top—*la crème de la crème*—the light to which we should all aspire?

The top has truth, beauty, and goodness and plenty of wealth for
mind and body—but I think no soul. The bottom lies, is ugly, often violent and murderous, and poor. But it wants to burst out from the bottom,
go somewhere, anywhere, and so acquires soul. In the scheme of things
laid out here, the bottom is with God, just as Jesus was with the publicans;
just as Moses was when he sought out the Israelite slaves; just as Buddha
was when he made himself look like the most hideous, sore-covered
beggar in Magadha; just as Muhammad, peace be upon him, was when
he killed his own people, the Quraishis, in the battle of Badr; just as
Confucius was when he wandered, unemployed, over barren Shandong
hills. The prophets all rose to the bottom.

There is no denying the poor their vision of entering into the light
of the civilization we have created, just as barbarians were drawn from
Asia and even the borders of China whence came the Huns. The poor
will become individuals, have more sex, fewer children. The ballooning
of population will cease.

Revolution means death, which is at the heart of all religions, and it
means soul and God. Revolution is movement. So is capitalism, but only
of mind and body. Revolution is movement of the soul, going so often
together with destruction of body and degradation of mind. Christ hanging on the cross, suffering and dying a hideous death, said: Follow me!

The message that forces itself out of my mind is a Catholic one: try
as you will, you cannot escape suffering, and if you seek soul and God,
and are drawn, as a pilgrim or a servant, into the world, then the suffering
will come, but also a sense of wholeness, of oneness with God, the world,
and your soul, of directions that take you beyond the pain in your body

and mind onto another road beyond the mountains toward a new domain.

In spite of all my travels and the fact that so much of what I write professionally is about the world, I have a fear of the world. The world is full of movement; I crave whatever minuscule rest I can find around me. I almost never watch television, American civilization's door to the world. Buddhism regards the world—people—as illusion. Cut your attachments to the world and you shall be free.

I am conservative, and like many environmentalists with their localistic obsessions, want my corner. The great Buddhist missionary to Japan Dengō Daishi (circa 800) taught that all one needed to do in the world was "shed light on a corner of the world." Does that mean it's okay to stay home? Other voices say to me I should go forth and be a pilgrim, a nomad pilgrim, which is what one must be to be in the world. And those who rise to the bottom become pilgrims, like Mother Teresa.

Lots of people who have made it in this civilization are rediscovering biology. They have kids, something that always gives direction. Or they seek out their roots, which also gives direction. Many are turning to community (somebody even made up the term "intentional community," meaning, I guess, people who come together and have longer-than-short-term ties to each other).

It is just a few steps from the belief that at least two of us exist to a belief in the world. It is just a matter of going from lovers to family to tribe to nation and finally to world. We know—even if we disapprove of their exclusivity—of the deep feelings many people have toward their tribes and nations. Not so long ago nations were considered too big for such loyalties. But as the world became more modern broader national loyalties grew up. It is only a matter of time before deeply felt world loyalties arise on a large scale.

Neither Christianity nor Islam nor their ancestor, the faith of the children of Israel, can by themselves provide a vision for the world. Nor can the other great religions, Buddhism and Hinduism. One reason the Marxist vision was so successful (so successful that millions died for it,

as they would have for a religion) was that it offered to people going in
circles a vision of the world. "Workers of the world unite," followed by
a call for revolution, a most powerful direction-giving force in the modern world: "You have nothing to lose but your chains."

A vision of the world is at its core a realization in mind and by body
that God, soul, and world are three in one and one in three.

Such a vision will give you what Buddhism promises its followers:
wisdom, rest, and discipline. That is to say, you will know about the world
and its swirlings. Your direction-seeking soul will be at rest with itself
and at peace with the world. And your body will be whole and pure even
as you age and become ill and you are like the leaves on an oak tree in
New England that turn red and golden in autumn. The three God-
religions, however, seek movement more than rest. So do Confucianism
and even Taoism. Their trajectories are moral because they operate in
the world. They want to shape and change your behavior to make it a
better world. In the secular world of American civilization, success is
knowledge and skills. What is going to be needed in the next century is
wisdom and morality. For the *I*, these may come from philosophy, but
for the *we*, they will come from religion.

A NEW PILGRIMAGE

As a child I was terrified of being without a home. Why did I decide to
wander? It wasn't rebellion. Something drew me out into the world, and
the world entered into me as I learned more and more languages. Then
I went to different places, intrigued especially by the lights, the smells,
the sights of people and things. When I traveled I was lonely. But I never
stopped. And though I did settle down to a "normal" home life (wife,
children, dogs), thoughts of the world filled my mind, and my body still
sought places like Chinatowns or old American houses. I go into Catholic
churches and Buddhist temples wherever I find them and would go into
mosques if there were more of them in the United States.

The world is our Israel. It is the land God promised us. We are the
chosen people. There are no other people in the entire vast universe, and

if there were they would simply be aliens, like goyim for the Jews. God commanded Moses to lead the children of Israel out of Egypt, and they have been wandering ever since. All people wander now.

Every religion promises ultimate rest. We all build houses; even nomads do. Those who die are put to rest. Yet rest is movement, and movement is rest. God is both the beginning and the final unity. Soul is direction and turns movement into a journey that eventually arrives, even if only at a Ramada Inn for an overnight rest.

When I travel, I like to think of myself as a pilgrim. The root meaning of *pilgrim* is "to cross boundaries." Pilgrims leave their homes and fields to seek out a distant place where they can meet God. Places of pilgrimage are, and long have been, tourist centers with all kinds of shops hawking all kinds of things to all kinds of people. Bethlehem, I have read, is full of small shops that provide a living to Arab families. The boundaries between tourism and pilgrimage have always been fuzzy. But the religious feeling that comes from pilgrimage is of oneness. I remember many years ago standing in front of the tomb of Jalaluddin Rumi, the Muslim mystic, in Konya. There was a large, bright green turban on the stone. Green is the color of Islam. I was a kind of atheist then. I went with my professor at Istanbul University, an exile from Soviet Bashkiria, to the tomb. He was then rediscovering his Muslim faith, and, standing in front of the tomb, I felt his prayers. Later I learned of the Islamic idea of *tauheed*, which means a sense of being one with God, or what an American might call belonging, in the highest sense of the word. Such feelings of oneness are transient, maybe so flimsy as to be trivial. Yet they are very different from the twoness every tourist feels who wants to get his or her money's worth on a long trek.

Pilgrims seek oneness—some kind, any kind, of oneness. When I read of the tidal wave of religion pouring back over the human scene, I also note the bloodshed that follows. I also note how murderously exclusive these religions are, showing deep love for their own coupled with fierce hatred of the enemies of their own.

All that is true and discouraging. Yet it is a sign that God is returning to the world and, more practically, that these are the horrors that accompany the emergence of the world as a world—a world where North and South both are a part of this new *tauheed*.

That has to be the pilgrim's vision of the world to come.

As states battle each other over national vanities, the movement toward unity comes from diversity. God has shifted his wand, which anointed the state two hundred years ago, to point it toward society. The waves of religion that are spreading throughout the world flow at the bottom, at the lowest points of the earth's social surface. Heaven is down here, and hell is up there.

If that be so, heaven is hardly paradise, nor is hell hell considering that those at the top enjoy such fabulous lives. Wherever there be heaven, that is where direction is, and wherever there be hell, that is where life goes around in circles, which means hell's punishments for circularity will afflict the vain and power-hungry.

If God is down here, then this is where the action is and we shall witness the suffering that became incarnate in Christ's crucifixion, and in the sufferings that are the core of every religious story in every religion. Was not Abraham ready to plunge a knife into the heart of his beloved son Isaac in obedience to God's will?

I have for many years now seen similarities between the world today, especially America's role in it, and that of Rome in the first century of the Christian reckoning. America decided to play God in the world ever since it created itself as the United States of America. No other modern country has had that ambition. Russia came closest to embracing such an ambition, but it retreated when the wily Stalin succeeded in getting rid of the messianic Trotsky. Nazi Germany and imperial Japan were just powerful pagan gods who knew they had lost to God.

Asia's empires began the practice of deifying their rulers. Then Augustus, under whom the Roman Empire began, had Julius Caesar deified. Empires and God-religions go together. The grand Chinese empire too began as a "mandate from heaven," and its emperors were called sons of heaven (the Chinese word should be translated as "God"). All empires have sought wider and wider unities. So has America. Now even in Congress, both liberals and conservatives demand that other countries become democratic as grounds for being in America's good graces.

As the American state becomes more and more imperial, religions are spreading at the level of society throughout the world. In ancient Rome, Christianity eventually displaced all other religions. It became a force for unity rising from the bottom, and in the empire's western regions it eventually displaced the existing imperial system. But in the first century, Christians were only one of many religious sects that had sprung up throughout the empire.

Among the Roman elites who were riddled with gloom and doom forebodings, austere Stoic doctrines spread to replace the circular life of Rome's rich. Stoics had a sense of a God greater than the apotheosized gods of the empire. At the time, Cleanthes' "Hymn to Zeus" was popular: "We are the children, we alone, of all on earth's broad ways that wander to and fro, bearing thine image whereso'er we go." Stoics, however, never looked downward.

The Roman Empire arose in the western Mediterranean and then gained control of the eastern Mediterranean. Latin tongues were spoken in the west, and Greek in the east. The civilization was the same, but the cultures were different. That too has suggested to me a contemporary analogy: an Anglo culture north of the Rio Grande and a Hispanic culture south of the Rio Bravo.

But the civilization throughout the Americas—and generally in the world—is increasingly the same. In the nineteenth century, Enlightenment civilization was European and spread to Latin America. Now a single worldwide civilization exists that combines roots in the European Enlightenment with other roots in Anglo-American culture. That civilization is spreading throughout Hispanic America, as Rome's civilization, shaped from Hellenistic civilization and Roman culture, spread throughout the Mediterranean world.

✧

Over the years I have begun to sense that my soul is tugging me south-ward. I read novels in Spanish, and the words of Spanish seem first fa-miliar but then distant, more distant than Chinese or Arabic words. They seem more distant than Russian or Italian words, and even though German and French words to me are cold, they seem quite familiar. But Spanish seems grand and ominous—and the novels all deal with death.

Meanwhile, life is routine, as it has to be when one lives with other minds and bodies, and with "so many things to do." As I write, things of mind and body do not come to mind, and if they did they would be another book I would never write. The room where I write is where our family of four humans and two dogs slept (until the boys grew up), on the floor, smothered by blankets, each to his or her or its own pillow. I felt all alone under the covers. I think the others did as well.

There are no two planes or two rooms neatly segregated one from the other. We are all together in one room, and we are all alone from each other in that room. Souls can never know each other, only sense each other, and so, rightly, communal life has to be mostly the sharing of minds and bodies.

So as I peck away at these smooth, astonishingly obedient plastic computer keys, I somehow sense that it is the beginning of a journey on the continuum of life-death.

I have always liked being a tourist, and now I want to be a pilgrim. I want to go, like the seventh-century Chinese Buddhist pilgrim Hsüan Tsang, who went, sandal-shod, crossing the Himalayas all over India several times, to where God, I guess, was leading him. He went south and then back north and then south again.

When I was a child I looked east past the cemetery to Europe. From my early twenties on, I always wanted a room with a window facing west where I could work. But in recent years I have consorted with more and more people from the south. I have been looking south.

Maybe my road leads south.

✧

Author photograph © George Korejko

Sinologist, historian, and sociologist Franz Schurmann has taught at the University of California, Berkeley for more than thirty years. Author of *The Organization and Ideology of Communist China* and *The Logic of World Power,* among other books, he has studied and travelled in Asia, Europe, and Latin America. A cofounder of Pacific News Service, he reads widely in the Chinese, Arabic, and European presses, and writes a weekly newspaper column.

Richard Rodriguez, the author of *Hunger of Memory, Mexico's Children,* and *Days of Obligation: An Argument with My Mexican Father,* is among America's leading essayists. He is an editor at Pacific News Service, a contributing editor of *Harper's Magazine,* and a commentator on the "McNeil-Lehrer News Hour."